INSTITUTION BUILDING AND DEVELOPMENT:
FROM CONCEPTS TO APPLICATION

Published with the cooperation of the

INTER-UNIVERSITY RESEARCH PROGRAM IN INSTITUTION BUILDING

MEMBERS: *The International Development Research Center, Indiana University*
The Office of the Dean of International Programs, Michigan State University
The Graduate School of Public and International Affairs, University of Pittsburgh
The Maxwell School of Citizenship and Public Affairs, Syracuse University

Institution Building and Development

FROM CONCEPTS TO APPLICATION

Joseph W. Eaton, *Editor*

University of Pittsburgh

 **S A G E PUBLICATIONS** Beverly Hills / London

For information address:

SAGE PUBLICATIONS, INC.
275 South Beverly Drive
Beverly Hills, California 90212

SAGE PUBLICATIONS LTD
St George's House / 44 Hatton Garden
London E C 1

Printed in the United States of America

International Standard Book Number 0-8039-0165-8

Library of Congress Catalog Card No. 72-82842

FIRST PRINTING

INSTITUTION BUILDING AND DEVELOPMENT
From Concepts to Application

Joseph W. Eaton, *Editor*

ERRATA

1. Page 52, line 5 of paragraph beginning "A Prescriptive Model": delete word "not."

2. Page 168, "Institution Building Matrix" figure: add "Figure 3."

SAGE PUBLICATIONS, INC.   SAGE PUBLICATIONS LTD
275 S. Beverly Dr. / Beverly Hills, CA. 90212   44 Hatton Garden, London E C 1

ACKNOWLEDGMENT

The preparation of this book and the chapters of the participating office were greatly facilitated by a grant of the Ford Foundation to the Inter-University Research Program in Institution Building. This consortium includes participants from the University of Indiana, Michigan State University, Syracuse University and the University of Pittsburgh, where the research headquarters are located. Neither the associated universities nor the Foundation necessarily endorse or are associated with the views expressed by the collaborators of this volume.

Mrs. Belle Stock, the Secretary of the Institution Building office, nursed this publication through its many growing pains and prepared the index. The authors of this book are much indebted to her.

Joseph W. Eaton

Pittsburgh, Pennsylvania
May 1, 1972

CONTENTS

INSTITUTION BUILDING AND DEVELOPMENT:
FROM CONCEPTS TO APPLICATION

INSTITUTION BUILDING AS PLANNED CHANGE

JOSEPH W. EATON

University of Pittsburgh

The idea that man can determine his own destiny is gathering momentum. Fewer and fewer people want to leave the future to prophets or to the happenstance of fate. Personal, local and national planners have staked their claim to making events happen somewhat according to a model. New cities or the rebuilding of slums move from a drawing board to reality. Education is not only left to the discretion of parents and teachers; there are programs to affect school systems at local, state, and national levels.

The standards of rationality that are applied in the planning for social change by Americans overseas often seem more professional than many of those advocated for similar domestic projects. In the U.S. domestic scene, technically trained experts usually have staff posts. Few become involved in policy-level planning. Experts tend to be suspect by the politician. The latter feel that their role requires them to adjust long-range planning objectives to the day-to-day short-range perceptions of interest of their constituency. Politicians more often than planners decide when and how to compromise, to adjust what they *want* to what they think they can *get*.

In the foreign aid field, social scientists are more often trusted to perform both planning roles. They come up with blueprints but also function at policy levels. Developing countries have their domestic politicians, but often turn to foreign experts to help set political priorities for development and modernization especially if such advisors come "cost-free" or bring added dollar resources in the form of project grants. Reasons for the more trusted acceptance of academicians may be their high prestige overseas plus the fact that the foreign

[11]

experts do not compete with local people for *permanent* jobs. They come as temporary technical "missionaries," assigned by interests in their own government to aid the cause of development and modernization of a host country. The professional model of the overseas "developer" is that he:

> "employs the skills and insights of all the behavioral sciences for the deliberate encouragement of constructive economic, social and political change. 'Developers' are increasingly in demand, not only in the developing countries, but in this country. The universities have only begun to train people for development as such. The need for talent will grow."[1]

The Inter-University Consortium

This book is the outcome of a joint effort of scholars concerned with the training of such development specialists. All of them have been engaged as field personnel consultants and/or researchers on overseas development projects. They found, as have others who made systematic studies of foreign assistance programs, that there is not enough knowledge which can be taught to others. After a few informal conferences, scholars at the universities of Pittsburgh, Michigan State, Indiana, and Syracuse decided to work out a common strategy. They began to apply selected concepts to the analysis of institution-building processes, hoping thereby to increase their ability to fill their manifold roles as teachers, researchers, and policy reviewers. In a world where foreign aid and domestic social engineering are often performed by new organizational entities, a series of controlled studies of institution-building processes might also in time lead to noteworthy contributions to social science theory. The development of innovative organizations, their modes of counteracting opposition, and the circumstances that support or retard their institutionalization thus became the primary focus of a consortium with headquarters at the University of Pittsburgh called the Inter-University Research Program in Institution Building.

In October 1964, the Ford Foundation agreed to assist this consortium with a grant. A series of studies was financed on the basis of an agreement to apply, when feasible, a joint conceptual framework. Following the Foundation's action, the U.S. government, through AID, contracted for the conduct of a series of four case studies. Each of the universities also contributed support, much of it in faculty time to design field studies that used part or all of the central concepts. The participants were trained in a variety of disciplines and professions, including public administration, sociology, political science, agricultural economics, social work, and psychology.

The writer participated in one of the early meetings of the group when the idea of developing an inter-university consortium was discussed, but he was an observer, then preoccupied with other tasks. He was not part of the creative effort that led to the formulation of the institution-building conceptual framework. In this sense, he is an outsider, now entrusted with the task of editing the efforts of an in-group of creative scholars.

Their ideas are being presented as the authors want to express them, but the editor was given freedom to ask questions and raise issues that might provide a basis for continued intellectual development of this analytic framework. The ultimate aim is the development of a set of hypotheses and theories which can guide those engaged in planned social change with a mutualistic or expert role.

Excluded from consideration are the planning roles that would be performed by men with dictatorial power within the framework of a social Darwinist philosophy.[2] Members of the Inter-university Research Program in Institution Building consortium accepted the viewpoint that planners could use such powers as are inherent in the persuasiveness of data-related reasoning, economic incentives, political support, and national service ideals. Planners who think that the long-run objectives of their effort justify the threat or the use of banishment, imprisonment, and terror will find that these methodological alternatives were not considered. Planners must often proceed without guidance from prior experience. Certainly no man involved in futuristic explorations can have had all the experience he might wish to have had. The conceptual framework that was adopted had the function of facilitating comparative study of planful institution building within the restraints of a democratic political philosophy.

Refinement of Categories

What is the scientific utility of a set of concepts? As mere words, they add nothing to the data. It matters little whether a new school of public administration is described as an organization or an institution; nor if those in positions of responsibility are called leaders or administrators. What does matter is a precise definition of these concepts, in terms that are sufficiently operational and reliable so that different investigators will apply them in a roughly comparable manner to comparable data.

These considerations help to explain why the Inter-University Institution Building Research Consortium, which sponsors this volume, was organized. It became a cooperative enterprise of field research. IB, as its originators often abbreviate their conceptual framework, defined as its central objective the study of *institution building as planful establishment of new organizations to serve purposes which are judged by those in power to require autonomous administrative intervention and special linkages to the larger social system, different from those which can be provided by already existing administrative units.*

This approach to the analysis of planned change focuses attention on two dimensions:

Micro-system Changes:

"The planning, structuring and guidance of new or reconstituted organizations which advocate and embody changes in values, function, physical and/or social technologies."

Macro-system Changes:

"The establishment, protection and fostering normative relationships and action patterns with linked organizations in the larger social system and the attainment of normative acceptance in the environment (complementarity)."[3]

Those who first formulated the IB paradigm did not think (nor do they now claim) to have evolved a perfect conceptual scheme for the analysis of institution building. The practical aspects of planned social change involve such diverse disciplines as economics, political science, sociology, and psychology. They have relevance to such professions as public administration, social work, and public health. The IB concepts are focused on the commonplace reality that planned social change involves the use of organizations, public and private, to implement plans. They also monitor the implementation process in order to initiate changes whenever the outcome fails to conform to what had been theoretically anticipated.

IB proposes the use of a set of concepts or of logical abstractions, which identify organization variables in a complex social process, such as leadership and doctrine. The concepts are a nomenclature, the utility of which is the fact that different investigators found it useful in describing their observations.

IB is sometimes referred to as a theory—a network of ideas about how two or more variables are related. Theoretical formulation about planning change through organizational operations are found in every study sponsored by the IB consortium. But there is at this time no interrelated network of propositions that would justify being designated as IB theory. Until now, research has come up with only isolated propositions about the process of institution building.

IB has a normative dimension. Milton Esman clearly indicates in Chapter 1 that the viewpoint he represents envisions development (guided or induced innovation) as a process within a relatively democratic system of management. Some principles are set forth, which are designated as elements of a theory, but they express moral rather than scientific prerequisites. They would make less sense in a dictatorship which can handle dissidents by shooting them.

The original conceptual framework is systematic because it brings into focus a number of analytic variables of the development process, such as leadership and doctrine. But as Esman points out, it does not lend itself to the analysis of the gradual adaptation of organizations to ongoing internal and external pressures and conflicts, nor to the problems of organizational maintenance over time. Thus, while this analytical framework claims to be generic in that it can be used to analyze deliberate efforts to induce change through the vehicle of organizations in *any* culture and for activities in *any* sector, "its utility is confined to the institution-*building* process and it probably will be of more limited utility in analyzing processes of organizational maintenance of well-entrenched bureaucracies or the unplanned adaptation of institutions to changing circumstances."[4]

With all its limitations, the IB set of concepts offers practical tools to the lonely planner with responsibility for guiding change through administrative procedures. As Ralph Smuckler elaborates in the final chapter of this book, the concepts facilitate the asking of relevant questions. They help identify needs for data already in existence or being sought through new research. Some of the many complex variables of planned change, when formulated in terms of the IB nomenclature, makes it possible to examine already documented experience from comparable situations in order to apply it to reduce the uncertainty quotient of planned social change. It will always exist when men try to influence the future by anticipating it on the basis of an organizational blueprint that can, at best, consider only part of the relevant data and which must embrace ideological assumptions. Such blueprints are subject to inherent limitations, all too little understood by the public that tends to expect from social planners the perfection expected from a bridge builder.

1. Data Insufficiency. Organizational plans for managed change can, at best, collect only some of the required data. This is not only true in developing countries. In the most developed areas, planners never have all the facts that would be required. In deciding the street layout of a new section of the University of Pittsburgh, currently on the drawing board, it would be helpful to know what types of automobile will be in production in 1980, or the number of persons who will want to attend the University of Pittsburgh. At best, some educated guesses can be made.

2. Priority Conflicts. Social planning also requires the setting of public priorities among competing objectives, many of them reasonable. Often, one objective must be sacrificed—at least in part—to attain another. If the new campus area is to have green space between buildings and relative freedom from traffic, students will have to walk a good deal or expensive underground transportation facilities must be provided. No one can build a new campus area at low cost, with optimum access for students having less than ten minutes to rush from one class to another and with lots of scenic green space!

3. Social Planning and Politics. Whenever priorities are proposed in a social plan, the responsible organization must be prepared to encounter opposition, both from within and without, from persons who would prefer different priorities. Planning, unless the process is secret, has the inherent consequence of alerting potential opposition elements to organize to advocate a change in the plan.

These and other social realities give institution building a high *uncertainty quotient.* If it is undertaken, nevertheless, it is because most men prefer a degree of planning and the public setting of priorities to leaving the future to chance and to the political manipulation of non-public—at times even anti-public—power groups.

NOTES

1. Joint Committee of the National Association of State Universities and Land Grant Colleges (NASULGS) and the Agency for International Development (AID), *The Institutional Aid Agreement: A New Operational Framework for AID and the University,* Place of publication not listed: 1970, p. 5.

2. Joseph W. Eaton, "Community Development Ideologies," International Review of Community Development, No. 11, 1963: 37-50.

3. Milton J. Esman, "Institution Building Concepts—An Interim Appraisal," Pittsburgh: Inter-University Research Program in Institution Building, University of Pittsburgh, 1967, p. 1.

4. Milton J. Esman, *The Institution Building Concept—An Interim Appraisal,* Pittsburgh: Inter-University Research Program in Institution Building, University of Pittsburgh, 1967. The ideas were originally set forth by Professor Esman in a paper presented to this conference which was published in abbreviated form as "Institution Building in National Development," International Development Review, December 1962: 6.

Part I.

CONCEPTS

THE ELEMENTS OF INSTITUTION BUILDING

MILTON J. ESMAN

Cornell University

MILTON J. ESMAN is the John S. Knight Professor of International Studies, Director of the Center for International Studies, and Professor of Government at Cornell University. He was the organizer and first Research Director of the Inter-University Research Program in Institution Building and the principal architect of the "Pittsburgh" model of institution building. He has written extensively on comparative and development administration, foreign aid, and institution building. His book, *Development Administration in a Plural Society: Institution Building and Reform in Malaysia,* was published in 1971 by Cornell University Press.

THE ELEMENTS OF INSTITUTION BUILDING

M I L T O N J. E S M A N

Cornell University

Institution building (IB) is a perspective on planned and guided social change.[1] It is concerned with innovations that imply qualitative changes in norms, in behavior patterns, in individual and group relationships, in new perceptions of goals as well as means. It is not concerned with reproducing familiar patterns, with marginal deviations from previous practices, or with incremental improvements in efficiency. The dominant theme is innovation.

The IB perspective posits purposeful social innovation induced by change-oriented elites who work through formal organizations. Their objective is to build viable and effective organizations which develop support and complementarities in their environment. This support permits the innovations to take root, gain acceptance, become normative and thus institutionalized in society. IB is a generic process, in that it can apply to any form of non-coercive social innovation in any sector of society in any culture at any time. It is not, however, an exclusive model of social change, for it does not explain changes that occur by random processes or unplanned diffusion, nor those imposed by sheer coercion, nor those that occur through revolutionary action. In the IB model, an institution is conceived as a change-producing and change-protecting formal organization and the network of support it develops in the environment is *not* conceived (as elsewhere in the literature) as normative action patterns (e.g., marriage, contract) or as a sector of society (e.g., business, religion).

[21]

I. DEFINITION AND GUIDING CONCEPTS

The point of departure for the IB model is the following definition:

"Institution-building may be defined as the planning, structuring, and guidance of new or reconstituted organizations which (a) embody changes in values, functions, physical, and/or social technologies, (b) establish, foster, and protect new normative relationships and actions patterns, and (c) obtain support and complementarity in the environment."[2]

The concepts composing the model are summed up in the following diagram:

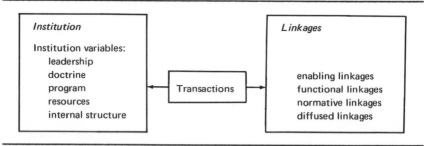

Figure 1. THE INSTITUTION-BUILDING UNIVERSE.

This conceptual framework provides a means for identifying operational methods and action strategies that could be helpful to practitioners and to persons actively engaged as change agents, particularly in cross-cultural situations. The five clusters of "institution" variables have been defined in the following way:

(a) Leadership refers to "the group of persons who are actively engaged in the formulation of the doctrine and program of the institution and who direct its operations and relationships with the environment." Leadership is considered to be the single most critical element in institution building because deliberately induced change processes require intensive, skillful, and highly committed management both of internal and of environmental relationships. Leadership is considered primarily as a group process in which various roles such as representation, decision-making, and operational control can be distributed in a variety of patterns among the leadership group. The leadership group comprises both the holders of formally designated leadership positions and others who exercise important continuing influence over the institution's activities.

(b) Doctrine is defined as "the specification of values, objectives, and operational methods underlying social action." Doctrine is regarded as a series of themes which project, both within the organization itself and in its external

environment, a set of images and expectations of institutional goals and styles of action.

(c) Program refers to "those actions which are related to the performance of functions and services constituting the output of the institution." The program thus is the translation of doctrine into concrete patterns of action and the allocation of energies and other resources within the institution itself and in relation to the external environment.

(d) Resources are "the financial, physical, human, technological and informational inputs of the institution." Quite obviously the problems involved in mobilizing and in ensuring the steady and reliable availability of these resources affect every aspect of the institution's activities and represent an important preoccupation of all institutional leadership.

(e) Internal Structure is defined as "the structure and processes established for the operation of the institution and for its maintenance." The distribution of roles within the organization, its internal authority patterns and communication systems, the commitment of personnel to the doctrine and program of the organization, affect its capacity to carry out programmatic commitments.

The second major category of variables are the "linkages"—"the interdependencies which exist between an institution and other relevant parts of the society." The institutionalized organization does not exist in isolation; it must establish and maintain a network of complementarities in its environment in order to survive and to function. The environment, in turn, is not regarded as a generalized mass, but rather as a set of discrete structures with which the subject institution must interact. The institution must maintain a network of exchange relationships with a limited number of organizations and engage in transactions for the purposes of gaining support, overcoming resistance, exchanging resources, structuring the environment, and transferring norms and values. Particularly significant are the strategies and tactics by which institutional leadership attempts to manipulate or accommodate to these linkage relationships. To facilitate analysis, four type of linkages are identified:

(a) Enabling linkages, "with organizations and social groups which control the allocation of authority and resources needed by the institution to function."

(b) Functional linkages, "with those organizations performing functions and services which are complementary in a production sense, which supply the inputs and which use the outputs of the institution."

(c) Normative linkages, "with institutions which incorporate norms and values (positive or negative) which are relevant to the doctrine and program of the institution."

(d) Diffused linkages, "with elements in the society which cannot clearly be identified by membership in formal organization."

"Institutionality" as the end state is an evaluative variable—a standard for appraising the success of institution-building efforts. The concept of institutionality denotes that "at least certain relationships and action patterns incorporated in the organization are normative both within the organization and for other social units, and that some support and complementarity in the environment have been attained."

Underlying these concepts and their interrelationship is a series of theory-related perspectives on social change:

1. The developmental process involves the introduction and acceptance of numerous changes or innovations in modernizing societies. Many of these changes are technological. They concern ways of manipulating the physical environment (water control systems, fertilizers) or of regulating social relationships (merit systems or patterns of university organization) which are new to the host society. Many of these innovations combine elements of both physical and social technologies (family planning, agricultural extension). Many such changes which seem to be purely technical and rational to foreign change agents and even to domestic leaders and innovators may, however, be perceived by local people as damaging or threatening to their material interests, their occupational or social status, familiar relationships or well-entrenched habits. Those who resist innovations are not necessarily only the rich and powerful or the poor or illiterate; they may be found also among the most "enlightened" and educated, such as professors who resist curriculum changes or civil servants who fight organizational improvements. Because innovations often involve important changes in attitudes and behavior and do not readily fit into local practices and institutions, they are inevitably implicated in social change. Innovations should thus be conceived both by domestic and external change agents as *induced social and behavioral changes.*

2. In the contemporary context, most such changes do not occur by autonomous diffusion or by evolution. They do not just happen. They are *deliberately induced* by individuals or groups who see such changes as beneficial both to themselves and to society. Thus IB has a pronounced social engineering basis. But there is much uncertainty in the introduction of changes into any social system, many consequences that are unexpected and responses that are unpredictable, even in well-planned experiments in social change. Indeed, induced innovations should be looked upon as experiments. These experimental ventures must be *guided* by individuals or groups who are consciously prepared to engage in *organizational learning* from the data of experience and to *adapt* their technological innovations and their original plans for introducing them to what proves to be feasible in the environment—but without abandoning their innovations as the price of survival. IB is thus a guidance and social learning process, not the "installation" of prepackaged technologies. It thus excludes both autonomous and coercively imposed innovations.

3. Induced innovations require the vehicle of complex formal *organizations*. As societies modernize, the number of functionally specific formal organizations multiplies and only through such organizations and networks of organizations can complex modern technologies be managed and integrated. Important changes depend on centers of competence which bring together, combine, develop, and activate the variety of skills required for the technical phases of the job, the commitment to specific innovations, and the political abilities needed to guide change processes in an uncertain and perhaps friendly environment. It is formal organizations which promote and protect innovations and which represent and symbolize them to their clients and to society as a whole.

IB is thus a double-barreled activity. Change agents must both (a) build technically viable and socially effective organizations which can be vehicles for innovation, and (b) manage relationships (linkages) with other organizations and groups on whom they depend for complementarities and support and whose behavior they are attempting to influence. Building viable organizations and managing their linkages are closely interrelated aspects of a single institution-building process.

4. The object is to achieve *institutionality*—meaning that innovative norms and action patterns are valued within the organization and by the larger society and are incorporated into the behavior of linked organizations and groups. The environment becomes supportive of the innovations; the organization and the innovations it represents become valued and meaningful elements in the surrounding society. At this point, the institution has been built. The model does not deal with subsequent stages in the life-cycle of an institutionalized organization, with organizational maintenance through time, including the tendency to become resistant to subsequent innovations, or the process by which an institutionalized organization may sustain and renew its innovative thrust.

II. A GUIDANCE MODEL

While IB is not a universal model of social change, it does apply to innumerable situations in contemporary societies in which (1) change agents, usually enjoying some measure of official sponsorship or indulgence, attempt to impress their goals, their preferred norms and action patterns on society; (2) the components of the society that are relevant to the proposed innovations must be induced—they cannot be merely coerced—to accept the innovations and have the capacity to resist or to reject them if the inducements fail; (3) formal organizations are employed as the media or vehicles through which change agents develop the technical capacities and the normative commitment needed to guide, sustain, and protect the intended innovations.

IB is thus a learning and political rather than a coercive process, but the innovations are deliberately induced and guided by persons attempting to extend their influence. Changes attempted by most non-totalitarian governments in all sectors of activity from agriculture to industry, health, education, urban affairs, public administration, and welfare policy are amenable to guided change in the form visualized by the IB model. This applies especially to activities in which foreign technical assistance is a factor.

The IB model is an elitist theory with an explicit social engineering bias. Changes occur from the top down, not from the bottom up, and they are guided by persons enjoying a measure of official authority or sanction. The vehicle of change is a formal and probably bureaucratic organization, which aggregates the technical capabilities and the value commitments required to innovate and to promote and protect them in the environment that is relevant to the organization. Its environment is a set of organizations or groups, each operating in its own substantive domain and pursuing its own interests. With these organizations and groups the innovating organization must establish and maintain a set of transactional and exchange relationships which insure its access to resources, outlets for its products, and environmental support for its activities.

Like any system functioning in a changing environment under conditions of uncertainty, the organization and the change processes to which its leadership is committed must be *guided* or *managed*. However thorough and skillful the initial design and the planning, IB is never a self-executing or self-fulfilling process. It is a continuous game of coping with uncertainty and contingencies, with human and technological shortcomings, and with competitive interests. Thus the leadership must be continuously learning and adjusting, not only correcting variances from an original design, but making major changes in tactics, in timing, in programming, in resource allocation, and even in redefining institutional goals. Continuous and active management is thus indispensable. Since IB is an instrumental model, it does not provide criteria for determining what innovations are desirable; but it does speak to the feasibility of alternative choices of means for meeting perceived needs and of methods of managing induced change processes.

III. SOME UNDERLYING ASSUMPTIONS

The IB model makes a number of assumptions about environment, about organization, about change processes, about institutionalization.

About *environment,* it posits not a vacuum into which innovations can be poured and absorbed, but an ongoing pattern of relationships in which individuals, groups, and especially organizations, each participating in an area of activity, promote and protect their own interests which are sanctioned by the larger system of which they are a part. Environments, however, are not closed and static systems, nor are they monolithic. They, too, are changing and differ in their change readiness and change resistance both to generalized change and to specific innovations. The managers of different organizations may perceive their interests differently and thus vary in their readiness or resistance to proposed innovations. It is the first task of change agents to assess these environmental realities in detail. They cannot assume that there is an active demand in the environment for their product, however meritorious they conceive it to be. They have to expect and identify environmental hostility to innovations. Even when this is minimal, other organizations may compete for control of the market which the change agents are seeking to enter and may attempt to preempt proposed innovations by adopting changes on their own. The environment is essentially political and may present a broad spectrum of generalized change readiness and change resistance as well as receptivity and hostility to specific innovations. The environment also presents a complex of intellectual, normative, technical, and resource constraints, opportunities, and capabilities to provide the inputs or accept the outputs of the organization, regardless of the political factors already referred to.

About *organization,* the model assumes the capacity of formal organizations to socialize those who come within its boundaries to new norms and action patterns, so long as the contact is long enough in duration, and socialization is an explicit concern. Thus organization can decisively influence the behavior of staff members and of clients. Organizations are not merely conversion or service-providing structures, though they do both. They do not merely reflect the values of the environmental system in which they participate. They have the capacity to act on their environment, particularly on the specific subsystems with which they carry on transactions and maintain linkage relationships. Thus organizations can be dynamic vehicles through which change agents can impress their values both on persons within their boundaries and on external contacts. The type of organization implicitly assumed in the IB model is bureaucratic, with specialization of roles, formal rules, and hierarchical authority structures. Not only is this the most common form of organization in modern societies, but it is the one through which guidance methods of management can most readily function. Within this form of organization, there may be many degrees of centralization and decentralization, of authoritarian or collegial decision-making, of permissiveness and of control, but the form is essentially bureaucratic, not constitutive.

Institution builders invest in organizations. This implies the continuity of organizations and the willingness of change agents to sacrifice current outputs for future capacity. One invests not only in physical facilities but also in the technical and managerial capabilities of staff, in access to informational resources that are processed and stored for future use, in internal communications capabilities so that information may move quickly and thus facilitate more prompt and rational action, and in sources of social support. One invests normatively in the organization so that its component units and individuals may be motivated by similar goals and expectations, bring the same value premises to bear on problems that arise, develop a high degree of interpersonal trust and thus put forth greater effort than their salaries alone could evoke, because they derive part of their rewards from the psychic satisfactions of serving an organization and a set of purposes in which they believe. Organization is more than an aggregation of individuals and equipment, and both the technical performance and the commitments it evokes result from what has been invested in it.

About *change processes,* the model implies induced rather than spontaneous initiation and guided rather than autonomous diffusion. Unanticipated events, some favorable and some unfavorable to change agent goals, will inevitably crop up and these must at times be dealt with expediently; but in this rationalistic guidance model, the main reliance is on planned and managed change. The three main change processes are technological, cultural, and political. *Cultural* or normative methods rely on efforts to change individual or group values, attitudes, or role perceptions using ideological, indoctrinative, emotional, symbolic, group dynamic, and other subcognitive methods. *Technological* methods rely on cognitive information or on new practices or services to induce fresh action patterns and intellectual commitments to changed roles and activities. *Political* methods rely on the redistribution of power, redefinition of rewards, manipulation of resources, or the use of influence and bargaining to produce behavioral change. In any major IB effort, all three methods must be used in a variety of sequences and combinations.

About *institutionality,* the end product of IB effort, the model stipulates a series of tests, that will be discussed later in this paper. The fundamental principles are that (1) new norms and action patterns must be established both within the organization and in its relevant environment, and (2) both the organization and the innovations for which it stands must become institutionalized, prized in the environment. This means that both the organization and the innovations it fosters are "infuse(d) with value beyond the technical requirements of the task at hand," to use Selznik's celebrated phrase.[3] The intrinsic value so achieved can be conceived as a resource that enables change agents to accomplish their objectives at reduced cost because of the commitment of staff and the favorable image projected in the environment.

IV. INSTITUTION VARIABLES, LINKAGE VARIABLES AND TRANSACTIONS

As we have previously indicated in Figure 1, two groups of variables or factors are important to understanding and guiding institution-building activity. These are the "institution variables," which are essentially concerned with the organization itself, and the "linkage variables," which relate mainly to external relations.

The most important variable is *leadership.* Guidance requires leadership, and this is especially true where the problem is not to maintain the status quo but rather to achieve behavioral changes within an organization and in an environment which may impose obstacles to the intended changes. An organization without leadership may be out of control and unless the leadership is both technically and politically competent both for its internal and external responsibilities, and committed to innovation, the enterprise may be in trouble—even though its opportunities are otherwise favorable.

Leadership in complex organizations is usually a collective process in which various roles—such as external political contacts, internal management, program development—are divided among members of a leadership group. Alternative leadership styles may significantly affect the performance of a new or reconstituted organization committed to innovation. In many cases one man is the dominant personality and if he has innovative commitments, organizational capability, and political skills, the enterprise is equipped with a precious resource. He should be able to induce key staff members to identify their own interests with the welfare of the organization and the innovations it represents. Where these qualities are not present in the top man it may be possible to compensate for them among other members of the leadership cadre. Where this is not possible, there is a built-in ceiling—independent of environmental limitations—on the prospects that the institution can be built. Those concerned with the institution must, under such circumstances, work for leadership change or emphasize those activities which are consistent with the commitments and capabilities of the existing leadership group.

Doctrine is the most elusive of the institution variables. It is the expression of what the organization stands for, what it hopes to achieve, and the styles of action it intends to use. Men are motivated to act partly by the expression of ideas and symbols. Clear, consistent, confident, and oft-repeated expressions of doctrine can develop consensus on common objectives among members of an organization, establish the premises for effective communication, develop a strong sense of collective purpose of cohesion, thus increasing both the satisfactions of its members and the effectiveness of the organization in dealing with the external environment.

Doctrine also acts on the external environment projecting an image of the organization, the values for which it stands, and the services or benefits that it can be expected to deliver to its various linkages or clients. Doctrine is not a single concept but rather a group of themes which are projected by the leadership to its internal and external audiences in order to gain and maintain support for the organization and its purposes. There is a degree of flexibility in doctrine. Themes can be differentially emphasized for different clienteles and they can be modified over time as the organization faces new problems and learns from experience.[4] Doctrine thus motivates personnel, establishes expectations about organizational performance, provides standards for decision-making and for evaluating results, and helps to prepare the ground and to rationalize shifts in the organization's emphasis, activities, and outputs.

Thus, the elaboration, expression, and manipulation of doctrine is an important responsibility of those who are guiding IB activities. It is a phase of institutional management in which time, thought, and effort must be invested, yet it is frequently neglected. Failure to deal with doctrine means that the organization will lack credibility, it may drift opportunistically into activities which are easy because its sense of purpose is obscure. Leadership will thus fail to use the power of ideas and symbols to guide the organization in its internal development and in interaction with its external environment.

The organization's *program* is the set of activities it undertakes, the translation of doctrine into action. This involves a set of choices about how the organization will apply the resources it has available and what stream of products or services it intends to provide. It is through its programs of action that the technological and social innovations for which the institution stands are converted into specific products or services.

Programs of action tend to be formulated in response to legal mandates, environmental demands, opportunities, or the priorities held by leadership. Their priorities are usually instrumental to the innovations to which leadership is committed. But programs are not formulated in a vacuum. They must be so designed and managed that they build support for the organization among prospective "publics" and minimize opposition. The dilemma is that some innovative programs tend to generate opposition among important groups in the environment, while others that respond to felt needs or are easily accepted in the society contribute little innovation. Effective programs must be perceived by clients to deliver substantially more benefits than dissatisfactions in order to draw their support. Therefore, those who shape an organization's programs must carefully assess what its prospective publics are prepared to accept and develop a program mix which combines innovations with responses to "felt needs," invests some of the organization's energies in preparing the environment for additional innovations in the future, and adapts program outputs to feedback, to what is learned from the responses of clients. Programming, especially for an innovative organization, is thus a dynamic process; it cannot be determined once and for all.

Yet initial decisions about the organization's programs or outputs are critical because they help to determine what kinds of resources in staff, facilities, equipment, and information sources the organization will assemble. These, in turn, militate against rapid shifts in program content because such resources can only partially and gradually be directed to new operating activities. Program development must be consistent with the resources available to the organization at any time, or it will be unable to deliver services. At the same time, the effective delivery of services helps the organization to win support in its environment and thus to claim and mobilize additional resources which, in turn, provide the wherewithal for improved and expanded services in the future.

The magnitude and quality of the *resources* available to leadership are important determinants of the organization's effectiveness. Resources may be regarded as inputs that the organization either converts into products or services or into increasing its own capabilities. Resources can be classified as legal and political authority, personnel, funds, equipment, facilities, and information. The problem of the institution builder is to mobilize—that is, to attract these resources to the organization and to mount programs of action consistent with the capabilities of these resources at any time. These programs of action should product benefits and satisfactions for individuals and groups in the society that maintain and enhance the organization's continued access to such resources.[5] Resources being scarce and having alternative uses, they are available to an organization over time only at a price. The price is usually the organization's ability to produce valued services to those in society who control or influence the flow of resources. The organization must thus earn its way in the world, though it may be vested early in its life with access to resources because of future expectations rather than the requirement for immediate performance. Thus, it may be accorded some time to prove itself before its performance is evaluated in terms of future access to resources.

Resources are not inert. They must be developed, combined, and deployed before they produce useful outputs. Perhaps the most important resource to an organization is its *staff*. Staff development is a continuing function of institution builders because personnel are rarely available in the labor market with the precise skills, knowledge, and programmatic commitments that effective performance requires in an innovative organization. The development of appropriate skills may require long-term investments during which time inadequately skilled personnel can perform only at a modest level or on a limited range of activities—despite the high expectations of some important publics. The organization must be prepared to sacrifice current output because it is investing in the more advanced training of its staff. Moreover, the capacity to function effectively in formal organizations is severely limited in many societies by a pervasive individualism and absence of interpresonal trust, which can only be compensated by intensive training and the search for effective patterns of interpersonal relationships—which would constitute innovations in that society. The development and maintenance of a value commitment in its personnel is a continuing function of leadership through the deployment of doctrine. This staff commitment to the innovative values of the organization must be supported by other material, status, and psychic rewards to staff members which reinforce their value commitments and thus enhance the organization's effectiveness. These commitments may be designated as the "withinputs"[6] of the organization.

Likewise, *information* about its external environment and about new technologies must be collected, analyzed, processed, stored, retrieved, and disseminated when needed, for an organization operating in an informational vacuum cannot make rational decisions. It is also necessary for an organization to continuously scan its external environment for signs of changes which represent potential dangers or new opportunities to which it can adapt its programs before it is confronted with crises. Thus, leadership must invest energy in establishing an information system and maintaining its informational resources at a high level of efficiency.

Though it is not the only resource that organizations need, *funds* are indispensable to finance facilities and equipment as well as current operations. Whatever sources provide money—sales of products, national or local budgets, voluntary contributions, or foreign assistance—leadership must work at meeting expectations and catering to demands that insure the reliable flow of funds and do so without sacrificing the crucial innovative objectives of the organization. One of the important tests of the success of technical assistance and the depth of institutional development is the capacity of an innovating organization to attract and continue to mobilize funds from national sources when technical assistance is withdrawn.

Any organization, including an organization that is becoming an institution, must achieve technical competence in all of its components and effective cohesion among them. The need to insure such integration is incorporated in a cluster of variables called *internal structure*. This includes formal and informal patterns of authority, division of labor among components, channels of communication between them, and the methods of mediating and resolving the disputes that inevitably break out over policies, priorities, resource allocations, and, indeed, personalities in any complex social structure. The organization is the most valuable resource of the institution builder, for it is the vehicle through which he extends his innovative influence into the society. Shaping the internal structure is likely to call for different tactics in new and in reconstituted organizations. Much of the knowledge in modern organization theory and administrative management practices which focus on the internal problems of enterprises is applicable to the situations that institution builders encounter in developing and sustaining viable internal structures.

Some leaders are more interested and more effective in the internal management of their organizations than in guiding their external relations. Yet, effective institutional leadership requires simultaneous attention to building the organization and to managing its environmental relations. Every organization is engaged in a network of interactions with other organizations, at a minimum to exchange goods and services. Aside from these business-like transactions, an innovative organization is concerned with gaining support and overcoming resistance, and in bringing about changes in other organizations with which it interacts. This net work of inter-organizational relationships is designated as linkages.

To simplify this concept, four kinds of institutional linkages have been identified:

Enabling linkages provide authority to operate and access to essential resources. Enabling linkages may also be used to protect the organization against attack and to guarantee its access to resources during the critical period while it is developing its capabilities but is not yet strong enough to deal with its external environment on its own terms. Needless to say, prudent institutional leaders cultivate their enabling linkages—but not to the point that they damage or fail to develop more broadly based sources of support.[7]

Functional linkages provide the needed inputs into the organization and take its outputs. In addition to complementary relationships, this category of linkages includes those institutions which are real or potential competitors, which perform or seek to perform similar functions or services. Among the functional linkages of a national planning institution are other government departments which provide the planning institution with information and requests for approval of projects (inputs) and in turn receive allocations of funds or requests for information (outputs). An agricultural extension agency will have functional linkages with the research agency which provides it with inputs and with farm organizations which take its outputs.

Normative linkages are relationships with other organizations which share an overlapping interest in the objectives or the methods of the new institution. These may be reinforcing or hostile. Thus, a family-planning institution may have a normative link with a church group which may be either supportive or hostile, and a school of public health may have normative linkages with the organized medical profession.

Diffuse linkages are relationships with individuals and groups not aggregated in formal organizations or collectivities but able to influence the standing of the innovative organization in its environment. An example might be the parents of present or prospective students of an educational institution or the "clients" of a tax collection agency.

Institutional leadership must at all times take account of the network of linkages with which it is implicated. Some of these linkages are critical, others are relatively less important at any time period. Leadership should identify and evaluate these linkages, assess the present status and future prospects of such relationships, develop appropriate tactics for dealing with each of them, and allocate their energies accordingly. Since the environment of any organization, especially an innovative one, is always more or less competitive, and since there are many uncertainties that cannot be predicted in advance, prudent leadership must continuously maintain surveillance of these relationships to anticipate problems or new opportunities and be prepared to modify tactics accordingly.

The leaders of linked organizations have their own interests to promote and defend and they may do so actively. Therefore, the management of these linkage relationships is a dynamic process involving transactions, exchanges, give and take with other organizations and groups. Some of these actions are initiated by the innovative organization which may be required, in other cases, to respond to the initiatives of others. In this real world of competitive power and influence, an organization must often defer the promotion of some innovations until they are better understood or otherwise more acceptable to other organizations whose cooperation or acquiescence are essential. In some cases it may be necessary for innovators to sacrifice some of the things they want in order to protect other things they want even more. While seeking satisfactory working arrangements with other organizations—at minimum cost to their own change goal—they may at times be required to fight other organizations or groups which are blocking their objectives, to form coalitions, and otherwise devise and carry out strategies that protect and promote their objectives in a competitive environment. Timidity and caution may result in an organization that loses its effectiveness as an agent of change even though it survives on terms that others set. Foolhardy aggressiveness, on the other hand, may lead to swift destruction.

Thus, the rational management of an organization's linkages requires a cool and continuous assessment of the environment, broken down by the specific relationships which are important for its purposes. Appropriate tactics must be devised to deal with each of them—consistent with the organization's operational capabilities. The leadership has available doctrine and programmatic outputs as instruments to cope with external linkages. It must be prepared to adjust both to what it learns from experience and to emergent needs that it discovers, at some cost perhaps to its preferences, but at least cost to its major innovative purposes. Success means improved access to resources and additional opportunities to provide services that effectively move the environment in the directions contemplated by the leadership of the innovative institution.

V. STRATEGIC PLANNING AND MONITORING

One of the main implications of IB theory is the active role of leadership. Building a viable organization—the internal focus—and managing its social linkages—the external focus—involve the guidance of a complex system through uncertainty. This is possible only if leaders have a clear idea of the innovations they are attempting to introduce (a doctrine), an operating strategy, and a capacity for organizational learning. Pragmatic improvising, though often a necessity, is no substitute for strategic planning and operational monitoring of the content of induced social change.

Strategic planning [8] ought to precede and inform any institution-building enterprise, particularly any decision by a foreign agency, to participate in a technical assistance capacity. It is equally valid for the creation of a new organization or the attempt to regenerate and redirect an existing one.

Among the strategic issues that might be accounted for in planning and IB venture are the following:

   (a) what innovations are most suitable to the needs and circumstances—a decision that depends on the preferences and commitments of change agents, their knowledge of available alternatives, and their assessment in detail of the elements of change readiness and change resistance and of specific sources of support in the environment;

   (b) what organization should be the vehicle—an existing one that can be restructured, or a new one;

   (c) what leadership patterns are suitable—centralized or pluralistic; what are the desired qualifications of leadership; who are available as the initial incumbents;

   (d) what sources of essential resources can be relied on for such inputs as funds, personnel, information, authority, and at what price; who are likely to take the organization's outputs on acceptable terms;

(e) what shall be the initial operating program and tactics, and how should activities be phased over time; what shall be the relative priorities between building the organization, providing useful services, and extending innovations;

(f) how shall the organization be designed and staff requirements determined so that operating programs may be consistent with organizational capacities and synchronized with staff development activities;

(g) what are the significant linkages and how can doctrine and program help to influence the behavior of each linkage in the desired direction;

(h) what combination of survival, service, and change tactics should be employed at successive points in time;

(i) what control mechanisms should be employed to monitor current performance and to evaluate institutional progress;

(k) what shall be the role of technical assistance in this venture, the specific relationship of foreign and domestic personnel in the various internal and linkage management activities of the organization.

To maintain the relevance of a strategic plan once it is adopted, formal or informal monitoring mechanisms are needed. *Operational monitoring*[9] is charting what the organization actually does against a set of original intentions or expectations. Otherwise the organization tends to drift away from its original design as it responds to unanticipated pressures, events, and opportunities. Monitoring does not mean that an organization cleaves to an original design, regardless of its experience. It does mean that the organization is learning from its experience but is relating that experience to an original plan and set of purposes. Thus, there are base lines for describing and evaluating performance in the main dimensions of the organization's activities. Operational monitoring can thus provide the data and the assessments that inform inevitable changes and continual updating in the organization's operational plans. It enhances the quality of decisions and tends to insure that changes in the organization's program, doctrine, or internal structure are deliberately calculated in relation to original plans, organizational learning, and alternative possibilities rather than by opportunistic drift or pressures.

Informal monitoring is attempted by all responsible administrators, but the pressures of daily operations and the complexity of their tasks often relegate this activity to low priority. It is therefore desirable, if the scale of the activity permits, to attach a monitoring staff member or unit to the leadership group to perform this research and evaluation function. Its utility will depend on the quality of its data gathering and analysis, its capacity to scan the environment for new and prospective developments, its ability to formulate and present alternative courses of action, and its access to the leadership group.

VI. INSTITUTIONALITY—THE END STATE

Institutionalization means that the organization and its innovations are accepted and supported by the external environment. The environment has accommodated to its innovations more than the organization has accommodated to the original environment. But accommodation in the real world is usually a reciprocal process, so that the operative question is how much A accommodates to B and on what issues. This adjustment process involves functional, normative, and power relationships. Institution builders must sometimes sacrifice or defer indefinitely one whole program in order to save another. Accommodation is often less dramatic—a set of incremental concessions that results in much accommodation and little innovation; the organization survives, perhaps to fight tomorrow's battle, but no new institution has been built. The IB model implies a relatively stable, non-revolutionary environment. Too radical a set of deviations from familiar norms and practices will attract unmanageable and destructive opposition. Thus the managers of substantive and procedural innovations must make concessions to the local milieu, identify with well-established popular themes, symbols, and slogans so that the venture starts with a maximum of legitimacy, supplementary to the services it can render and the power it can generate and deploy.

What are the end states of the IB process—the directions toward which ventures should be moving? These must be distinctive for each activity but in general they should meet the following criteria:

1. Technical capacity: the ability to deliver technical services which are innovations to the society at an increasing level of competence, whether they be teaching agricultural sciences, enforcing income taxes, or providing family-planning services.

2. Normative commitments: the extent to which the innovative ideas, relationships, and practices for which the organization stands have been internalized by its staff—for example, the merit system for personnel selection or participative roles for students.

3. Innovative thrust: the ability of the institution to continue to innovate so that the new technologies and behavior patterns which it introduces may not be frozen in their original form, but the institution can continually learn and adapt to new technological and political opportunities.

4. Environmental image: the extent to which the institution is valued or favorably regarded in the society. This can be demonstrated by its ability to (a) acquire resources without paying a high price in its change objective, (b) operate in ways that deviate from traditional patterns, (c) defend itself against attack and criticism, (d) influence decisions in its functional areas, and (e) enlarge and expand its sphere of action.

5. Spread effect: the degree to which the innovative technologies, norms, or behavior patterns for which the institution stands have been taken up and integrated into the ongoing activities of other organizations.

Mere survival is a necessary but not sufficient test of institutionality. An organization may survive, but the price—due to incompetent or uncommitted leadership, to technical inadequacy, or to environmental hostility—may be the abandonment of its innovative objectives. It may survive as an additional organization but not an innovating one, and, thus, would be of little interest to institution builders. On the other hand, though the organization may go under, its technical and behavioral innovations might be taken on by other structures and thus survive and prosper in other organizational settings. But in the overwhelming majority of cases, innovations depend on the survival and success of the organization or group of organizations responsible for protecting and promoting them. This is the reason that in the IB perspective, both the organization and the innovations it represents must be fostered and both must achieve societal acceptance.

VII. TECHNICAL ASSISTANCE IN INSTITUTION BUILDING

Technical assistance or external intervention is not an explicit variable in the IB model. The assumption is that non-coercive social change (as opposed, for example, to military government or the Stalinist pattern of collectivization) is essentially an indigenous phenomenon, and that particular instances of deliberate or guided change may or may not involve external participation. The IB perspective explicitly rejects the notion that meaningful change can be a straightforward transfer of technology or the installation of prepackaged know-how or organizational forms from one culture to another whether managed entirely by indigenous innovators or assisted by foreign advisors. Nevertheless, a large number of ventures in induced change in less developed countries since World War II have involved external technical assistance change agents. Most of the researchers working in IB research have been drawn to the subject in order to strengthen technical assistance performance, and most of the sponsors of this work have clearly hoped for a payoff in this area.

It is clear that technical assistance can influence IB at any point, including strategic intervention with enabling linkages in a manner that may be closed to indigenous change agents. (The latter must usually work within the styles and the channels of the indigenous system, while external interveners need not be so restricted.) The optimal roles of technical assistance personnel no doubt vary at different stages in the IB process, but it appears that technical assistance is most critical in five types of activities:

1. As the providers of change models. Technical assistance implies, on the part of the indigenous elites, a recognition of inadequacies in the structure or performance of their own institutions. They are looking for better models and they rely on the experience or the intellectual achievements of other societies to supply these models, as well as the technical and managerial know-how to help local people use these instruments and fit them to local conditions.

2. As participants in the leadership function, in the framing of doctrine and priorities, the development of programs, and especially the building of the internal organization.

3. As providers and allocators of valuable resources (advisors, participant training opportunities, equipment, money, information, and prestige) which facilitate the process of induced change by providing both inducements and independence for domestic change agents. Resources also legitimatize and increase the influence of foreign TA (technical assistance) personnel.

4. The traditional Point Four and agricultural extension functions of *transferring and adapting technology* through teaching, training, and demonstration is only one of the functions of technical assistance in an IB situation. In addition to its intrinsic importance, their technical contribution helps TA advisors to build confidence among local personnel and this is indispensable to their major IB purposes.

5. An emergent but increasingly important function for IB forms of technical assistance is to incorporate *evaluative research* into projects, research that will help local change agents to appraise their performance, adjust their programs to changing conditions and new information produced through organizational learning, and to contribute new knowledge to the science and to the art of guided social change.

VIII. IB AS A GUIDE TO RESEARCH AND TO PRACTICE

With the elaboration of this model, the concept of institution building has graduated from a slogan to a complex and sophisticated intellectual construct capable of orienting both analysts and practitioners to important problems of action. It compels organization theorists and practicing administrators to look outside the boundaries of the formal organization and to focus on the external linkages which determine the social relevance and effectiveness of their efforts. It forces social change theorists to come to grips with the phenomenon of the complex organization as a necessary instrument in purposeful social innovation. It focuses directly on the relationship of leaders and of ideas to purposeful group action; of resource inputs to programmatic outputs in the context of social exchange; and the political as well as the learning dimensions of guided social change.

The objective is not only to provide useful perspectives but also to generate insights about tactics of intervention that will reduce the uncertainty facing practitioners of planned social change and increase the probability that their efforts will yield greater success than would be likely in the absence of this model. Its utility for researchers and analysts as well as for practitioners, even at the current rudimentary stage of its development, has been amply demonstrated by the testimony that appears in the subsequent chapters of this volume. [10]

NOTES

1. The ideas presented in this chapter are drawn from materials which have appeared in a number of published and unpublished articles. Among them are: Milton J. Esman, "Institution Building in National Development," International Development Review,

December 1962; Milton J. Esman and Hans C. Blaise, "Institution-Building Research—The Guiding Concepts," Pittsburgh: Inter-University Research Program in Institution Building, 1966 (mimeo). Milton J. Esman and Fred C. Bruhns, "Institutional Building and National Development, An Approach to Induced Social Change in Transitional Societies," in Hollis Peter (ed.), *Comparative Theories of Social Change,* Ann Arbor: Foundation for Research in Human Behavior, 1966; Milton J. Esman, "Some Issues in Institutional Building Theory," Purdue University, International Agricultural Development Program July 1969 (mimeo); and Milton J. Esman, "Institution Building as a Guide to Action," prepared for AID Conference on Institution Building, November 1969 (mimeo). The original concepts were developed by members of the Executive Board of the Inter-University Research Program in Institution Building consisting of the author, Hans C. Blaise, and Saul M. Katz of the University of Pittsburgh; Ralph Smuckler and Eugene Jacobson of Michigan State University; William Siffin and Fred Riggs of Indiana University; and Irving Swerdlow and Julian Friedman of Syracuse University.

2. Milton J. Esman and Hans C. Blaise, "Institution-Building Research—The Guiding Concepts," Pittsburgh: Inter-University Research Program in Institution Building, 1966 (mimeo). The subsequent diagram and definitions are drawn from this basic source document.

3. Philip Selznik, *Leadership in Administration,* Evanston: 1957, p. 17.

4. This theme is developed in detail by Fred C. Bruhns in "The Role of Values in the Management of Institutional Doctrine: The Institution Building Experience of an African Regional Organization." Ph.D. dissertation, University of Pittsburgh, 1968.

5. For further development of this theme, see Norman Uphoff and Warren Ilchman, "The Time Dimension in Institution Building," Pittsburgh: Inter-University Research Program in Institution Building, n.d. (mimeo).

6. This concept was provided by Frank Sherwood, "Social Exchange in the Institution Building Process," Pittsburgh: Inter-University Research Program in Institution Building, 1967 (mimeo).

7. See Gilbert Siegel, "Development of the Institution Building Model: Administrative Department of Public Service in Brasil." Pittsburgh: Inter-University Research Program in Institution Building, 1966 (mimeo).

8. This concept is further developed by Warren Haynes and Tom Hill in their forthcoming study on building institutions for management education in India.

9. See Eugene Jacobson, "Research in Institution Building, Lessons from the Field," prepared for the Committee on Institutional Cooperation—AID Conference on Institution Building Overseas, French Lick, Indiana, August 1968 (mimeo).

10. Its utility has been further confirmed by the extensive output of the Committee on Institutional Cooperation, which used the IB model to examine the uses of technical assistance in building agricultural research and educational institutions overseas. The main findings of this research enterprise appear in its summary report: *Building Institutions to Serve Agriculture,* Purdue University, 1968. Some of its more significant findings are included in J. A. Rigney, J. K. McDermott, and R. W. Roselley, "Strategies in Technical Assistance," Technical Bulletin 189, North Carolina, Agricultural Experiment Station, December 1968.

INSTITUTION BUILDING AS VISION AND VENTURE: A CRITIQUE

WILLIAM J. SIFFIN

U.S. Agency for International Development

WILLIAM J. SIFFIN is Director of the Office of Development Administration of the United States Agency for International Development in Washington. He is on leave from his regular academic post as Professor of Political Science at Indiana University. He has been a member of the Board of Directors of the Inter-University Research Program in Institution Building and served as its Chairman for several years. He has written extensively on institutional change and social, and economic development, especially in Thailand, where he served between 1957 and 1960. His most recent publication, with W. G. Thrombley, deals with *Thailand: Politics, Economy and Social Cultural Setting—A Selected Guide to the Literature,* Bloomington: Indiana University Press, 1971.

INSTITUTION BUILDING AS VISION AND VENTURE: A CRITIQUE

WILLIAM J. SIFFIN

U.S. Agency for International Development

The institution-building perspective is presented as the outline of a strategy of directed social change: "Innovations should . . . be conceived as *induced social changes*. . . . Institution-building is thus a double-barreled activity. Change agents must both (a) build technically . . . and socially effective organizations as the vehicles for innovations; and (b) they must manage relationships (linkages) with other organizations and groups on whom they depend for support and whose behavior they are attempting to influence. Building viable organizations and managing their linkages are closely interrelated aspects of a single institution-building process."[1] Institution building is described as "a generic model of induced change . . . [one that] . . . comprises a very large number of technical assistance activities."[2]

INSTITUTION BUILDING AS AN ARGUMENT ABOUT PERSPECTIVE

What follows is an effort to put the perspective in perspective—to examine and assess the institution-building argument, and to note and consider some of the implications and possible extensions of that argument. "Argument" is an appropriate label for the institution-building perspective. IB argues that (a) technology is a key if not *the* key to development, (b) the establishment of

[43]

effective organizations is the essential instrumental problem of delivering technology, and (c) normative factors are the critical concern in building organizations to deliver technology and its developmental fruits. In short, "institution building" means "organization building"—although it specifies the problem of organization building in an unconventional way.

The conventional literature on organization has dealt with such issues as efficiency, rationality, and manageability, reflecting concern with "best ways" to specialize, integrate, and make organization work. It has addressed the problems of decision-making under conditions of complexity and indeterminacy, and of inducing participants to behave appropriately. In the broad reaches of this literature there is also considerable attention to organization-environment relations. The "theory of the firm" is a theory of the economic interactions of organizations and their environments; "the politics of bureaucracy" labels efforts to study the claim-making and behavior-inducing activities of public sector organizations. Yet much of the knowledge of organization-environment relations to be found in economics, political science, sociology, and anthropology has been systematically ignored in a variety of organization-building efforts—for understandable reasons.

The problem of those who would create organizations is in part the usual one of "finding relatively simple descriptions for complex systems."[3] In the real world of satisfycing behavior, one prime source of solutions to this problem is experience. A complex problem can often be attacked by reducing it to the equivalent of a problem previously solved. The lessons of past experience shape the selection of what matters and what does not. As long as the problem at hand falls into the class of situations to which that experience applies, well and good. The difficulty arises when the established perspective fails to serve its intended end—when the case to which it is applied falls outside the established class. Sometimes this is discovered only retrospectively, and at considerable cost.

The institution-building perspective holds that the conventional experience-based simplifications about organization building are inadequate and misleading guides to social change efforts. They ignore crucial considerations. They fail to take account of the normative aspects of organization-environment relations. The perspective is formally divided into two general elements—a set of statements about intrinsic features of an organization, and another about "linkages." But the whole view reduces to a set of concerns with the latter—i.e., with getting appropriate qualities instilled within the organization, given their absence in the environment and their inconsistency with environmental qualities, and otherwise engaging in appropriate transactions with that environment. The IB "problem," then, is in the final analysis a problem of organization-environment relations.

How is it that tried-and-true perspectives for specifying organizational problems in the West, renowned as they are for their organizational attributes, do not seem to fit the needs of development? And why is it that fuller use has not been made of some of the established lodes of knowledge of the interactions of organizations and their settings?

It is an administered age."[4] Organization itself is a potent institutional feature of our modern cultures. By and large, our prevalent kinds of organizations swim like fish in compatible culture-rivers. Congenial values have been well institutionalized in a rich and supple range of supportive structures. Together, institutional and other ecological circumstances have afforded nigh unique capacities to organize. In the United States even crime gets organized— the fullest flowering of illicit endeavors occurs in enterprises that use the conventional tools for promoting efficiency, rationality, and responsibility.

Given this ambience, the perceived problems of organizations have not much been "institution-building" problems. More often than not, they have been those of tinkering, adjusting, and sometimes even radically reforming organizations or sets thereof into an appropriate compatibility with hallowed culture themes. In the enterprise sector, such problems have to a considerable extent been met through the working of market forces. In the public sector, unending efforts are made to bring bureaucracy to heel by appeal to the virtuous trinity of efficiency, economy, and responsibility, through the application of an organizational-managerial technology that has grown relentlessly since those first portentous shovellings at the Midvale steel plant in 1880. Until recently there have been no intensely felt needs for bringing forth organizations to thrive in culturally hostile, alien settings.

The developmental efforts of the past twenty years, initially in the "new nations" but increasingly within some of the so-called developed countries, have stirred such needs. The simplifications that have generally worked in places such as the United States do not work in a lot of other places, or even here, when people try to deal with the problems of creating certain kinds of organizations to induce change. The institution-building perspective is one response to this frustration. It is an effort to provide a relatively simple description of a class of situations that fall outside a long-established category.

The institution-building perspective draws selectively, adaptively, and implicitly from some of the established middenheaps of knowledge about organizations and their environments. An immediate antecedent is Philip Selznick's brief discussion of the somewhat elusive idea of the valuing of an organization "for itself," as distinguished from its "value" or utility as a substitutable instrument.[5] The institution-building formulation does not use the term "institution" precisely as did Talcott Parsons when he wrote of "generalized patterns of norms which define categories of prescribed, permitted, and prohibited behavior in social relationships, for people in interaction with each other as members of their society and its various subsystems and groups."[6] But this is the kernel of the concern of the institution builders. They see the task of organization building for social change as one of getting appropriate patterns of norms established in a specified field of action.

From the institution-building perspective, these patterns include much more than the norms embedded in a particular technology per se. Presumably the place of technology in the organization-and-environment view of IB is that initially sketched by Talcott Parsons and powerfully elaborated by James Thompson.[7] In this plausible perspective technologies are not invariably self-institutionalizing As John D. Montgomery has observed: "Introducing new technologies into the less-developed countries has proven to be a task beyond the capabilities of technicians alone"[8] —including organizational and managerial technicians. Seeking to redress the inadequacy of a conventional view of the problem of establishing viable organizations, the institution-building perspective has gazed into the waters of sociology to find the tenet that is its core. The result is offered as a more useful "relatively simple description" of those complex systems: organizations made to exist and to foster development in uncongenial—even downright hostile—organizational climates.

About this perspective only one question really matters: how good is it?

Were we to answer that question by appeal to faith or authority, this examination would be briefer than it is. Quite a number of experienced practitioners of the latter-day art of the change agent have said, "It describes my problem." And they have proceeded with exegesis, extension, and exhortation. But this is not enough. Validation by faith suffers from the fact, among others, that some supporters can be found for almost any view. We know that the devotees of institution building are a doughty band of doers who have found other simplifications of their problem inadequate. Unless and until the IB perspective is clearly found to fail them, they are by force of circumstance predisposed to be supportive. We shall therefore apply our own tests. To begin, it will be useful to say just what the institution-building perspective is, and something about what it is not.

IB AS THEORY

Institution building is not a theory (save in the loosest and most metaphorical sense of that much maligned word). One useful conventional conceptualization of a theory is that of "an empirical generalization"—a general statement of some regular, predictable relationships between two or more types of things.[9] Newton's generalization about gravitation is an example. This broad and basic statement, this axiom, explains a lot of things, including Galileo's law about the behavior of falling bodies, which is one of the statements that can be deduced from Newton's theory. The Newtonian theory and its derivations explain countless individual occurrences that are the instances of a general pattern of observable regularity. The institution-building perspective does not explain institutionality as a quality related to some other quality or qualities in a regular, determinate (or probabilistic) fashion that can be observed.

The perspective holds that there is something that can be labelled "institutionality." It asserts that this quality can be a feature of organizations viewed as open systems. It notes that to achieve this valued quality, the "right kind" of leadership, linkages, and so forth, must be had. The perspective does appear to posit certain relationships as if they were interacting variables to be staked out and perhaps reduced to determinateness. But calling the elements of the institution-building perspective "variables" is more a figure of speech. They are the broad and general labels of qualities, relationships, and categories of action. Empirical referents cannot be delineated in a neat, discrete fashion to sustain a systematic examination and precise analysis of their interaction.

The phenomena addressed by institution building are of a different class than the materials of the physical sciences. This is not to deny that assumptions about regularity and interaction can readily apply to social phenomena. Nor is it to deny the possibility of theorizing about institutionalization. All that is being claimed is that there is a difference between "as if" statements and "if/then" statements; and that statements about institution building, formulated as if they were theoretical, are not necessarily the sort of "if/then" statements that do proffer a certain kind of explanation—a theoretical explanation.

In use, the IB perspective is apt to be self-fulfilling—i.e., the outcomes of efforts described in institution-building terms can be retrospectively explained as manifestations of adequacies or inadequacies in the elements and relations that make up the perspective. Viz, "Institutionalization did not occur because the leadership was maladroit." If this means that an organization-building goal was not achieved, and that some people in leadership roles were dunderheads, and that there seems to be a prima facie relationship between these two particular events—then nothing is added to an understanding of the situation by describing it in institution-building terms. Rather, this is but one of several ways to tell what happened. The choice of one particular language or set of labels in preference to another does not necessarily add to the power of an explanation.

If institution building were an empirical theory, it would necessarily include indices of "institutionalization"—the discrete state or condition that is intended to be attained through a certain quality of intervention. But the IB literature is not clear and precise on this point. It offers a debatable set of stipulations, along with some latitude for choice. In the absence of a clear and unequivocal index of the state to be achieved by the appropriate interaction of the variables, it is rather obviously impossible to subject the theory to the test of validation—or falsification.

Institution building involves too many possible kinds of interaction among too many complex and elusive variables to be evolvable into a relatively general theory—one with explicit rules by which to operationalize its variables to analyze a specifiable class of phenomena.

These observations do not seek to fault a sow because it is not a silk purse. Sows, like "explanation sketches," can be eminently useful things, provided they are understood for what they are and for what they are not. The utility of the institution-building perspective does not depend on its proclamation as a potent and parsimonious theory. It does depend in part upon an understanding of the nature of the perspective, lest false expectations be made of it. Theory is the admissible and appropriate objective of general explanation-oriented scholarship, and theory building is not to be knocked in principle. But systematic empirical theory is only one type of tool for the problem and solution-seeking efforts that compel the men of action who do not live by theory alone. Many of the interesting and some of the crucial questions are simply (or otherwise) not susceptible to solutions drawn directly from tested and demonstrated theory, and this will probably always be the case. Only simple-minded men will yearn to attack such situations through some magic theory that would print out concrete plans of action by which to immutably and artlessly transform given circumstances into other more desirable circumstances.

If the IB perspective is to have power, that power must stem from its use by reasoning, analytical, and adroit individuals. The IB perspective is explanatorily sterile—but this does not keep it from being suggestive. It possesses what Anatole Rapoport has called "explanatory appeal."[10] The source of this explanatory appeal lies in a sense of recognition—"the transformation of something unexpected into something expected."[11]

IB AS A MODEL: QUALITIES AND LIMITATIONS

The appeal of the IB perspective stems from the uncertainty consciously faced by the organization-building change agent. If he is aware of the need to map a novel task-environment, he will want a tool for identifying what matters and what does not matter. He will seek the perceptual foci and the filters that promise to produce a manageably simplified view of an empirically inchoate condition.

In other words, he will seek a *model* of some sort. At the least this will be a static analogy, allowing him to pick out the apparently relevant elements of his situation. If it is a more powerful dynamic model, it will not only identify salient circumstances; it will indicate at least some of the ways in which they interact.

> "Each of us uses models constantly. Every person in his private life and in his business life instinctively uses models for decision making. The mental image of the world around you which you carry in your head is a model. . . . A mental image [of any kind] is a model. All of our laws are passed on the basis of models. All executive actions are taken on the basis of models. The question is not to use or ignore models. The question is only a choice among alternative models."[12]

There is also another question about models—an important question about their intrinsic qualities.[13]

A "model" may be to a practitioner as a "heurism" is to a scholar. A heurism is not a theory and a heurism is not "true." It is a speculative statement that lays out a set of categories in terms of which to attempt to perceive and analyze phenomena of interest. A heurism per se is intended to specify no innate empirical or ontological commitment. It is a lens as distinguished from the things that may be seen through a lens. A workable heurism leads to hypotheses, and hypotheses—which do have empirical content—can be tested. This, in turn, can lead to valid new knowledge.

A model may be a heurism in this sense, or it may not. A heuristic model consists of a set of categories, abstract labels of classes of things, and some formal statements about them, in terms of which to mediate certain desired encounters with reality. It is the medium, not the message, in a logic of inquiry wherein the utmost effort is made to separate the two. If the model short-circuits the gap between instrument of analysis and object of analysis, it becomes an a priori "explanation" of an intended object of inquiry and is no longer a heurism in the pure sense of that term.

Admittedly, significant philosophical problems lurk in this logic of inquiry. But when the aim of the intended game is careful and systematic explanation, a basic rule of that game is to maintain a distinction between the instruments and the objects of inquiry.

This is where practitioner-oriented models usually vary from heurisms. Practical models commonly contain sets of premises that intend to say something about empirical features of a relevant field of reality, such as a task environment. They may at the same time contain pure heuristic elements. Thus, logically speaking, practical models can be real bastards. This does not necessarily make them bad, but it can make them tricky things to use. Even in an age that does not subscribe to guilt by ancestry, it is important to know the relevant qualities of our tools—because of the effects they can have. Inadequate heurisms may only send their scholarly perpetrators back to the drawing board, bad models can have unfortunate effects on the lives of people.

The fact that practical models mix heuristic and hypothetical elements does not make them automatically bad. It does make them dangerous, simply because they contain unassessed (and in a sense unidentified) elements of a priori explanation. They are loaded but not tested, so the buyer had better beware.

Change agents, however, must take what tools they can get. As practical souls, motivated to find, analyze, and attack concrete problems with beneficial consequences, they are less concerned with logical purity than with efficacious action. Their modeling exercises tend to be as practical as possible, and their images are to a considerable degree drawn from experience. The endless quest for practical models goes a long way toward explaining the "Sarawak syndrome," the incessant tendency of practitioners of the change agent role to exchange accounts of their endeavors. Ego may impel the raconteurs, but at least some of the listeners are interested in acquiring, refining, or validating the pragmatic lore upon which they draw to form their own models.

The most vivid and compelling examples of lore building and lore transfer are, interestingly enough, found in traditional societies. Thus a recent study of

Eskimos explores the oral tradition by which Eskimo survival is sustained.[14] During long winter nights, hunting stories are swapped and the lessons embedded in an ancestral legacy are passed down across the generations. Vital and hard-won information is assessed and transmitted. A coherent core of knowledge is maintained and adapted within a viable institutional framework—the framework of a community living consciously on close terms with ever-possible disaster, and nurturing its ability to keep on doing so through mechanisms including the ruthless ridicule of deviance from and disrespect for established norms, and the understandable veneration of those who have managed to become elders. So long as the task environment of the Eskimos remains more or less congruent with their model, their prospects for survival seem good. The lore-seeking change agent, alas, has no comparable institutional base. And his problem is essentially that of coming to terms with a novel task environment, rather than a traditional one.

The problems of the Eskimo and the change agent are poles apart. The Eskimo really has no modeling problem. Long before self-conscious social science, the Eskimo world achieved a viable means for mediating and managing its encounters with the given realities. The change agent, on the other hand, is faced with the need for figuring out what the system is and what he might do to rearrange it.

The lore of the Eskimo is validated in the way that matters most—by the continuing survival of the Eskimo. The same cannot be said of would-be change agents. Their continuing presence reflects the sensed existence of some needs, more than anything else. That they accumulate and exchange lore in the form of practical models is likewise more a manifestation of need than an assurance that what they say is valid. Neither the established credentials nor the earnest discourse of blind philosophers make them good sources of knowledge of the nature of the elephant. The artist's discourse on his art is not the practice of that art. Unless he has access to a mediating symbolism that both delineates and conveys the import of his efforts, he will not manage to say much about the thing he does, and how and why he does it.

Hence the quest for other, better solutions to the modeling problem. For the qualities of the models that men use to manage their encounters with reality are the prime boundaries of their ability to deliberately modify that reality. If hunch and intuition and unvalidated "parallels" are the chief sources of the views of change agents, then efforts to build organizations for development are bound to be matters of art, luck, and perhaps a bit of magic. These are all too often not enough.

From the practitioner view, the institution-building perspective offer the appeal of a promising model, a new and better lens through which to see what needs to be seen. Part of this appeal is exactly the sort of which Rapoport speaks—the appeal that comes from the naming of things to make them seem familiar, understandable, and manageable. For change agent, the perspective surfaces and spells out perceptions that he has himself sensed in a more implicit, less deliberate manner. This response is one source of validation for the model—the validation of credence and credibility.

The IB perspective does more. It offers a certain amount of information about its elements—some knowledge of how leadership works, some thoughts of what doctrine is (not much, but enough to set the customer thinking and thus perhaps to shape some working premises of his own). Most of all, it tells him something about linkages, offering a broad functional typology and thus a set of categories in terms of which to order empirical information as well as judgments and decisions.

As a practical model, the institution-building perspective has a number of notable characteristics. It is static. It is a priori. It is unoriented. And it is generally focused upon solution-seeking concerns.

A Static Model. The perspective is static in the sense that it identifies a set of topical areas without (a) saying how they are interrelated, or (b) saying what to do about the respective categories. The perspective does, of course, claim that its categories intend to encompass the necessary and sufficient concerns of the institution/organization builder, and in that gross sense the model posits that all its categories are interacting. Each presumably affects the others.

Each of the categories amounts to a statement that "Here is something you had better do something about." The IB perspective is essentially static, however, in the sense that it does not say what to do—how to fulfill the implicit categorical imperative, or how to determine when an action meets some standard of the necessary and sufficient.

This staticity is an inevitable consequence of the generality of the perspective. As a generic model it aims to cover a vast range of possible circumstances. The empirical referents of its global categories are larger than the varieties of Elizabeth Barrett Browning's love for her poet husband. The ways of their working, assuming one does solve the problem of applying the categories to particular phenomena, approach infinity. The model has no choice but to be static.

An A Priori Model. The institution-building perspective is an a priori view. It did not evolve, was not built, by the sifting, sorting, and aggregating of large numbers of cases or experiences. Because its categories were not evolved in this fashion, they are not capable of being justified by reference to the evidence. As noted earlier, the IB perspective is something of a synthesis of the lessons of pragmatic experience and certain sociological concepts. In this sense, it might be termed a synthetic model. It is in any case more a model "before the fact" than "after the fact," as suggested by the concerns of those who built it with testing to see if it could indeed be used to marshal data and to generate interpretations and explanations.

An Unoriented Model. The model is unoriented in that it does not specify the circumstances of its applicability. This statement does require qualification: the institution-building perspective claims applicability to the broad group of cases involving the creation of purposive, non-voluntary organizations for social change objectives. The IB perspective is offered to would-be change agents for whom the task of building an organization is a given. Under such conditions, it can be argued that there is no need for specifying the model's limits of relevance—it applies to all the cases in which it is intended for use, or in which there are likely to be users. In this simple sense, its relevance and the limits thereof are given, and thus the model is oriented.

But this is too simplistic. Unless all the cases in which change agents set out to build organizations are without question instances in which the IB perspective fits the task environment, then there is an inescapable question of orientation—a question that asks: "By what test can one tell if IB is the right lens for viewing and interpreting the situation?"

A variant of this question is: "How can I tell if 'institution building' is likely to work?" From the practitioner's viewpoint, this is an entirely admissible query, to which the model does not speak. In this sense the IB perspective is unoriented. It does not include a specification of the limiting conditions of its pertinence. And there are a number of interesting questions about this pertinence. They include the possibility that alternative models of a social-change task environment might apply. After all, institutionalization is not necessarily a linear process. Assertions to the effect that the right or sufficient amounts and qualities of leadership, doctrine, structure, linkages, and so forth, will invariably lead to an institutionalized outcome are not entirely persuasive. It can even be argued that, under certain conditions, institutionalization itself might be an undesirable outcome of an effort to inculcate a technology into an environment as a means of development. The model, as explicated, acknowledges this, in part, by its emphasis upon a certain kind of institutionalization— that of adaptive and innovative organizations. It does not, however, specify how this particular sort of outcome can be differentially pursued in institution-building efforts, and notes that here is a problem and a danger.

A Prescriptive Model. The institution-building model avoids the false allure of magic formulae. Its static and general qualities keep it quite free of procedures and routines. Claiming to offer a valid and useful view of a broad class of situations, the institution-building perspective does not really promise success in dealing with any one of them. Yet the model does not have a perscriptive cast—a solution-seeking and solution-specifying orientation. At the last, one might say it is proto-prognostic. It is, in other words, somewhat loaded.

At the outset the IB view posits that purposive, non-voluntary organizations with certain technical and normative features are the generally necessary means to the improvement of a wide variety of conditions. It also posits institution/ organization building as a relatively linear process, and one that can be deliberately rational. Its deus ex machina is the change agent, that manager-entrepreneur of the process by whom and through whom the developmental process is seen and steered. Finally, the perspective proffers a set of categories—categories of action, the things about which something must be done. These become the categories within which praxiological knowledge is to be acquired, for use in "doing it." Some of the problems or difficulties inherent in this prescriptive bent have been mentioned in the above discussion of the chief characteristics of the IB model.

The Residual Question of Utility. This litany of limitations is not an implicit argument that the institution-building perspective is no good. It is an argument that, like practically everything else, institution building is something of limited utility. Understanding the limitations can help enhance the value of what remains. It has been said that, "There is no lie so foul as an ill-stated problem." The institution-building perspective is neither foul lie nor fair verity. [15] It can be either. Which it shall be depends upon a number of things—notably the limitations of the model, and the ways in which they are honored and/or overcome. Unacknowledged, they are likely to be neither honored nor overcome.

In the final analysis, the value of any model such as this will always be affected by subjective factors—by the intelligence and discernment of its users, not to mention some luck. The problem of modeling is not, and is not ever going to be, one of "programming the world" to eliminate the need for interpretation and judgment. Good models do not supplant the driver; they do remove his blindfold and sharpen his vision.

PRACTICAL USES OF THE PRACTICAL MODEL

A full appreciation of the institution-building perspective requires something more than an analysis of its intrinsic features; the actual and potential uses of the perspective must also be considered.

As the bibliography in this book indicates, the institution-building model has been put to practical use. It has been applied in descriptions and evaluations of organization-building efforts and in quests for lessons about the processes and circumstances of institutionalized organization building. These applications are the practical payoffs from the practical uses of an intendedly practical model. They need to be assessed, both for their immediate utility, and for clues to ways to build upon what has been done so far.

In Case Studies. Some years ago this writer used the institution-building perspective as the framework of a study of the development of the Thai Institute of Public Administration over a period of about ten years. [16] The IB view generated the central set of questions explored in the case—questions about an avowed effort to build an organization with certain desired institutional features: what did get institutionalized; what particular set of interacting factors seemed to explain how and why; and what tentative lessons might be drawn from the analyzed experience?

The study was an analytical history of a particular case. With some exceptions the procedures for "operationalizing" the key terms in the IB perspective were also specific to the given enterprise, although generally established conventions were used to describe such factors as organization structure and leadership. The study turned out to be relatively satisfying—to the author, at any rate. It dealt with some questions that might have been overlooked in the absence of the perspective. And it generated a few interesting hypotheses that could have been explored in a relatively general fashion. In short, the IB view was a useful practical tool for a relatively simple and straightforward inquiry. Its value did not stem from the power of a systematic methodology of institution-building analysis; it derived from the questions that the IB perspective posed, and the answers that were sought and to some extent found.

In Analyzing Development Strategy. The institution-building perspective was recently used as one of the tools of a broad and trenchant analysis of the results of United States assistance to agricultural extension services in Central and South America.[17] The author, Edward Rice, asked: Had the efforts resulted in "viable" extension institutions? He concluded that they had not. About a quarter-century after the work of assistance began, in settings where governmental services are never well off, "extension is probably in worse shape than any other." Rice found that the extension services had developed favorable attitudes among their diffuse client populations and among the interested professionals. But they built no strong working links with other institutions— "really an incredible situation." He offers a succinct description and an acute explanation of how this came about. He notes that the American advisors who helped establish the organizations certainly had a clear sense of doctrine, and that this doctrine became something of an ideology within the indigenous leadership. But that doctrine was not really translated into an effective program, for the program was process- rather than purpose-oriented, and it was utterly defective in its provisions for evaluation and training.

Rice looked into the matter of leadership. He found it difficult "to get a good hold on this variable, since . . . visits with the leaders were too short to form impressions about their political viability, professional status, technical competence and organizational competence, all of which are elements of leadership emphasized in the IB model." On one count, he found the leadership impressive—continuity. He found the services had little or no autonomy of control over resources, but lots of autonomy in programming their activities—a circumstance that seemed more of a liability than an asset, for it was the autonomy of organizations without working interdependencies, in circumstances where effectiveness depends upon such linkages.

The key to Rice's assessment is suggested, if not summed, in this statement: "The extension school seems to have gotten hooked on a method, rather than on the objective." The critical question, from this view, is not one about institutionalizing something, but rather about what something ought to be institutionalized. Exploring this question is beyond the capability of the IB perspective as it stands.

Rice concludes: "The attempt to build extension institutions in the study area appears not to have been successful. Part of the reason is because the institution building process was poorly designed and executed. Part of the reason is because the extension process, as conceived in the 1940's and 1950's, should not have been institutionalized at all in most of the twelve countries." In reaching these conclusions, the IB perspective gave Rice some targets of inquiry, some categories within which to make judgments, and some general guides to those judgments. IB served useful, if limited purposes. For the more fundamental facet of his analysis, Rice could not get guidance from the institution-building view, because it is not equipped to handle the sorts of questions he had to ask—questions about the relevance and utility of a given kind of institution/ organization as a vehicle of developmental change in a particular setting.[18] This particular practical limitation illustrates a finding of the earlier intrinsic analysis of the model.

In Training Change Agents. The institution-building view has also been used as a guide by change agents, and as a framework for training people who create and run developmental organizations. It has, in other words, been applied in pedagogic and praxiological efforts to inform and sensitize operators, as well as in research.

A good example of this sort of application is found in the *Report On The Asian Agricultural College and University Seminar* issued by North Carolina State University, Raleigh, after a seminar in Thailand and India in the fall of 1970. The key participants were twenty-four Asians from ten countries—ranking officers of agricultural colleges and universities and of ministries of agriculture and education. There were also five observers from international agencies. The relevance of the institution-building model to agricultural development was a major theme of the meetings.[19]

The seminar's leaders saw the model as a means of focusing the attention of participants upon important problems and issues. According to the report, "The reaction to the model on institution building was one of genuine appreciation for an analytic outline which permits people to think about the important aspects of institution building in an orderly fashion. It articulated those intuitive feelings about institution building which most administrators develop with experience. It was agreed here, as in various earlier seminars, that there was little new in the model; rather, its uniqueness is in the way it brings ideas together in an understandable fashion."[20]

Within the IB framework, the participants talked about leadership styles and procedures, about student participation, and about doctrine. "Thus, the Land Grant Model was accepted by the participants almost universally as the modern, innovative and productive doctrine in building institutions to serve agriculture."[21] Under the IB category of program they explored a series of problems of relating teaching, research, and extension. They discussed the internal structural problems of personnel administration, as well as ubiquitous resource problems. "The term 'linkages' became a useful addition to everyone's vocabulary almost from the first day of the Seminar," and a lot of linkage problems were examined. "Many questions were asked about the cooperation between university and farmers or farm groups, and the influence this cooperation has on public support. The direct farmer contact that was in evidence, both at the U.P. Agricultural University and the Punjab Agricultural University, provided strong evidence that this is a necessary source of support in any cultural setting."[22]

In concluding the conferees agreed that the institution-building perspective was one of the most important things they had learned from the seminar. It had led them to "a renewed understanding of the importance of the linkages among the institutions serving agriculture, particularly those dealing with teaching, research and extension," and it had provided an "opportunity to see different administrative patterns for encouraging and strengthening these linkages and for integrating them into the common service of the rural people."[23] And the seminar was judged a success.

It is not exactly easy to present a detached and discerning perspective on this pedagogic and indoctrinational use of the institution-building approach, for the circumstances and characteristics of such application are not simple. The justification for the approach might be put in these terms:

> The agricultural organizations represented in the seminar, and others like them, are crucial contributors to development. Those organizations have all sorts of problems—problems that can be identified, described, and assessed in institution-building terms. It is imperative that the leaders understand those problems and develop strategies for managing them.
>
> In practice, the individual problems are complicated and tricky. There is obviously no general formula for solving them. But they can't be solved at all unless they are understood; and the IB perspective is a useful tool for promoting that understanding. It provides a set of categories; we can use them to help impose order on what would otherwise be an overwhelmingly confused and inchoate universe. More than that, we can use these categories to put the focus on the *right* factors—factors that appear to affect the fulfillment of commitments to the building of organizations for social change. Thus we can avoid diversions into misleading and irrelevant problem definitions.
>
> More than this one can hardly ask. For our purposes the fact that the perspective is explanatorily sterile is irrelevant. So is the fact that the perspective is "unoriented." We get our orientation from the shared concerns of the participants, and from our interest in the land grant college as the key instrument to be promoted. The generally prescriptive orientation of the model is quite appropriate to our aims;

and the fact that it's an a priori model is irrelevant—unless you can furnish us with a better model more substantially based upon evidence.

Finally, for us the sheer simplicity of the IB perspective is a source of strength. In a limited pedagogic exercise we can only do so much—and not very much at that. A seminar like this can only make a broad and simple cut into a problem area, with the hope that the participants will move further and deeper into their own analyses as they shape their own strategies. Anyone who would fault the institution-building perspective as we have used it must fail to understand the nature of our efforts, the limited utility, for our purposes, of esoteric academic analysis, and the vast constraints that face us in our attempts to accomplish something in the resistant atmosphere of the real world.

A PRACTICAL RESPONSE TO THE PRACTICAL
PROBLEMS AND OPPORTUNITIES

These are honorable and appealing arguments. They are the arguments of people for whom the earlier sections of this paper seem turgid, tendentious and tangential—a tangle of academic pontifications that simply do not say much to the laborer in the vineyard. Yet certain significant difficulties are involved in—and related to—these practical arguments in favor of the existing institution-building perspective. The difficulties should be noted. They point out needs and offer opportunities to enhance and enlarge our useful knowledge of institution building as a potential social change strategy. Here are the important difficulties embedded in the efforts at practical applications of the existing institution-building perspective, along with their implications:

First, there is the problem of saying more about linkages. As a pedagogic and would-be praxiological device, the practical application of the linkage aspect of the IB perspective does demonstrate more explanatory appeal than explanatory power. It calls to mind the voluptuous young lady who knocks on your door, enters, and then only wants to sell you a new model of a toothbrush, when you already have a lot of toothbrushes.

The participants in the Asian Seminar quickly latched onto the word "linkages," and felt it a most useful word. They then used it to label a number of quite familiar problems, and it does not appear that they said much that is new about those problems. Yet we must grant that the IB perspective's disaggregation of the idea of linkages into four types may well have stirred the participants to more discerning thinking about their linkage problems, thus moving them one step toward better managing those problems. The evidence is not clear, and one can always be hopeful.

But one who would be hopeful had better be careful. The participants agreed that direct farmer contact for the developing country's agricultural university "is a necessary source of support in any cultural setting." This judgment is unsustained by the specific evidence that was presented to support it. As long as it remains unqualified and unelaborated it is an ingenuous observation, a leap from IB's prefatory linkage statements to a generalization that papers over complex and differential biases about the roles and linkages of Asian (and other) agricultural schools in the extension function.

Whether or not this leap did occur is not so important as the fact that it *can* occur, given the explanatory limitations of the existing institution-building model. If the model is to be used practically, to talk about real-world problems, it must be made better by filling in the relatively empty boxes labelled "linkages" with certain important knowledge.

Some of it would inform us about strategies for mapping and making linkages. This knowledge addresses the ways in which task environment characteristics affect linkage planning and strategy. This knowledge also gives us practical understanding of the kinds of environmental conditions that make certain kinds of linkages sensible in the first place. A tangible (and tentative) example of what I have in mind is the above-cited work of Hunter. It presents interesting hypotheses about the feasibility of certain kinds of linkages under given task-environment conditions or stages of agricultural development. Hunter's hypotheses may be debatable, but his approach is compelling. The fruit of this kind of knowledge is explanatory power to back up the explanatory appeal of the linkage element of the institution-building perspective. Without such knowledge the initially elevated expectations of the recipients of the model may soon fade to disenchantment. Also, as things now stand, talk about linkages can inspire logical leaps into ignorant assertions about what ought to be. The existing practical model does open the door to more perceptive thinking about organizational problems of development. The need is to illuminate the room inside.

Second, the problem just mentioned is one aspect of a larger practical problem of the perspective—one that can be attacked with large prospects for success. It is the problem of moving the model from a gross prescriptive "it will work" orientation toward one that explores and more fully states the conditions under which it is likely to work—or not. To assume that there are conditions under which institution-building efforts are likely to succeed is both plausible and wise. Knowledge of those conditions is imperative to improving the model as a practical model. Quite a bit of that knowledge is available. Essays into this area have been made in the work of Rigney and associates that examines aspects of the strategy and tactics of change agent interventions, in the Pooler article in this volume, and elsewhere. These efforts offer valuable lessons.

Others would flow from the linkage analyses suggested above. But linkage questions and questions about change agent strategies do not begin to exhaust the needs. There is an interesting set of questions about technology—questions about ways in which, and circumstances under which, various kinds of technologized activities are prone to institutionalization. Technologies have output specifications and performance norms embedded in them. As noted earlier, there is clear evidence that technologies are not self-institutionalizing: they do not automatically transfer from one setting to another. But the degree to which an activity is technologically centered in all likelihood does affect the probability of its being institutionalized as an organized effort at social change. The ways in which this works will be affected by intrinsic characteristics of given technologies, intrinsic characteristics of particular kinds of task environments, and the possible relations between them.

The needed studies will never tell us of the inherent goodness or badness of any particular institution-building social change strategy. The institution-building perspective is inherently and inately instrumental; assigning values to social goals will always be beyond its competence. Institution-building premises will never settle arguments about the desirability of building land-grant-type agricultural colleges. But a developed and dynamic model can provide knowledge for *some* of the judgments that must be made about social change goals and strategies. Information about the probable feasibility or infeasibility of given aims can reduce the number of efforts that turn out badly simply because they did not stand a chance of working.

People do promote institution building, so it is essential that the gross prescriptive bias of the existing model be refined. As things stand, the practitioner who claims knowledge of institution building, who professes to use it, and who fails, may be unduly indicted for the disaster. It might not have been his fault, for his tool is not very sharp. Even so, the fullest imaginable development of the institution-building model will only reduce indeterminacy. An institution-building effort involves the establishment and operation of a rather novel open system, one that is subject to a host of exogenous influences, some of which are bound to be fortuitous and unpredictable.

Third, one more problem—one very real danger—must be noted in considering the practical use and development of the institution-building perspective. This is the danger that the perspective, as a rather general but unoriented solution to a large but not delineated set of problems, may capture the game by winning the struggle to define the problem in solution-seeking circumstances wherein the institution-building specification turns out to be wrong. This danger is inherent in the combination of two things: the inherent qualities of the present model, plus the ways in which it can be put to practical use.

The practical arguments that have been offered in support of the existing institution-building model are the powerful arguments of men with a mission. If they have faith that moves mountains, they also know that faith without works is nothing, and that works require tools. Institutional building is a tool.

Effective men of faith have achieved monumental results. But men of faith and good will have also perpetrated some monumental disasters and even greater numbers of less spectacular failures. Their visions are usually simple, sometimes faulty, and always grievously difficult of a priori validation. The current institution-building perspective does not address this validation problem. The most it could ever do would be to address and answer questions about probable feasibility. It is a purely instrumental perspective.

But it is an instrument that does not now specify the conditions and limitations of its use. And it is a problem-oriented instrument—one that sketches or at least suggests a praxiology, a line of solution-serving action.

Men of good will, men of action, men impelled to do something about some of the problems of the world, practical men with an intuitive sense of the utility of institution building—such men are entirely capable of powerful assaults on the goal-setting and resource-allocating mechanisms of the world—with unpredictable consequences, some of which are bound to be unfortunate. The Rice study of extension in the Andes is an illustration of what can happen, and there is much other evidence. The existing state of institution-building knowledge might have reduced the likelihood of the Latin American misfortune, but not very much.

To this problem there are three lines of response. The first and most immediate is to realize the limitations of the current state of the institution-building perspective. The second is to systematically identify and develop knowledge about institution-building processes and strategies. The third is to produce strategically useful knowledge about alternative interventions for social change—knowledge of other positive developmental strategies.

This third point is vital. Without work of this sort, effective practical decisions to use the institution-building approach can only be made with a fuzzy awareness of the alternatives. Just as there are task environments in the real world that must be understood in plotting and pursuing deliberate developmental strategies, there is a social change strategy knowledge environment. The institution-building perspective is but one element of that environment, an element whose meaning and utility much depends upon our ability to assess it in comparison with others.

Practical pursuit of this third response does not require a shotgun approach to all the conceivable strategies. Promising lines of inquiry proceed rather directly from the point at which we are today. One is to look at institutionalization that occurs in other ways than direct institution-building interventions. An example in Glynn Wood's brief study of "Educational Entrepreneurship in India: A Study of Institution Building in a Transitional Society."[24] He found that the growth of higher educational organizations in Mysore outran Indian plan targets as a result of forces that were certainly not programmed, and with somewhat appalling consequences. This sort of phenomenon is an essential subject for analysis and a promising source of lessons. Work currently being done by S. N. Eisenstadt at Hebrew University, Jerusalem, may offer a useful framework for such study. Eisenstadt examining institution building in processes of Modernization, with field studies in Malaysia and the Philippines, to probe the ways in which the aims, characteristics, and resources of different social groups affect tendencies toward modernizing institutional development.

Also on the periphery of the current institution-building perspective are concerns with "the institutional infrastructure of development." Institution building has so far focused upon the building of an organization. It can and should be oriented within the context of a concern for interacting sets of organizations. It should also evolve multidimensional perspectives to take account of networks of organizations and the institutional themes that run through them, sustain them, and affect them in other ways. The idea is not new, but a systematic approach to its content and ramifications is needed. A recent essay by Melvin G. Blaise, "The Role of Institutions in Agricultural Development," briefly addresses this topic;[25] and the entire book containing his work seeks to present the concept of layered institutional interactions and constraints as they affect agricultural development. Studies of salient institutions that are not particular organizations or types of organizations (in the sense that the IB perspective uses the word organization) are also important. The legal institutional apparatus is particularly germane; it impinges upon a vast variety of developmental efforts, and has some direct relevance to practically any kind of enterprise that fits within the compass of the current IB model.[26]

On a related front, Douglas S. Paaw and John C. H. Fei have opened up the argument that "long-run economic development is at least as much a process of improvement of economic agents and their organizational efficiency as it is a matter of increasing supplies of physical factor inputs."[27] It is the implications of this not very novel premise, as explored by Paaw and Fei, that are germane to a broadened orientation to institution building. They argue for the transformation of the vague conceptual apparatus of the institutional economists and its integration with the more systematically analytical approaches employed in economics. The results of their thinking are displayed in *The Transition in Open Dualistic Economies.* [28]

Along with all of this is a need for studying other manageable strategies of social change. Meeting this need involves efforts to build typologies of strategies, then to make them potent by finding out how they work under specified environmental conditions.

There is no end to the visions of what is needed and what might be done. But the guiding principle for expanding the ambit of our knowledge is clear. In the first place, it is to provide an orienting context for understanding and using institution building. Beyond that, it is to enlarge our ability to meet the needs that inspire a concern with institution building in the first place. (If I could lay down one rule to influence such an enterprise, it would be a rule against original research, a rule calling initially for the careful mining and refining of the vast middenheaps of existing relevant knowledge. Only then might the original rule be modified.)

CONCLUSION

The broadest form of the relevant question is: how can better models be developed as the tools of efforts to manage social change—models that afford portentous perspectives on the task environments of social change efforts—so that promising interventionist strategies can be contrived? One subordinate element of this compelling question is: how can better models of institutional development be devised for efforts to manage social change?

The compass of even this lesser question is enormous, although the idea of institutionalization does give it a certain increment of focus. The IB perspective does not address the subject of political development, yet some of the interesting and suggestive literature in this field is conceptualized in institutional terms.[29] Thus Huntington has asserted that the strength of political organization depends upon the amount of its support plus the "level of its institutionalization." By level, he means degree of adaptability, complexity, autonomy, and coherence of organization and procedures; by institutionalization, he means the degree to which entities manifesting some version of these qualities are valued and accepted in a stable fashion. Huntington is striking for a comprehensive portrait of the processes and probabilities of political change. For him, institutionalization is a salient and variable quality of a highly complex state of affairs, and not something deliberately achievable by the wise and conscious efforts of a managing force with considerable control over the system.

The IB perspective is much less ambitious in its concerns than those which would deal with whole systems of society or with their political subsystems. But the ways in which institutionalization is viewed in these studies has a suggestive relevance. It lies in questions such as: how are characteristics of the initial-state conditions likely to affect the possibility that a given (or desired) kind of entity might be institutionalized? This question is addressed by Martin Landau's chapter in this volume. Its further exploration will go a long way toward meeting some of the felt needs of would-be institution builders.

Let us assume that institution building is the name of one of the games. Let us assume too that this means creating viable organizations to hopefully serve social betterment. Finally, let us assume that men of good will have rather compelling drives to play this game. Then, at the very least, let us ask how the existing state of the lore might be improved along two related lines: one is to provide the parties to such games with better perceptions of the task environments in which they might wish to play; the other is to provide them with more discriminating knowledge of the strategies and tactics for playing. If these two lines of inquiry are pursued in tandem, they should cross-fertilize. Strategies can be selected and shaped to fit goals, given the salient features of a task environment; and the crucial features of task environments can guide speculation and the analysis of strategic possibilities. As it stands, the IB perspective begins to address concerns about task environments and strategies. Now we must go further—not to build a science of institution building or any other such foolishness, but to enlarge our capacity to respond to compelling questions about the ways and means of social change.

NOTES

1. Milton Esman, "Institution Building as a Guide to Action," *Proceedings, Conference on Institution Building and Technical Assistance, December 4 and 5, 1969,* Washington, D.C. and Evanston, Ill.: Agency for International Development and Committee on Institutional Cooperation, n.d. pp. 10-11.

2. Ibid., pp. 11-12.

3. Herbert A. Simon, *The Sciences of the Artificial,* Cambridge: M.I.T. Press, 1969, p. 112.

4. John Gardner, *The Recovery of Confidence,* New York: Norton, 1970, p. 28.

5. *Leadership in Administration,* Evanston: Row, Peterson, 1957.

6. *Structure and Process in Modern Societies,* New York: Free Press, 1960, p. 177.

7. *Organizations in Action,* New York: McGraw-Hill, 1967. Thus perceived, an organization has three distinct levels of functions and control—technical, managerial, and institutional. The organization is also seen as an open system, interactive with its environment, faced with uncertainty, but subject to rationality criteria. Such organizations can also be differentiated on the basis of both technology involved and environmental characteristics.

8. "The Challenge of Change," International Development Review, March 1967: 2.

9. There are also formal theories, the tautologies of arithmetic, that do not refer to empirical phenomena, but such theories are patently outside the domain addressed by the institution-building perspective.

10. Anatole Rapoport, "Explanatory Power and Explanatory Appeal of Theories," Ann Arbor: Mental Health Research Institute, University of Michigan, 1968, p. 7.

11. "Explanatory Power and Explanatory Appeal for Theories," Ann Arbor: Mental Health Research Institute, University of Michigan, January 30, 1068. See especially discussion pp. 24-30.

12. Jay W. Forrester, "Counterintuitive Behavior of Social Systems," Technology Review, January 1971: 54.

13. I am indebted to my colleague, Professor Martin Landau, for comments upon which the following observation is based.

14. Richard K. Nelson, *Hunters of the Northern Ice,* Chicago: University of Chicago Press, 1969.

15. It is only fair to note that the IB perspective, as developed in IRPIB, the Inter-university Research Program in Institution Building, was consciously perceived as a priori and tentative as well. The object of that program was to apply and assess the perspective, mostly by using it in case studies. IRPIB fades away, but not before bringing its findings and its pending issues before whatever audience chooses to take them up.

16. W. J. Siffin, "The Thai Institute of Public Administration; A Case Study in Institution Building," Pittsburgh: Inter-university Research Program in Institution Building, 1966 (mimeo).

17. Edward B. Rice, *Extension in the Andes,* Washington, D.C.: U.S. Agency for International Development, 1971.

18. Some of the work of Guy Hunter of the Institute for Overseas Development seeks to move toward a systematic perspective on questions of this sort. Compare his *The Administration of Agricultural Development* Oxford: Oxford University Press, 1970.

19. To quote the *report:* "Specific objectives of the Seminar were to provide for a carefully selected group of Asian agricultural leaders a formal exposure to the newly formulated institution building concepts, and then in a series of visits to Asian institutions to use those concepts as an analytical frame for viewing institutional development strategies and progress." (p. 3)

20. Ibid., p. 23.

21. p. 26.

22. p. 31.

23. p. 49.

24. Washington, D.C.: American University, 1970 (offset).

25. Chapter 1 of *Institutions in Agricultural Development,* Ames: Iowa State University Press, 1971.

26. Wm. V. Skidmore, Jr., "Technical Assistance in Building Legal Infrastructure: Description of an Experimental A.I.D. Project in Central America," Journal of Developing Areas, July 1969.

27. "The Institutional Approach to Economic Growth," Washington, D.C.: National Planning Association Working Paper M-9422, November 1968, p. 9.

28. Washington, D.C.: National Planning Association, Center for Development Planning, July 1970. This report (2 volumes, 715 pages), prepared under an AID contract, should be forthcoming soon in book form.

29. E.g., Samuel P. Huntington's *Political Order in Changing Societies,* New Haven: Yale, 1968; S. N. Eisenstadt's work beginning with *The Political System of Empires,* New York: Free Press, 1963; and much of the work in the Princeton series of studies in political development.

METHODOLOGICAL ISSUES IN INSTITUTION-BUILDING RESEARCH

J I R I   N E H N E V A J S A

University of Pittsburgh

JIRI NEHNEVAJSA is Professor of Sociology and Professor of Social and Economic Development at the University of Pittsburgh. He was Chairman of the Sociology Department from 1962-1966 and in 1968-1969. Dr. Nehnevajsa was a member of the Board of Directors in 1964-1966 and Research Director in 1966-1967 of the Inter-University Research Program in Institution Building. He has served as Visiting Professor at the University of Heidelberg and the University of Mannheim. In 1970 he began serving for one year as Acting Dean of Social Science and Commerce and as Professor of Sociology at the Chinese University of Hong Kong. He has carried out research on processes of change in Brazil, India, Japan, Spain, Germany, and Finland, and he has studied likely economic and political developments in Colombia. His publications include contributions to such volumes as the *Industrialization and Development,* Hoelscher and Hawk, editors and others.

METHODOLOGICAL ISSUES IN INSTITUTION-BUILDING RESEARCH

JIRI NEHNEVAJSA

University of Pittsburgh

1. INTRODUCTION

Whenever an innovative organization is studied to determine what can be learned about the process by which innovations get institutionalized, the investigator must deal with a number of common methodological issues. This paper is an attempt to outline some of the main points, and to generate a kind of research "map" in which various elements can be systematically anticipated and located.

The first part of the paper suggests a general frame of reference. The interrelatedness of research and development practice can be thought of as a local cycle beginning with evaluation of the performance of some ongoing institutional arrangement, such as, for example, a school or a bank. The evaluative activities are followed by efforts to redesign the institution as needed. In turn, a reevaluation of the new program can then begin. This evaluation cycle addresses itself to the process of setting up an institution, and then evaluating both the plan (design) and the way it actually operates.

The second part of the paper is concerned with the conceptual mapping or logical patterning of the normative structure and functioning of an institution (blueprint mapping), of its operations (operations mapping), and the kind of perceptions salient segments of the population have regarding the institution (image mapping). For each of these mappings, certain substantive concepts are identified to cast further light on what it is that requires description and analysis. These mapping dimensions have been the major common substantive orientation of researchers who have been involved in institution-building research. Thus they relate to, and are basically adapted from, the seminal work of Esman. Intra-institutional components (such as doctrine, themes, program, leadership, personnel, resources, organization) as well as inter-institutional ones (such as enabling, functional, normative and diffuse linkages) are considered aspects of the pattern.

Time itself is a highly salient dimension of analysis, in that emphasis is placed on mappings not only in the present, but also an antecedent and anticipated states of affairs.

In the last section of the paper, the major research requirements are summarized.

2. THE IDEA OF INSTITUTION BUILDING

Organized human effort is purposive. This means that there exist some "intended results" for the attainment of which the organization, if only initially, is set up. Institutionalization may be said to occur when the values, technologies, and actions which form the fabric of the organized effort become *norms*. Human performances and the interactions among them become *social roles* and the *division of labor,* respectively.

The intended results, in turn, can be construed as satisfaction of needs, satisfaction of desires, or both. How particular needs come to be recognized as such, and how particular desires get identified and legitimized, are questions beyond the scope of this discussion. Four major categories of problems are of particular relevance.

(1) Some existing needs or desires may not be satisfactorily (adequately) met.
(2) Some existing needs or desires may be met relatively satisfactorily now, but there are indications that they may not continue being adequately met in the future.
(3) New needs or desires may emerge (hence, come to be recognized and legitimized).
(4) New needs and desires may be expected to emerge in the future.

To say that existing needs or desires are not being adequately met implies that some operating institutional arrangement (hereinafter referred to as institution) has not been attaining its intended results sufficiently well. This presupposes that some form of observation of the performance has taken place such as to lead to the conclusion that a discrepancy exists between actual and intended outputs.

The purpose of analysis under these conditions is to determine the sources of (the reasons for) the difference. Also, to provide insight which will lead to such alteration in the institution and in its relation to other aspects of the larger system as will enhance the probability that the objectives will be attained "better," "more fully," or "faster."

The analysis of the reasons for underperformance leads to differentiating among (1) those sources of the discrepancy (between intended and actual results) which are internal to the institution, (2) those which are attributable to the institution's linkages with other system, and (3) those which are diffuse effects of the total imbedding environment—both human and physical.

In principle, it is easier to induce desirable changes when the reasons for the discrepancy are predominantly (if not exclusively) intra-institutional, than it is when the difficulties lie in the linkages with other segments and institutions of society or in the total environmental context. In turn, it is easier to induce changes when the discrepancy sources have to do with the linkages with other institutions, especially those which are functionally related (in providing inputs or absorbing outputs), than when evidence suggests that the total environment accounts for the problem.

The postulated explanation of this has to do with the fact that there is more control over the institution as such, somewhat less control over its linkages (because this entails some control over the functioning of other institutions and segments of society), and even less control over the environmental ambience viewed as an overall impact upon the institution in question. By way of simple illustration, it is easier to alter the curriculum of a university than it is to alter the educational or personal backgrounds of incoming students (since this involves also making some alterations in secondary education); and this, in turn, is easier than to affect all those forces in society which provide or withdraw support (including finances).

This differential in manipulability might suggest that the environment operates largely as a constraint because it cannot be readily altered. This is not strictly correct. More often than not, manipulation of the environment can occur on the basis of planned effort to change the patterns of support or opposition by formulating or modifying extant values so that the institution can be compatibly incorporated in a larger system.

Now when some needs or desires are not satisfactorily met, it is obviously possible to attempt to alter existing institutions by inducing some mix of new values, technologies, or actions (within the institution and in its relation to other institutions in the linkage sense). Such alterations amount to organizational redesign; but their viability, even if the changes improve performance, depends on their gradual *institutionalization* in the organization, in its linkages, and in its (social) environment.

It is similarly possible to set up new organizations on the premise that existing institutional arrangements do not lend themselves to alteration or, if altered, would still fail to manifest improved performance. This then is an issue in organizational design and, as before, such new organizations also have to be institutionalized if they are to be more than single-shot (or one-cycle from inception to output) affairs.

It is then appropriate to argue that organization building has to do with all induced changes (in values, technologies, and actions) aimed at improved performance, whether by modifying an existing institution or setting up a new organization. In turn, institution building implies the objective—in the redesign or design of organizations—of integration into normal societal existence; indeed, that the induced changes become part of the institutional fabric of society.

In other words, if changes, no matter how beneficial, fail to become institutionalized, the resulting improvement in performance may be of only short duration; and the organizational innovations will tend to vanish with the disappearance (by death, transfer, and all other dynamics which produce this effect) of the individuals who have been the carriers or catalysts of change. Hence, institution building, rather than organization building, needs to be the overriding objective in efforts to induce change.

Now, *development* (social, economic, political) is precisely an effort to induce change(s) so that better "performance"—relative to needs and desires of men in any particular domain of life and in all of them—is the consequence. Hence, the idea of institution building is linked with the concept of development in the following manner: the objective of development is to build institutions by redesigning existing ones or designing new ones so as to contribute to an ever-improving performance of society for the benefit of its members; that is, for the satisfaction of their needs and their legitimized desires.

But a final problem remains: it is always necessary to judge whether the probable (or expected) amount of improvement (the bringing closer of intended and actual results) will be worth the cost of introducing the particular change—both monetary and human cost.

This, indeed, adds to the difficulties. For the human (social) and often the fiscal costs can be assessed only *predictively,* and there are considerable risks associated with being wrong about such cost estimates. In other terms, the "costs" (consequences for the social system as well as the actual human effort which has to be expended) have to be taken explicitly into account in the redesign or design process, but such costs can really be evaluated only after the alterations have been induced.

3. ANTICIPATING THE FUTURE

One of the key points then is that decisions in the present time (and certainly those decisions which involve the process of induced change, e.g., development = institution building) are significantly determined by anticipations regarding the future. This is so because changes can be introduced into the fabric of societal institutions only when some perspective exists, no matter how intuitive or unsystematic it may be, about the anticipated costs (again social consequences, human and monetary costs) which will be incurred.

Anticipation is also required due to the fact that inducing any change involves some "lead time"; that is to say, it takes y-years or m-months or w-weeks between the time a need for change is recognized, a plan for inducing change is formulated, the suggested change is approved and implemented, and its effects are actually identifiable. It may take three to four years to conceive, plan, build, and populate a new, elementary school for example.

Thus, starting an effort of this kind today (1971) involves a lead time which stretches into 1975, and the new school will really operate in the environment of 1975 and not in the context of the intervening years. This lead time varies from problem to problem, but it is always there (e.g., in applying brakes when driving an automobile, there is at least a fraction of a second between the decision and the physical impact of the braking action upon the vehicle). The future, as a significant dimension in any decision function, is even more important when it comes to societies or societal institutions in which *planning* is expected or rewarded, and in which the objectives are, to begin with, of a more long-range than short-range variety.

Many institutions may be regarded as adequate (e.g., the difference between intended and actual results is acceptable) for the purposes for which they were initially set up. Thus a local coal mine may be producing a supply sufficient for the local steel industry and for (all) other requirements. But long-range planners must be concerned with the question of the industrial requirements of the future, and this calls for anticipations or predictions regarding the exhaustion of the mine's supply in relation to expanding or contracting industrial needs. New, usually more expensive veins may have to be tapped, alternative sources of fuel must be developed or utilized, and so on. This process then leads to an evaluation of an organization in terms of criteria that are not yet most relevant: on the basis of future rather than contemporary adequacy.

Several special problems need to be taken into account in any such futuristic evaluation. The further removed the future is from the present when underperformance can be expected, or new needs or desires are expected to arise, the less likely is the problem to be viewed as acute. There is more time over which to monitor performance, to observe whether the anticipated underperformance is, in fact, in the making.

On the whole, confidence in evaluations which deal with short-range forecasts is higher because such forecasts can soon be pitted against changing reality. Indeed, if an organization were to be altered now to fit long-range anticipations regarding the future, there is always the risk that original forecasts will turn out to be erroneous; or that values, technologies, and actions of the present will enter into the specifications and these may not be any longer appropriate in the future for which such changes were instituted.

Thus there exists a strong tendency in all societies to attach high priority to short-range planning. In fact, quite often nothing is done about a future societal problem until it becomes quite acute. The present concern about pollution and about the very rapid depletion of nonreplenishable resources in the United States, and increasingly so elsewhere, is among the more dramatic illustrations which could be cited.

Much less effort, sometimes none at all, goes into the identification of solutions to problems which are already here but which have not yet become manifest in a manner that will get them accepted as altogether critical. The population problem, long in the making, did not receive the kind of attention at a time when action might have had effects that today can no longer be obtained, or can be obtained only at excessive, and often intolerable costs. It is being dealt with, if slowly, now that the excessive increments in population have already occurred in many of the countries that are in most need of some population control due to the discrepancy between their birth rates and the capacity of their institutions to provide the necessary goods and services. Thus many societies respond to crises as they come about, but rarely in circumstances and at times which might have prevented such crises to begin with.

These special features of long-range planning (especially relative to the rather short temporal horizons of decision makers) account for the fact that problems often most in need of study are least likely to get the attention required in time. When a problem gets truly recognized as such, it may already be out of hand or extremely critical. In such a situation, the demand for action tends to be immediate, and there is little patience left to postpone dealing with it until more information, via research, will have been obtained. One of the major tasks of the social researcher is to participate in the process of forecasting future events, so that more time can be made available to explore alternative solutions before the social climate compels action on the basis of insufficient information.

Finally, it must be recognized that planning always involves the determination of priorities among alternative ways of utilizing public and private resources. Priorities are an inherently controversial issue. The preference of politicians to avoid controversy is understandable in a democracy where their power is based, to an extent at least, on public support. This also is a variable favoring short-range rather than long-range planning. Why engage in a complex controversy about a problem that will not occur until our grandchildren will be in charge, or may possibly not occur at all due to errors in forecasting?

Futuristic evaluation data need to be collected in the design of long-range change. Thus the researcher is involved in applying his knowledge to something that goes beyond the writing of a report. He must know that the findings are likely to be utilized in institution building. He needs to provide evidence which can substantiate why one solution is to be preferred over alternate possibilities that also seem plausible in view of some of the information which is available. In order to decide which of these alternatives should be given top priority, it is necessary to make the following determinations:

(a) Which institutional alterations or innovations appear to be practicable: alterations internal to the institution, in its linkages with other institutions, and in its total environmental context?

(b) Which of these feasible changes are most likely to achieve the effect sought, or are, at least, likely to come close to achieving such intended effects;

(c) Which of the alterations can be induced at the lowest cost in human and material resources?

(d) Which alterations will have the least detrimental consequences and side-effects for other institutions?

(e) If changes are actually introduced, it is clearly necessary to schedule reevaluations from time to time to see if the anticipated effects actually occur. This implies the notion of an ongoing monitoring of the process of institution building and rebuilding.

4. THE EVALUATION CYCLE

The steps which have been outlined in the previous discussion can be summed up in the following paradigm:

(1) Goal analysis: Identification of objectives.

(2) Realization analysis: Observation of actual attainment or realization of the objectives.
  (a) If no discrepancy, "no problem" at the time of study is observed and no further research or action required; after some lapse of time, Steps 1 and 2 would be repeated for reassessment.
  (b) But: If there is a discrepancy between intended and actual goals, the evaluation continues with Step 3.

(3) Underperformance analysis: Explanation of sources of, or reasons for, deviation between intended and actual results—search for sources of degradation.
  (a) Decision whether to do anything when a discrepancy exists. This depends on a "boundary" statement defining the threshold of tolerable discrepancies.

(4) Problem-solving analysis: Identification of alternative solutions.

(5) Feasibility analysis: Identification of solutions which are possible given the state of values, technologies and actions, and given the expected state of values, technologies, and actions at the time when the solutions might be actually operative in the institution itself.

(6) Effectiveness analysis: Identification of solutions which are likely to lead to desired improvements.

(7) Cost-effectiveness analysis: Identification of those feasible solutions which have both best effectiveness and least cost (money as well as social cost).

(8) Impact analysis: Identification of the probable effects which the implementation of the solution will have upon other institutions, and upon the social system in general (social consequences).
  (a) Decision whether to implement solutions which may emerge from Step 8, if any, or if social consequences can be disregarded, from Step 7, or if cost can be ignored (such as when one seeks improvement at "almost any cost") from Step 4.

(9) Realization analysis: Observation of whether the adopted solution improves the system as expected.
  (a) If it does, no further research or action is needed. After some lapse of time, reassessment is begun again with Step 1.
  (b) If it does not, the analysis returns to Step 3 with the new data from Step 8. (Step 8 is, of course, Step 2 but at a subsequent time period.)

Items (a) and (b) in this evaluation cycle involve political rather than technical decisions. Steps 1 through 9 also involve many research problems. To these we shall return in some detail.

The principal political decision that governs the evaluation cycle is the specification of operational objectives of the institution (Step 1). In a National Planning Commission, this may be the adoption of a development plan for the national economy for a certain time period. In an Agricultural Training Institute, this may be the graduation of a number of specialists with specified kinds of know-how per unit time, such as a year.

These normative decisions reflect latent larger social goals. In the National Planning Commission, the implicit general goal may be the improvement in the standard of living as measured by the per capita income, or by some particular percentage, or by a change in the distribution of existing national resources. In the Training Institute example, the larger operational objective may be agricultural technology and, through it, improved agricultural output; or it may be the goal of decreased illiteracy to enhance still more abstract social values such as "increasing the level of enlightenment."

The third major issue has to do with objectives which an institution has vis-a-vis other institutions with which it is directly linked. These objectives may have to do with institutional maintenance, justified as needed for the attainment of the operational goals. This, in turn, may be seen as a prerequisite to the attainment of larger social goals to insure that the needed inputs and other supports are actually obtained, or that the outputs required by other institutions are generated.

The fourth major issue has to do with by-product effects of the institution and its functioning. Thus nationwide planning may indeed generate an adequate plan, so that the analysis may stop at Step 2 above. It may be supportive of enhancement in material well being, as intended, but also it may entail regimentation in political or social terms. In turn, this would affect national stability or democratic governmental forms in general, or civil liberties in particular, or relations with neighboring nations, and so on. Similarly, training of agricultural technicians might yield the desired number and quality of personnel. This in turn, would increase agricultural output but unless other conditions are also met, this manpower may lead to overproduction with the resultant change to declining prices of agricultural commodities with unstabling effects on the total economy and social system as a whole.

The basic eight-step analysis previously mentioned, in principle, requires review along at least four dimensions:

(1) relative to operational objectives of the institution under study;
(2) relative to social goals which the institutional objectives support or are instrumental toward;
(3) relative to inter-institutional linkages from the vantage point of (a) boundary maintenance, (b) input and support acquisition, (c) output and support production;
(4) relative to consequences for other aspects of social, political, and economic life of the society.

Hence, a given institution-building research study, when it deals with an already existing institutional structure and function, may concern itself with any one of the steps and any one of the dimensions, or cut across steps within a dimension, or deal with one step with respect to several dimensions, or finally, deal with several steps with respect to several dimensions.

5. THE DESIGN CYCLE

If particular social needs are not met, or there is an anticipated problem to which no existing institutional framework addresses itself, the building of a new institution is called for. A plan is needed, spelling out the objectives, the kinds of material and human components which are probably needed, the type of organizational format (institutional structure) which might best provide the facilitative organ, and the kinds of inter-institutional arrangements which will be most likely to enable the institution-building process to succeed. The lessons from large-scale systems design are, therefore, directly applicable.

How does one develop an institution which will do what is expected of it? How can it accomplish its objectives with the fewest possible detrimental consequences, some of which seem inevitable in any social innovation? Until a plan has been implemented, for a while, the question arises again and again whether the new institution is accomplishing its intended ends. Hence, there is a need for successive evaluation of the design during the process of implementation. This entails the notion of monitoring the degree to which planned and actual measures coincide or fail to agree, and the extent to which they are converging or diverging over time. If major discrepancies exist between institutional design and the achievement of intended objectives, a need for redesign will emerge once the sources of the discrepancy have been identified.

The logical steps of the cycle previously discussed are essentially the same, except that its starting point is different. Therefore the order of business, including research, is somewhat different in the design cycle than in the evaluation cycle:

(1) Goal requirements: Identification of objectives which the new institution is to have.
    (a) Decision whether an institution is to be designed (built) with a view to attain these objectives.
    (b) Institution design effort, including at least:
(2) Design requirements:
    (a) Functional requirements: Identification of functions required to attain the objectives.
    (b) Resource requirements: Identification of resources which are needed to support the functions, specifically money, supplies, equipment, materials, facilities.
    (c) Human action requirements: Identification of actions which humans have to take in order to perform the required functions.

    (d) Personnel requirements: Identification of social roles into which the human action requirements may be clustered so as to determine the types of personnel and their numbers and qualifications which might be needed.

    (e) Organizational requirements: Identification of alternative ways in which the social roles can be linked with one another into an organizational format.

    (f) Interface requirements: Identification of ways in which the total institution may be interconnected with other institutions and the social system as a whole; specifically to note which inputs are needed and where from, which outputs are required and by whom, and which constraints exist upon the designed institution due to its linkage to the environment.

(3) Feasibility analysis: Identification of technically feasible institution designs.

(4) Effectiveness analysis: Identification of effectiveness, relative to objectives of Step 1, of alternative designs.

(5) Cost-effectiveness analysis: Identification of feasible designs which have both adequate effectiveness and least cost (money as well as social cost).

    (a) Decision whether to implement institution design, that is whether to build an institution according to the design specifications.

(6) Realization analysis: Observation whether the adopted design leads to attaining the intended objectives.

    (a) If it does, no further research or action are needed. Go back to evaluation-design-reevaluation cycle Step 1 inasmuch as the new institution can now be treated as if it were an operational one.

    (b) If it does not, go to Step 7.

(7) Underperformance: Explanation of sources of, or reasons for, deviation between planned for and actual results—search for sources of degradation.

    (a) Back to Step 2 for redesign effort.

In the evaluation cycle, we were concerned with four normative dimensions in terms of which the data analysis can be performed, and must be performed if we wish to deal with total institutional performance within its larger environment. In the design cycle, which calls for the setting up of new institutional forms to meet some new actual or probable needs, the same kinds of considerations apply. But the dimensions of analysis are different.

The design is affected by the mission of the newly developed institution and proposed objectives. There also is a constraint by larger social goals which the new institution is supposed to support. The outcome will also be affected by already existing missions of other institutions and the requirements for inter-institutional linkages. For instance, the proposed degree of institutional autonomy will be affected by the authority of already existing institutions whose inputs and outputs will be needed to accomplish the new goal.

Finally, the plan is constrained by anticipations regarding probable consequences of introducing the new institution into the social system, even if it seems adequate as a technical solution (feasible, effective, and not too costly). In other words, the induction of new institutions into society produces a kind of chain reaction with some effects noticeable almost immediately, some delayed; some effects of considerable magnitude, and others relatively minor in scope (affecting few people only); some effects perceived as distinctly salutary and others considered detrimental to social values other than those which the institution directly incorporates.

6. INTERACTION OF THE CYCLES

The evaluation cycle is concerned with assessment of ongoing operations and their improvement, so that it blends into design problems when improvement is required and decided upon. The design cycle blends into the evaluation issue when a particular design is decided upon and implemented, so that a new institution is built to satisfy hitherto unmet social needs.

Another interaction between the cycles is relevant: if the evaluations in the realization analysis phase (to be discussed later) are such as to lead to the detection of a very large discrepancy between intended and realized objectives, a society may act upon this difficulty as if the needs were not being met at all—and thus move into the design effort to generate a new institution to cope with the problem. Or a design effort may lead to solutions which approximate the functioning and organization of an already existing institution. In this instance, the society may move to locate the new institutional mission within an already existing institution.

The former is a strain toward differentiation of functions; the latter is a strain toward their fusion. Both are operative in a social system at any time, and the nature and implications of this particular strain establishes a crucial research domain in its own right. It deals mainly with the agencies which have the enabling or preventing powers with respect to the differentiation or fusion of institutional activity.

6.7. THE VALUE DIMENSION

Institution building is based on plans which are sanctioned politically and normatively. The underlying values have the following characteristics:

(a) They are multiple. There is always more than one value that justifies the development of an institution. When alternate values exist and the necessity arises for one rather than the other to be given preference, planners must decide on priorities—on the basis of which choices are made. Maximum education might conflict with the value of well-being which, for some people, is translated as traditional continuation of the status quo. Freedom may mean an opportunity to make choices irrespective of the wishes of others. Safety, on the other hand, may require a high degree of societal control.

(b) Values have both very general and operational implications. For instance, men value well being. They also value health, security, safety, love, affection, justice, enlightenment, and the like. Such general values can only be translated into action programs through operational indices. Well-being might mean a guaranteed annual wage; health, a prepaid medical system; enlightenment, a system of education.

(c) Researchers also have values. This need not affect their work. They are rarely in a position where they are required to decide which values should determine how institutions are built or the order of emphasis of values. But the researchers' own value orientation is likely to affect the kind of data that are sought and the manner in which they are interpreted.

8. THE MAPPING OF VARIABLES

Though institutions are planned, a number of perspectives need to be considered. They can be divided into three organizing schemes or mapping of variables:

(a) Blueprint mapping: the detailed elaboration of what the new institution should be like from the point of view of those officially responsible for the planning process. For instance, it is not enough to know the current budgeting requirements in order to develop an institution. It is also important to know how the money is to be used, and how much value will be attached by those who authorize the expenditure, so that there can be a high probability that the funds will be available even if they should be in short supply throughout the general system.

(b) Operations mapping: the detailed elaboration of how the institution actually develops. This includes details that may be quite different from the blueprint by virtue of the fact that in the actual development of a new organization, hopefully to become an institution, compromises are made between competing normative objectives. Also, new information may be discovered that will require a deviation from the idea pattern to one that is realistically possible. It involves the assessment of how a budget is actually spent, in contrast to the original allocation.

(c) Image mapping: the detailed elaboration of how participants in the institutional development process perceive the institution or what they think it should be. Since those involved in the development of an institution will include persons of varying social roles and represent many different interest groups, their images are rarely, in fact never, identical. It is useful to recognize that the images of decision makers vary. Some have direct authority to decide about the fate of the institution as a whole. Their views are likely to be somewhat different from those who are opinion leaders without actual power in the planning process. A secretary is not likely to have the same image of an organization and its mission as its director. The clients of a new institution will see it differently from the staff. Finally, there are images of the public and of public opinion which are likely to have some effect on what occurs.

The existence of multiple perspectives of a plan in the process of being implemented is something that needs to be anticipated. When this occurs, it becomes much less likely that important and required information will be ignored if it may affect the way in which the institution develops. Monitoring observations can be of two types, regular and special. Regular monitoring implies the notion that at specified intervals the plans are reevaluated in their new time context, thus permitting their assessment relative to the previously obtained mapping and the evaluation of the likely reasons for shifts which may be noticed.

On the other hand, provisions are desirable for monitoring on a special basis. This assumes a research capability to remap the institution at such times as may seem indicated because of crises, emergencies, or unforeseen consequences which the researcher has a good reason to suspect have an important direct effect upon the institution or indirectly through the institution's environment. Revolutions, upheavals, natural disasters are good examples of circumstances which call for reevaluation on an "as needed" basis, rather than waiting for the regular interval built in for ongoing monitoring.

9. THE TIME DIMENSION

Time itself is a critical variable in institution-building research. There is, of course, "time zero"—the present in which the study is undertaken. If an institution is mapped out along the blueprint, operations, and image lines as of a given time, its description as of time zero is generated. But there is, indeed, time which antedates the current state of affairs. There are antecedents. The historical depth in this frame of reference simply involves the idea of mapping out the institution in its context at some prior time(s) or over some prior durations, perhaps from its very origins. This kind of perspective is highly relevant in that the past has, somehow, produced the present. Through the present, time zero, it constrains the future.

Operationally, such successive mapping of antecedent (to time zero) processes is of extreme importance. It makes a great deal of difference whether a discrepancy between blueprint and operations, for instance, has just come about, or whether it has a history of some duration, and whether over its history the problem has remained about the same (the discrepancy being about the same), has been increasing, or declining.

And there is, above all, the future. Thus the researcher, and the planner as user of research, must be concerned with future states of affairs quite directly, simply because any action taken will have relevance *only* for, and in, the future. This concern with the future has two major meanings in this context. For one, it has to do with "guesstimating," forecasting, or predicting the future.

(a) "Guesstimating" is essentially a subjective interpretation of information and its application to conditions which do not exist as yet. At the time at which such "guesstimates" are made, the conclusions are of unknown reliability and unknown validity.

(b) Forecasting is reproducible if one accepts the assumptions in the data of the forecaster: it has reliability within these limits (of given assumptions and given data), but unknown validity.

(c) Predicting is both reproducible and valid, at least within the limits of the probable and specifiable error of the prediction.

In the behavioral sciences, there is hardly any predicting in this sense. Some forecasting is done, of course: population growth, voting behavior, parole prediction, marital success, and the like. In turn, examples of typical "guesstimating" include such speculations as those having to do with the year 2000, or the effects of automation upon society, the impact of educational curriculum change on society, the effects of space technology, and so on.

Thus the first way in which the researcher and planner are concerned with the future involves "guesstimating," forecasting, or predicting the trajectories of the innovations, and the larger societal reverberations of such changes. The concern with future states of affairs also means that monitoring routines need to be established to observe the future as it is coming about, as it is realized. This, in turn, permits the researcher to learn from "guesstimating," forecasting, or predicting errors. It also permits the continuous shifting of time zero, so that subsequent projections and anticipations of the future can incorporate the newly acquired information.

Time is an essential analytical variable for mapping in still another sense. Institutions are changing and developing with time, reaching various stages in their life-cycle. Often, provisions for such changes, such as phasing in new elements or deleting some elements, are built into the institutional blueprint itself. The plan may make explicit provisions as to the growth pattern of the institution, or the time-related changes in its relation to other institutions, and so on.

Alternatively, blueprint provisions regarding growth and development of the institution over time may not be explicit. Rather, patterns of growth become incorporated into the blueprint as time passes. Usually, the fabric of successes and failures—the degree to which operations coincide with the blueprint at least at the level of output—determines such issues as to whether the institution will: (a) absorb new objectives; (b) shift from its current objectives to different ones; (c) increase its resource base; (d) increase its personnel; and (e) increase its output capability and expectation.

The blueprint is thus in a continuous process of development. Certain patterns of development may well be an aspect of the institutional doctrine, or its leadership and personnel, or its resource acquisition, or its organizational structure, or its relations to other agencies, institutions, and individuals. In part, the blueprint is changing because experience with actual operations introduces new elements, and leads to the deletion of existing elements, and these become incorporated into the institutional norms. The plan is also changing because of its interaction with images to the extent that the beliefs regarding the institution and its functioning become expressed in actions, and these actions may have a supporting, retarding or constraining impact on both operations and blueprint.

10. MAPPING DIMENSIONS

We have not tackled the problem of the substantive meaning of blueprint, operations and image mapping. This task is now before us.

First of all, there is an institutional *doctrine.* It may be said to include: (a) operational objectives; (b) social goals which these objectives serve; (c) methods of operation as specification of the ways in which the objectives are to be attained, when and how frequently (actual *program* of the institution); and (d) value-related justifications of the institution which pertain to overall desires or goals of men (or their alleged or imputed desires and goals) which place the institution into the largest context of human aspirations.

Second, there are usually institutional *themes,* which include consideration of such aspects as: (a) translation of the institutional doctrine into readily understandable slogans that may be simple yet ambiguous statements of objectives, describe underlying goals, value-laden justifications, and general operating methods; and (b) institutional symbols which stand for the effort as a whole, or the most comprehensible aspects of it.

Third, there is *leadership.* Two types of leaders should be distinguished: (a) initiators—persons who are actively engaged in the formulation of the doctrine and program of the institution; (b) executors—persons who direct the operation of the institution. These leaders can be further described on the basis of their origin in the social structure, their quality attributes, as well as their achievements, their knowledge and skills.

Leaders are individuals with particular motivations and aspirations such as the desire to serve, to attain power, to attain wealth, to attain fame, to be instrumental to the institution, to make the institution instrumental to their ends, to find means for self-expression, or to find means of escape from some otherwise undesirable or threatening circumstances. Usually a combination of these motives can be identified.

Four, there is *personnel,* which is conceptually broader than leadership. The requirements for personnel are subject to the definition of leaders. The maintenance of personnel is similarly within the purview of leadership. The authority of individuals viewed as "personnel" is limited to the performance of specific and usually repetitive tasks. Personnel in an institution have such characteristics as: (a) size, as measured numerically and in budgetary costs; (b) a variety of skills and educational mix, the relative numbers of professionals, semi-professionals, white collar workers and others; and (c) a mixture of roles and the way in which their performance is related spatially, temporally, and functionally to the operation of the institution.

Some of the characterizations of leadership also apply to personnel. From which parts of the social structure do they come? What are their personal characteristics, their skills, their motivations? Since various configurations are possible, of course, it becomes relevant to consider: (a) homogeneity of personnel characteristics along any line—whether or not any degree of homogeneity or the lack of it is necessary relative to the institution blueprint or simply results from other considerations; (b) comparisons of characteristics of the personnel and the leadership; and (c) the issue of selectivity, as measured by comparing personnel of a given institution and other institutions with the population distribution in general.

Fifth, there are *resources.* These include: (a) money, as in the form of budgets or other (less usual) forms of revenue; (b) physical plant, (c) equipment (reusable upon use); (d) supplies (diminishing with use); (e) materials; and (f) other facilities.

In some sense, the concept of resources describes current institutional assets and their dispersion. The kinds of issues this may pose are exemplified by consideration of use factor of each resource, consideration of useful life of each resource, and consideration of replacement or augmentation cycles.

Sixth, though in importance quite central, there is an *organization.* The organizational fabric is a web of social roles, each normatively specified, such that the total division of labor produces an efficient concerted effort toward the institutional objectives. An organization is describable by its: (a) degree of autonomy from authority of those outside the institutional sanction system; (b) hierarchical layers; (c) degree of centralization of decision functions; (d) degree of geographic concentration or dispersion; (e) types of functional or administrative divisions; (f) lines of command through which directives are issued; (g) staff lines through which directives are implemented, and their implementation reported; (h) control lines which establish feedback about the pattern of implementing directives, and difficulties in implementation.

The control functions include determination of deviations in performance and also explicit provisions for sanctions that are to be applied in the event deviations occur or in the event of exceptionally good performance.

Seventh, there are links of the institution to those individuals and agencies who have authority over it. These have been referred to as *enabling linkages* by Milton Esman in Chapter I. These revolve particularly about the issues of: (a) whether the institution will be set up at all, or be maintained once set up; and (b) what kinds of resources, when and how, will be legitimately received and from whom. These enabling linkages therefore relate the institution to superordinated agencies or individuals. Hence, institutions of this type are themselves the focus of analysis if one seeks to understand an institution which they are related to in this enabling sense. This is so because the institution is accountable to them. Withdrawal of support not only makes the attainment of institutional objectives difficult, if not impossible, but threatens the identity of the institution as a separate entity. Indeed, with respect to the enabling linkages, the institution functions chiefly on the boundary maintenance level: it seeks to justify its existence as a prerequisite to some larger social goals of which the specific objectives are mere derivatives.

Eighth, there are *functional linkages* which relate the institution to those other institutions that provide it with support or legitimately expect support from it. This means in principle that there usually exist other institutions which: (a) provide some, if not all, inputs to the given institution; (b) expect some, if not all, outputs from the given institution; and (c) constrain it, for example, by competing for the same leadership, the same type of personnel, the same resources, or by competing to fulfill the same function or role.

From this vantage point, is it essential to consider the *centrality* of the various functional interrelations of the institution with other institutions. This is, how important to the institution are the various inter-institutional arrangements? They include: (a) centrality relative to the institution depends on the magnitude of effect which results if no inputs are obtained from an otherwise legitimately expected source; (b) centrality depends on the effect upon the institution of degraded inputs—whether they are insufficient in quantity, reliability, validity, or untimely; (c) centrality depends on the effect upon the institution of depriving some other correlated institution (which legitimately expects this) of the needed outputs; and (d) centrality depends on the effect upon the institution of providing some other correlated institution (which legitimately expects this) with degraded outputs—whether they are insufficient in quantity, reliability, validity, or untimely. In other words, we cannot postulate that all functional linkages are equally important. The concept of centrality and its operational specification such as that indicated above is a good indicator of the relative importance of the various linkages. In each instance, the "greater the effect" the "greater the centrality" and, in turn, "the greater the importance" to the institution.

Ninth, there are *normative linkages.* These are ideological and ethical constraints. But they are also part of the institutional problem. The institutional doctrine and other normative provisions explicitly or implicitly deal with major social values. But these are values which are usually institutionalized in some other domain of social life, such as religion or politics. Hence, it becomes important to consider at least: (a) which customs, how and where institutionalized, bear upon the values the institution incorporates, explicitly or implicity; (b) which mores, how and where institutionalized, bear upon the values the institution incorporates; and (c) which laws bear upon the values which the institution incorporates. Therefore, the central issues have to do with *compatibility* of institutional values with custom, mores, and law.

The last problem is rarely relevant on the blueprint level, but it may well have bearing upon institutional operation and upon image specifications. Nor is the point made that the institutional values must be compatible with either custom or mores or both; often, the issue is precisely to change either or both. Rather, the research mapping problem is one of identifying the dimensions of compatibility-incompatibility so that enhanced comprehension of possible difficulties which an institution encounters may be facilitated.

Tenth, there are other *diffuse linkages.* They pertain to generalized opposition or support throughout the society's body politic, or agencies neither enablingly, functionally, or normatively related to the institution. The identifying questions might be simply: (a) what are the sources of opposition and why; (b) what are the sources of support and why? In a more sophisticated manner, one may worry about the effectiveness that sources of opposition may have at a given time or over time; and one may be similarly interested in knowing what it is that sources of support may do at a particular time or over time.

11. USES OF MAPPING

What kinds of mapping have we spoken of? Ten conceptual clusters of issues were identified:

(1) institutional doctrine
(2) institutional themes
(3) institutional leadership
(4) institutional personnel
(5) institutional resources
(6) institutional organization
(7) enabling linkages
(8) functional linkages
(9) normative linkages
(10) diffuse linkages

For each of these ten concepts, the blueprint map as envisaged would contain answers to the specific questions; and it would, in fact, contain answers to many more questions not spelled out in this document, but which may be further derived from it. Similarly, the operations map identifies the actual functioning of the institution along the same major axes and the components of each axis. Finally, the image maps contain the same information as it is garnered from those who view the institution from a variety of vantage points.

Explanations of discrepancies between intended and actual results (or outputs), requires identification of areas within which the maps do not coincide. Inconsistencies may be:

(a) Internal in the blueprint, such as when too much is demanded of various people in too little time; or when overlapping areas of authority within the organization lead to no one performing a necessary task, or performing it with insufficient accuracy or promptness.

(b) Inconsistencies may be due to discrepancies between the operations and the blueprint either because the blueprint is unknown or misunderstood, or because actual behavior deviates from it knowingly or by default.

(c) Inconsistencies may be due to discrepancies between images and blueprint and, insofar as people act on the situations which they define, the result is noncompliance with otherwise adequate blueprint provisions.

(d) Inconsistencies may be due to discrepancies between what goes on (operations) and images such that difficulties between the two make implementation of institutional objectives either very difficult or impossible.

(e) Inconsistencies may be due to discrepancies among blueprint, operations, and images such that what is expected is not what happens; and neither what is expected nor what is going on is accurately perceived.

These are explanations on one level of analysis; they do not quite pinpoint the sources of difficulties. But they provide a clue to the category of difficulty, especially if these dimensions are combined with the specific axes of issues along which mapping is to be performed.

Even these explanations, fairly non-specific though they are, may suffice to locate classes of behaviors which might help remedy the situation. If inconsistencies were internal to the blueprint, for example, one might be tempted to consider redesigning the institution and modifying those areas in which incompatibilities and conflicts exist. If discrepancies between the operations and the blueprint were found, some procedural or organizational modifications would seem indicated. If images and blueprint conflict, enlightenment or persuasion might well bring the image structure into increased compatibility with the institutional norms. When operations differ from images, it might be necessary to consider solutions along both organizational and educational levels: both would seem necessary except for special conditions which we will not go into at this time. If discrepancies exist among all three maps, it would greatly depend on the distribution of images, and on the degree of discrepancy between operations and blueprint, whether the emphasis ought to be placed on educating the relevant segments of the public (and thus hopefully come closer to blueprint and change images) or on modifying the blueprint (such as reorganizing to bring operations more in keeping with blueprint and, thus, to affect images).

Each of these problems is only mentioned here. Each constitutes a major research domain, and each is quite interesting in its own right. The purpose of this paper is to be suggestive rather than exhaustive. In this light, even the above suggestions as to the kinds of solutions are certainly only indicative of lines of thought. Otherwise, we would be vitiating our own emphasis upon research to consider alternative solutions, to study their feasibility, effectiveness, and cost-effectiveness.

12. RESEARCH FRAMEWORK: A SUMMARY

What then emerges from these considerations in the way of a basic research design? A brief summary of the key points will be now provided.

1. There is a requirement to produce blueprint, operations and image maps of an institution at some given time zero, the present. The problem is one of description insofar as it is necessary to generate such maps in a systematic manner. The dimensions in terms of which the mapping needs to be minimally accomplished include doctrine, themes, leadership, personnel, organization, resources, enabling, functional, normative and diffuse linkages. The analytical issue in this regard has to do with superimposition of the maps upon each other in an effort to identify the sources of institutional strengths and weaknesses which rest in the differences among blueprint, operations, and image maps in each of the respective dimensions. The problem is related to action (to begin with: planning for action) as soon as, given such analyses, a concerted attempt is

made to identify solutions which would bring the maps into greater harmony with each other.

2. There is a requirement to generate blueprint, operations, and image maps, insofar as possible, in the antecedent (historical) stages of the institution. The descriptive thrust in this regard has to do with an effort to produce such antecedent maps in a manner which will make them directly comparable with the time-zero mapping. The problem is of analytical interest when the researcher seeks to identify the differences among the maps over time so as to derive changes in, for instance, the blueprint (organizations and reorganizations, fluctuations in personnel and its characteristics, leadership ascendencies and general turnover, changes in doctrine, themes, and so on). The issue becomes one of action (or planning for action) when the historical trajectories (or stabilities) are taken as a point of departure to generate "guesstimates", forecasts, or prediction by projecting the past-to-present patterns.

3. There is a requirement to consider the kinds of circumstances or events which may account for either historical stability or change. The problem is again one of description in that it is possible to identify a variety of events which may have had one or the other consequence for the institution as a whole, or for any of the specific mapping dimensions. The problem is analytical as soon as an effort is made to seek explanations for stabilities and change by postulating particular impacts of the intervening events; and as soon as the evidence is used to make associational, semi-causal or even causal statements to account for the changes. The action implications have to do with the tentative identification of the kinds of events (on the basis of precedents and trajectories) which are likely to have particular consequences in the institution's future. The actions (or plans for actions) involve attempts to produce events likely to be beneficial and to prevent or avoid events which can be expected to be detrimental.

4. There is a requirement to identify the kinds of futures which the institution may have as a whole and in the specific mapping dimensions, contingent upon persistence of already existing dynamics as well as upon deliberate introduction innovative alternatives. The descriptive issue is one of recognizing that the combinations of admissible ranges of the mapping dimensions can produce alternative future states of affairs. The analytical thrust concerns hypothetical identification of the actions, the actors, the timings, and the goals which may be conducive to triggering processes into one future state of affairs rather than some alternative one(s). The action perspective has to do with affecting the institution or institutions superordinated, lateral or subordinated to it, in such a way as to generate one (desired) future rather than another, or to prevent one (undesirable) future rather than another.

5. Under ideal research conditions, the previous step presupposes a similar futuristic analysis of those institutions and agencies whose actions and functioning is central to the institution under study, and whose behavior is thus a codeterminant of its future. This leads particularly to the identification of the

kinds of adaptations which may have to be made on the part of other institutions and agencies if the proposed innovations are introduced.

6. There is a requirement to provide for the monitoring of the institution-building process along blueprint, operations, and image-mapping lines so that the process of actualization can be observed, and the time-zero maps can be updated in light of (a) secular changes, (b) changes specifically induced as an aspect of the institution-building effort, and (c) changes induced deliberately or accidentally by others. The descriptive aspect of this effort means that it is necessary to keep up to date with changes as they are occurring and when they are occurring, so that the institution-in-context maps do not become obsolete by the time they are actually produced. This is an analytical problem in that the whole social process can be viewed relative to the present (time zero) state of affairs and over the full historical horizon (as considered in Step 2). The issue is one of action (or planning for action) insofar as the recognition that innovations are not producing the intended results may lead to the consideration of alternative measures (redesign), or to changing the specifications of the objectives (intended results) or, of course, both.

A number of studies of innovative institutions along the lines such as those sketched in this frame of reference may indeed make some contribution to our knowledge about factors which impede or facilitate the introduction of institutional innovations. Thus institution-building research is viewed as an *integral component of the process of institution building* (and therefore, of development efforts). And there are no shortcuts.

LINKAGE, CODING, AND INTERMEDIACY: A STRATEGY FOR INSTITUTION BUILDING

MARTIN LANDAU

University of California, Berkeley

MARTIN LANDAU is Distinguished Professor of Political Science at the City University of New York in Brooklyn. He has been a Visiting Professor at New York University, at the University of Michigan, and at the University of California at Berkeley, as well as Senior Scholar at the East-West Center's Institute of Advanced Projects. He is presently Chairman of the Comparative Administration Group's (ASPA) Committee on Organization Theory. He has been a consultant with New York State Commission on Government Operations of New York City and to several other public bodies.

In 1970 Professor Landau received the Danforth Foundation's Harbison Award and the William E. Mosher Award of the American Society for Public Administration. His latest of many publications will be *Studies in the Methodology of Political Science,* to be published in 1972 by the Macmillan Company.

LINKAGE, CODING, AND INTERMEDIACY:
A STRATEGY FOR INSTITUTION BUILDING

M A R T I N   L A N D A U

University of California, Berkeley

THE INSTITUTION-BUILDING PERSPECTIVE

Esman's appraisal of the "institution-building program" states the following as its basic propositions: a very large proportion of significant change in developing countries is deliberately planned—i.e., engineered; the introduction of such change takes place primarily in and through formal organizations; these, innovative in intent, seek to foster new normative relations and action patterns; as such, they symbolize, promote, sustain, and protect behaviors without which development could not occur. If the goal is the attaining of those conditions we usually refer to as developed or modernized, it is necessary that such organizations (change agents) be institutionalized—made meaningful and valued in the societies in which they function.[1]

Emphasis on building institutions derives from a historical record which indicates that mere technological transfer does not do. More often than not it fails to take hold, leaving in its wake dislocations which are more than episodic. Hence the thrust, not for an organization, but—as Siffin puts it—for "a set of continuing patterns of action that encompass both the organization and its transactional relations with its environment."[2] Nor is this any less prone to failure, for "institutionality involves a complex set of inter-actions between the organization and its environment, the organization being required to accom-

AUTHOR'S NOTE: This is a modified version of a paper originally prepared for the Conference on Institution Building, Committee on Institutional Cooperation.

modate to its environment in order to survive while simultaneously attempting to introduce and to guide significant changes in the same environment."[3] The magnitude of this task may be estimated when it is noted that the environments which are addressed are generally structured in terms of "tribal" rules, while the change agent operates on the foundations of "Cartesian" rules.

In any case, IB program formulations clearly exhibit an orientation which is systemic in character. In its formulation of strategies (it is primarily devoted to the engineering of social change), its major concept appears to be that of linkage. What I wish to do now is to employ linkage as a point of departure in the consideration of an action strategy, which merits attention as a development praxiology. It may be helpful, however, to offer a few preliminary remarks about system and institution.

System

Oftentimes we forget that the term "system" is a very old word and that its historical definitions are not too different from those in current use. That is, the concept itself possesses little novelty and has been around for centuries. Indeed, it was employed as a cardinal principle by those 19th century philosophers whom we usually refer to, not surprisingly, as "great system builders."

In the social sciences, it is this fact that enables us to understand the current popularity of systems approaches. For when—at least in the United States—the pragmatists revolted against formalism[4] and threw out the grand systems of the moral philosophers, they so segmented the universe of social science as to usher in the era of "hardening of the categories." Inquiry became specialized, differentiated (separate and autonomous disciplines emerged), and those profound and vital interconnections which are so important to us today were lost as each burgeoning discipline spent a good part of its energy guarding its purity and independence. This was the price we paid when our scholarship shifted from an exclusive concern with the moral properties of institutions to a search for their empirical foundations. The special merit of systems approaches today is that they compel attention to "vital interconnections," forcing us to take due account of the interrelationships of the things we investigate. We have, it seems, turned full circle—only now our systems are to be empirically warranted.

It would be helpful at this point to offer a clear definition of a systems approach, but any such attempt merits a full-scale paper in its own right. It may suffice, however, to present some of the major elements of an energy-transfer model, upon which much of our social systemic orientations rest. By now, these are quite familiar to all of us and we can note, rather briefly, that a living system is "open" (it maintains itself in a continuous exchange of matter and energy with its environment); that it is "self-regulating," acting always to keep both its internal state and external environment stable; that its regulatory processes are manifold, complex, and redundant and serve to protect against threat; and that it constitutes a set of processes that are functionally interdependent (all working to guarantee the maintenance of a steady state). What I want to emphasize, however, are the following:

(1) As a system develops, it tends to become specialized: its parts assume definite structures and functions.
(2) As a system develops, it tends toward centralization: differentiated structures and specialized functions become subject to a central control which operates to integrate the various behaviors in the system.
(3) The organizational form of a living system tends toward hierarchy: its various structures and functions are arranged in terms of levels, the higher levels comprehending the lower.[5]

These general properties carry many implications, a few of which are important for this discussion. Note immediately that boundary exchange and mutual interdependence point us to the crucial character of *linkage,* while those we have enumerated provide us with a concept of development. They instruct that systems move from the simple to the complex; that the process of change or growth is marked by the emergence of differentiated structures and specialized functions; that the problem of integration calls forth centralized control processes; that the organizational form of living systems inclines toward hierarchy.

From a systemic viewpoint, then, standards of development are to be constructed in terms of the rate and extent of differentiation, specialization, and integration, which are the properties of complexity.[6]

Institution Building

A word now on this notion.

Sociologically speaking, "institution" refers to "normative patterns which define . . . proper, legitimate or expected modes of action or social relationships."[7] As employed by the IB program, this concept is modified only slightly. Given its perspective, it takes institution as "a change-inducing and change-protecting formal organization." Institution building then becomes "the planning, structuring and guidance of new or reconstituted organizations which (a) embody changes in values, functions, physical and/or social technologies; (b) establish, foster and protect normative relationships and action patterns; and (c) attain support and complementarity in the environment."[8] The IB program's deviation from the sociological norm here is really not significant. What it hopes for is that its institutions (change-inducing and protecting formal organizations) will, in the sociological sense, be "institutionalized"—that they will be taken as proper, legitimate, and expected modes of social action. This is the goal.

It is not an easy goal. Apart from a lack of energy and material resources, underdeveloped societies (or simple or traditional—however we refer to them) are highly institutionalized. Their normative patterns (operational codes) are maintained so tightly as to be invested with a sacred character. Tribal decision rules are of this nature; and such norms and relationships, patterns of behavior, customs and practices, are not to be tampered with easily. A violation of a norm is apt to be regarded as sinful, and a questioning of the norm approaches heresy. Accordingly, critical habits and experimental modes are, at best, derogated. In such societies, the moral order so dominates as to transform the technical or empirical order into a domain of negligible practical importance. In this circumstance, the environment is completely coded—which is to say that the entire system is treated by its members as a "closed set of variables." Elsewhere, I have suggested that the process of development constitutes a transformation of the decision premises of a given cultural community so as to legitimate technical decisions.[9] All formulations having to do with development, modernization, and institution building rest upon this assumption in one way or another.[10]

When, therefore, the concept of institution building is employed, its special point may be taken to be the establishment of those normative relationships and action patterns which sustain the use of empirical variables as routine grounds for decision-making. Institutional practices which permit empirical variables to play a major role in the system are the necessary supports for the introduction of new physical and social technologies. For they "open the set," so to speak, and allow change to occur. Once this process has begun, the environment is no longer completely coded and boundary exchanges can no longer be handled by sacred formulae. On the contrary, they have become problematical—open to hypothesis and experiment. The institutionalization of such action dispositions serve to facilitate economic and social development by distributing the requisite properties for change over the entire system. In a systemic context, we have always to remember that the relationship between an institution and its environment is roughly the relation between a variable and a parameter.

Linkage and Coding

To place institutions and environments in the systemic relationship of mutual interchange or reciprocal exchange requires that attention be paid to the problem of linkage. Linkages are those points at which exchanges (information or energy transfers) actually take place. But exchanges will not occur unless they are properly coded. Insofar as any institution is concerned, transfer elements possess a stimulus function: they constitute messages which are presented in terms of sets of signs which are not necessarily (or likely, in the domain we are addressing) to be encoded or understood—i.e., transformed into sets of signs that capture the informational content of the message. A sign here is to be understood as a construct or event by means of which one entity affects the behavior of another. Encoding is, therefore, crucial for it constitutes the process of making a set of signs intelligible. A code, thus, is a set of rules which provides the means by which this is done. At the linkage points (assuming effective coupling), these codes mesh—i.e., both the rules governing the institution and those which operate in its task environment are paired. It is on this basis that an exchange can be effected, as in the case of a seller and a buyer. Mapping linkages is, therefore, the *strategic consideration in the analysis of the institution-building process* and requires close analysis of the codes which both parties to the transaction bring to bear upon each other.

System theorists often speak of inputs and outputs. Whether in a serial arrangement or not, inputs and outputs must always be coded if they are not to lose their character. When pairing is congruent, the output of one member of the system becomes the input of another, and so on. When not paired, outputs may be ignored altogether, having no perceived stimulus function; or they may so overload a receiving member as to cause considerable strain or dislocation to the point of imbalance or disruption. They may bypass the receiver or they may force it beyond its range of stability. In traditional societies, in ghetto areas, in underdeveloped communities, these effects are readily observable.

Accordingly, an organization will be able to operate effectively in its immediate task environment to the extent that its distinguishing properties are distributed throughout the system of which it is a member. This distribution must be a prime objective for any institution-building program and it is, quite literally, an educational objective. For when such properties (they are, in their most fundamental form, existential and evaluative premises) are widely distributed, there exists the basis for a matching, a pairing of codes, which renders the relationship between an organization and its environment less uncertain. If the system is tuned properly, which is to say that ends and means are correlated, communication can obtain, and the situation is relatively ordered at those points where linkages occur. When not, development programs are fraught with uncertainty and hazard. Uncertainty, it may be emphasized, arises when codes are impaired. Should such impairment persist, an ordered system has become random and, as we have sadly learned, subject to the disorder and violence that have marked so many contemporary scenes—both developed and underdeveloped. Recognition of this danger lies at the base of the oft-repeated caution that Western praxiologies (rules of efficient action) cannot be automatically and uncritically applied to developing states. To do so is not only to court mischief, as La Palombara has put it, but to risk the destruction of one social system without providing any constructive alternatives. It would be well for us to reflect upon Black's caution that "modernization has been accompanied by the greatest calamities that mankind has known."[11] If there is any hyperbole in this warning, it is a sobering thought nonetheless.

Problem-solving

It is wise, if only for purposes of emphasis, to restate the thought of the last paragraphs. For means-ends relationships, it must always be remembered, are problem-solving devices and all societies have their *trusted* recipes for meeting the untoward. Indeed, when it is said that members of a society are "socialized," what they have learned are problem-solving programs—sets of formulae, maps, mazeways, or codes by means of which they make sense of the life-space in which they find themselves. They know what stimuli to respond to, when and how to respond, and under what conditions they may alter or modify responses. They have no special difficulties encoding and they have little trouble in exchanging with their environments.

Trouble, however, is, as Dewey once pointed out,[12] the loss of correlation between means and ends, inputs and outputs. When there is a good "fit" between the two, when they are paired, things run more or less smoothly. They are, within acceptable limits, predictable. Outcomes are produced by regularly employed instruments and are generally within the range of normal (probable) expectation.

If, however, the unexpected appears; if there should arise persistent anomalies and sustained discrepancies between normal expectation and actual outcome, the fit has been broken. The usual things (codes) do not work anymore, the situation has become disordered, and we are in trouble. It is at this point that we begin to search for an explanation, that we seek correctives—agents capable of reordering the situation. In the developed world, it is not the mode to leave such circumstances to chance, to consider them as accidental, or to refer them to a divinity. On the contrary, we search out independent variables or change agents and, whether our disposition is incremental or synoptic, we move to eliminate the trouble—that is, to change an undesirable state to one which is desired. Indeed, we have a paradigm for this, which we have labeled "rationality": given a condition which is deemed unsatisfactory and a condition which constitutes a desirable solution, find the set of operations (the instruments, processes, organizations, institutions) that will produce the preferred state.

But the production of a desirable outcome is no easy task, especially as regards the underdeveloped scene. In the first place, clear knowledge or a correct description of the condition to be acted upon is not so easy to come by. Nevertheless, it is crucial. For inadequate description obscures prevailing codes and renders it difficult to locate or identify those linkage points which might profitably be exploited. A failure to produce a desired outcome or the unintended production of an undesirable outcome is as much the result of inadequate description of the initial state condition as it is of defective praxis. It is for this reason that we have asserted that the mapping of linkages is the prime strategic consideration of institution-building programs and that this, in turn, depends upon a knowledge of those codes which are employed in daily life.[13]

Nor is the problem of preferred outcome any less difficult. While we are often able to provide a clear description of what is to be attained, as problems grow more complicated we find it increasingly difficult to so clarify our goals as to enable the measurement of achievement. Then, too, goal-states are frequently the object of bitter conflict. But even in the absence of conflict, such ends as are postulated must still remain within reach—within the scope of available technologies. This is not to say that we cannot invent new technologies or extend those we have. Rather, it is to emphasize that outcomes must be systemically relevant, capable of being linked to the existing situation. If they cannot, they risk becoming idle fantasies.

Finally, there is the formidable problem of technology itself—the means by which the existent state is to be transformed into the end-state. Here, too, a systemic orientation and common sense mandate the "field-determined" character of the instruments that we choose. And, in fact, we have come to learn this. We now tend to move with greater care, greater deliberation, knowing full well that the epistemological premises which sustain our technologies are not widely distributed in the environments that make up the underdeveloped scene.

It can be stated, in summary, that any indiscriminate legislation of end-states is as foolhardy as the indiscriminate application of means. Unless we understand the field-determined character of both, there will be those to pay the price of our conceit: for it is no more than that to erect dream worlds even as we watch real ones collapse. A means-end relationship is an empirical proposition, a hypothesis. If we break its contextual limits, we not only transform the hypothesis into sheer speculation, but we lose the opportunity to observe consequences and, hence, to build the knowledge that is needed. Effective development strategies depend, therefore, on accurate descriptions of systemic conditions and upon the construction of means-ends arrangements that are contextually or systemically relevant. When "arrangements" exhibit these properties, they become "fit" candidates for "institutionalization."

Intermediate Organizations

In turning to the construction of such strategies, I want to propose a planning strategy which may be of considerable value in bridging the gap between existent states and end-states. I must note, however, that I have only begun investigation and my remarks are of necessity to be taken as preliminary and suggestive. With this caveat, let us turn to the role of intermediate organizations in the process of development and institution building.

For purposes of this discussion, I do not propose any precise definition of intermediate, but I think that all of us are aware of its conventional meanings and can denote such stages with some degree of accuracy as being located between two points of reference. In terms of the problem at hand, the reference points are "simple" and "complex"—and the distinctions to be made, however rough, rest upon the *quantity and type of linkage arrangements,* and their rates of change. The more simple the organizational stage, the less the number and variety of linkage points and the slower they change; the more complex, the larger the number and variety, and the greater the rate of change. What is to be classified as intermediate, of course, depends upon the particular concrete system with which we are dealing.

In the context of institution building, the system which is the purchase point is, of course, our own. Its history is one of rapidly increasing complexity: it has been marked by the continuous emergence, and expansion (at high speed) of differentiated structures and specialized functions; it has sought control and integration of such diverse behavior by means of centralized agencies; and its organization forms have increasingly assumed the property of hierarchy. These features, so familiar to us, are the standards we generally employ in establishing the concept of developed. That they are consonant with so popular a model as systems only gives them greater force. We, therefore, feel more certain when we create, however inexactly, models of a developed society. To be sure, we are ready to admit cultural variations; but the end-state, as near as we can envisage it and as we invariably propose it, is always described by these properties. So it is, then, that all students of development scale the process in terms of differentiation, specialization, and integration. These are the critical features of the modern, developed, urban societies.

If now we look at the institutional components of those societies which we have assigned to this class, the large-scale organization (bureaucracy) assumes prominence. We refer to it as formal, complex, centralized, monocratic, and the like. Its features are also well known—so well known as often to engender concern at the path we are taking. And while it may frighten to the point of reaction, it is rather clear, as Parsons has observed, that this type of organization is at the very least one of the "most salient structural characteristics" of modern society. It is also to be emphasized that when we intervene to engineer social change, to hasten development, the primary instrument we employ (certainly for the IB program) is the formal organization. Here we need to recall that it is achievement-oriented, technical, rational, specific, affectively neutral; that it is calculated, impersonal, and instrumental; that rules, means, matter-of-factness, and expertise "dominate its bearing"; that its structure is deterministic (centralized), its rules complete, its operational codes specific and precise, its channels formal, its offices exact (jurisdiction), and its authority is exercised "without regard to persons." If this is an ideal typification, we shall have to remember, along wit Max Weber, that the "more complicated and specialized modern culture becomes, the more its external supporting apparatus demands the personally detached and strictly 'objective' expert."[14] Formal organizations of this type displace "action orientations" which are based upon personal sympathy and favor, tradition, kinship, and the like.

With the complex organization as the high side of a scale (and the simple organization, the low), we can now assign some properties which may, perhaps, clarify our use of intermediate organization. In contrast to formal-complex organizations:

1. It is by design (intention) nondeterministic in structure. The extent to which its internal processes are predictable and controllable is limited. That is, its structure is *less complete procedurally*. Its basic processes are not fully established, rules are neither comprehensive nor exact, lines of authority are less formal—often equivocal and ambiguous, jurisdictions overlap, its communi-

cations are diverse and multichannelled, its categories are not mutually exclusive, and its codes are more natural[15] (less formal).

2. It is, therefore, much less differentiated structurally, and its degree of specialization is less pronounced. Assignment to roles is less dependent on merit criteria, and ascription operates with greater force and visibility.

3. Its ethos is more reflective of gemeinschaft than gesellschaft. Primary group involvements are high, and "informal" groupings are not treated as residual. There is no explicit effort to establish formal organization priority, and there exists a high degree of communication between natural leaders and intermediate organizational officials. Motivational unity is less pronounced than in complex organization, the intermediate unit being more openly pluralistic.

4. To these characteristics, we can also add that intermediates are smaller in size, operate in terms of lesser magnitudes, and permit a larger social space to their members. Time perspective is shorter, and their decision processes eschew synoptics and tend to be more analogous to free market behaviors.

Taken as a whole, an organization of this sort is much closer to the "probability texture" of the task environment of the underdeveloped scene than is the complex formal entity.

The sense of my position is that intermediate institutional forms "mediate" the stresses and strains of transfers and exchanges by providing codes which are much more congruent, much more effectively paired, to those of the problem state than are those of complex organization forms. That is, the discrepancy as to codes and linkages is not nearly as great between simple and intermediate institutions as between simple and complex systems. The range of variation is less dramatic and the task of pairing is rendered less difficult. They can, thus, be more easily reconciled.

Once stated, this appears so patent as to be rather trite. And this, curiously enough, only strengthens the proposal. For the lexicon of a language does more than report conventional meanings. *It is also a register of success and failure.* Many of the terms we employ have either a positive or negative value, and while such evaluations are usually implicit, they are indicative of our experience with their referents. When a term denotes a pattern of behavior and its connotations are favorable, we may regard this as a sign that this behavior pattern has had, on the average, a long and successful performance record. "Mediate" is a good word for precisely this reason. To mediate is to settle a dispute, reconcile differences, bridge gaps—i.e., solve problems that permit sensible actions to be pursued in the face of sharp difference. By way of contrast, "meddle" is a bad word: it carries negative connotations indicating that the record of this type of behavior is not all that happy. Our problem as regards institution building is to mediate, not to meddle.

Beyond this conventional use, however, it is even more impressive to find that this rule covers a very wide range of phenomena. Success in building complex and stable institutional forms seems to be so closely tied to the role of intermediate organizational forms as to indeed constitute a principle. We are already familiar with this in terms of biological evolution, which marks the emergence of complex organisms as dependent upon subsystems which are capable of being sustained by their environments. One also has to note that an apparent similarity between the evolution of biological organisms and the development of social systems has prompted the widespread use of biological metaphor in the social sciences generally. And not without good cause: for it seems that all of our durable institutions owe their survival to the presence of environmentally sustained intermediate forms of organizations. American federalism, e.g., has capitalized on this principle; and its very success in producing a complex and stable organizational entity—a strong national government—has prompted what we have called for a generation or more the "crisis of the states."

The development of our corporate giants has exhibited this property, as do their organizational forms and technological practices. They are composed of stable subassemblies which achieve a unity only in terms of a complex set of codes and linkages. Their history has been well documented and we know it as a story of pools, mergers, and consolidations. The large number of small manufacturing firms, characteristic of pre-Civil War days, were the units upon which the modern corporation was formed. In the first period of great consolidation (1897-1904), John Moody listed 318 organizations which represented an amalgamation of 5,300 originally distinct units. From the standpoint of industrial development, the large number of small producers constituted a key factor. Apart from consolidation, it should be quite clear that a well-developed capital goods industry is quite dependent on a large number of small, specialized producers capable of being linked to its operations in the same way, perhaps, that "dramatic" technical innovations are constituted of innumerable minor processes linked together in a complex pattern. And while no single, unambiguous institutional arrangement accounts for industrial development here, it is obvious that intermediates loomed large in this process. Indeed, if we look at Japan, "there were tens of thousands of small private enterprises, which contributed in the aggregate an important part of Japan's growing production and exports. They were generally linked in subordinate relationships, through sub-contracts, to larger manufacturing and trading firms," all the more important there because of the oligarchic, almost feudal, control of national life (see Staley, 1966: 299). Even more, we can extend this to national and international trade unions, to bureaucracies, to transport systems, to educational systems, to distribution systems—to empires.

And what is to be emphasized should be clear: when stable intermediate entities are the basis of complex organization, they provide against disintegration. When such organizations are overwhelmed, they are not necessarily annihilated: they are more likely to break down into their major sub-assemblies—which not only continue to function but provide the basis for reconstitution. Beyond this, we may note the probability, as Simon (1962) puts it, that complex systems evolve from simple systems more rapidly (and with greater durability) if there are stable intermediate forms than if not.

The problem which is to be extracted here stems from the fact that development in our time is a forced process. Nature is no longer permitted its free course; we intervene directly (we call this social engineering), but it is a question as to whether we mediate or meddle.

More particularly, it is, as we have noted above, highly formal and complex organizations that play the dominant role in initiating and directing development programs. But such organizations, by their very complexity and their need for internal controls, are described by codes that are often literally unintelligible to the ordinary person. In our own communities it is not difficult at all to demonstrate marked increases in impairment to the point of incomprehension. This is the condition which has prompted decentralization schemes which, by means of intermediate agencies, are to close the gap—i.e., to reestablish correlation between means and ends. Nor should we forget that in our first historic period of rapid and massive change, intermediates of all sorts naturally developed; and these ranged from the boss to the precinct captain, from the "fixer" to the "middleman," from the "jobber" to the "broker." It is also worth a reminder that our bureaucracy was then rather reflective of an intermediate organization as I have described it, that roles were not sharply delineated and were ambiguous to the point of "favors." Where now only legislators can *legimately* do favors, then—under the sanction of the spoils system—civil service roles were so constituted as to allow the bureaucrat to do what the modern politician does now. We often refer to these past developments in latent functional terms; and while I am not suggesting here that we eliminate the merit system, it is striking that the anti-professional stance of blacks and others (including students)—their demand for less differentiated and more ambiguous roles—is so widespread today. This is a demand for an intermediate stage in much the same manner that the present mayor of New York City calls for "little city halls." That this is no isolated phenomenon is to be seen in the fact that the Los Angeles City Charter Commission has proposed "the formation of self-initiating neighborhood organizations (with populations between 5,000 and 30,000) with an elected board and an appointed neighborman, as a new institutional mechanism for communicating neighborhood needs and goals, involving citizens in city affairs, and reducing feelings of alienation." Perhaps we are observing, amidst the strains of complexity and the impairment at linkage points, the emergence of a new transfer agent—the "neighborman."[18]

In the underdeveloped scene, of course, the situation is far more acute. There, where tribal rules predominate, routine behavioral expectancies are of so different a character as to constitute another world. Moreover, such rules, and the cultural maps or mazeways[19] they give expression to, are sanctified by an immemorial tradition. To interpose suddenly the requirements of technology is to so disrupt prevailing mazeways as to tranform determinate systems into indeterminate conditions. The behavioral states which then obtain can run from uncertainty, anxiety and loss of identity to a paralysis of behavior. The principle of the "conservation of cognitive structure," which instructs that an individual will not abandon his set of cognitive maps (i.e., his conception of reality and the associated recipes for social interaction), even if their inutility is apparent, without having had an opportunity to reconstruct a new set (mazeway), should alert us to the magnitude of the developmental problem in simple societies. And while it is always easier to abandon one concept when another is offered, that which is to be substituted must be within range, within the field, or havoc can result. Perhaps we should enlarge upon this.

By any of the usual definitions employed, a culturally organized society is one in which organization depends primarily on the *patterned meaning* of stimuli learned by its members. Each can receive the other's messages: codes are equivalent or congruent, and the situation is determinate within acceptable limits. Prevailing systems of stratification, of socialization, of kinship, of authority and warrant, of rewards are comfortably nonproblematical—which means that predictability is high and bewilderment is low. That is, the grounds for everyday behavior are unquestioned. Here, of course, reference is to the probability texture of a system which is relatively stable—one which changes, but within limits that are behaviorally acceptable (there is a normal range to these changes even though we do not know them precisely).

In modern societies, which we now tend to describe as open, these changes are constant and accelerating. When rates of change exceed normal limits, such societies are prone to severe dislocation. This can arise for many reasons: the force of natural disaster, war, acute mismanagement of resources, or an unduly accelerated series of innovations which are beyond the society's capacity to absorb. If we restrict ourselves just to the latter, it should be clear that innovation is not without its costs. Apart from latent consequences, there is a liability[20] to newness. We easily observe this in attempts to reorganize those institutions that, at least manifestly, are wholly instrumental and predicated upon change. Even our most advanced technological organizations pay a price: when old roles must be set aside, we are exchanging the known for the unknown—which is never very comfortable. Those decision criteria which we have mastered and with which we are secure may no longer be rules of adequate solution. And this is but another way of phrasing obsolescence. Our experience documents the fact that innovation proceeds against resistances that are naturally interposed. To generalize this to the macro-level is to suggest, and not idly, that the routine grounds of everyday life in modern societies can be more easily shattered than we have hitherto thought possible.

Consider, then, the circumstance in traditional societies. Note, first, that to call them traditional is to assert that they are not prone to change, that they are not open. When change agents are introduced here, novelty is even more threatening. For new roles defy those of sacred tradition, new decision criteria appear as heresy, and new systems of organization challenge the gods. Planning, directing, engineering a developmental program assaults the foundations of such societies, i.e., those principles on which it founds its organization and patterns its behavior.

Now when we point to structural differentiation and functional specificity as attributes of the modern condition, what we are saying is that technical relationships must replace personal relationships: kinship must yield to competence. And this means that contract must substitute for status, and merit for ascription. It is, therefore, one of the preconditions of development that strangers learn to be trusted; for newness in this context requires a reliance on impersonal relations, on relations among strangers. Banfield, e.g., attributes the backwardness of tradition-bound societies to their incapacity to trust strangers. [21]

But there is more involved here than accepting or legitimating outsiders. If new organizational modes are introduced willy nilly, and these, as they invariably do, require the trust conditions described above, the local, the indigenous man, may himself be converted into a stranger. (We sometimes refer to this as a loss of identity.) Where before he was at home, in his own setting, living by his trusted and reliable recipes—now these lose their relevance and power and he is at sea. Confidence in the validity of his habitual responses, in his whole unquestioned scheme for interpreting life (his mazeway), is lost. It cannot be used anymore, and the insider has become the outsider. Lacking any status in the new circumstance, he has become a borderline case, a marginal man, a cultural hybrid. His seeming unity has fallen to pieces. With the probability structure of the old system disrupted, "typicality" or "normalcy" has been lost but new modalities have not been gained. He no longer can grasp the sense of the system; he no longer can rely on automatic cultural response, on an accepted knowledge of what it is all about. He now has to ask why; he now has to define the situation. Which is to say that the new structure is not a shelter for him; it is a domain of uncertainty, not a matter of course, but a problematic matter. The point of his life has been displaced—and what a displacement this is. He is in a maze but he does not know its ways. [22] He is truly in an identity crisis. On the basis of this argument, nepotism and corruption—those conventional pejoratives—do indeed "provide a familiar oasis in a strange landscape of modernization and thus provide a cushion for more traditional people against the harshness of the transitional period." [23]

In proposing intermediate organizational strategy, however, more is involved than the easing of the harsh. For we are hypothesizing that the use of this praxiology will, at the same time, accelerate the process of development and permit expansion of task environments on the basis of successive levels of durable, flexible, and effective organizational structures.

Hence, it is rather interesting to observe that, by a process of trial and error, development programs of all sorts here and there have begun to assign very high priority to the construction of simplified community organizations that can be sustained by their environments and can provide intermediate linkages—thus, acting as transfer agents. Talk of comprehensive planning systems designed to move whole societies forward is very popular; but our researches (theoretical and applied) continue, in their own languages of course, to urge that only intermediate institutions can close the acknowledged gap between administrator and community, that they will pair more effectively with indigenous systems and that the close coupling they provide can generate the normative relations and action patterns that "open a closed set." This holds as well for the elusive phenomenon of political development, for "the lesson of Mali is that contemporary administrators and political leaders who can learn to enlist tradition in the service of innovation will indeed be contributing to successful political modernization." So, Apter continues, "innovation—i.e., extra-systemic action—has to be *mediated* within the [traditional] social system and charged to antecedent values."[24]

This recognition can be reinforced by studies which show that organizational invention is field-determined, that it occurs on the foundations of the social technology available at the time. "Organizations which have purposes that can be efficiently reached with the *socially possible* organizational forms tend to be founded in the period in which they become possible. Then, both because they can function effectively with these organizational forms, and because the forms tend to become *institutionalized,* the basic structure of the organization tends to remain stable."[25] The stage is now set for the next level of linkage and the gap between simple and complex has been reduced. Conversely, if organizational forms outstrip their field, if they cannot be sanctioned by their environment, then they will either do great damage or fail or both. Here, however, if there exists sufficient gain as to allow for some degree of institutionalization and some degree of pairing, dislocations may be attenuated by a decomposition process that introduces a new intermediate linkage.

Intermediate strategies, however, are still largely implicit. They have not been exposed to the critical analysis that will permit us to develop effective and reliable process laws. It is possible, therefore, if not likely, that even where the initial impulse is sound, and mediating organizations are proposed, the resultant programs will suffer from administrative and operational procedures that are wholly unsuited to the tasks at hand. The usual device of strong centralized control, the overwhelming tendency toward the displacement of goals, and the attempt to program prematurely, vitiate the potential for a close coupling between the change agent and the local community. Moreover, it is equally probable that the linkage between the intermediate institution and its sponsoring institution will also be impaired. The net result is often to be seen as the enlargement of a national bureaucracy and the weakening of indigenous institutions; but there is very little of the intermediate supports necessary for a sustained development. In fact, the gap between the initial state and the preferred state widens, and mediation grows more difficult as the distance between the cultural maps of distinctive social classes increases.

Hence it is that the concepts of coding and pairing direct us to distinguish stages of institutional forms in terms of linkage requisites, and to build programs accordingly. Institution building must be translated into the problem of coding and linkage arrangements. Initial states must be described accurately; end-states must be field-determined; and as regards the means by which the difference between these are to be reduced, it is a fair hypothesis that the use of intermediate institutional forms of organization will yield the greatest gain. If it should now be countered that the problems are critical, that time is pressing, and that we need rapid change and powerful measures, I would agree. And it is for this reason that I offer Simon's hypothesis that the time required for the development of complex stable institutional forms "depends critically on the numbers and distributions of potential intermediate stable forms." [26]

A Note on Redundancy [27]

In urging a concentration on intermediate organizations in formulating development programs, the object in mind is to promote linkages that are effective and reliable and capable of serving as the basis for more complex (i.e., more advanced or developed) institutional forms. To an open system, however, risk and uncertainty are constant companions—and the prospect of failure always is high. No system, no matter how highly developed, no matter how reliable, can escape this threat.

In the case of development programs, failure is made even more probable by the great discrepancies between the requisites for new physical and social technologies and the supports present in the community. If intermediate institutions tend to close this gap, they do so because of their redundant character.

That fact—namely, the existence of redundancy—is generally frowned upon. It appears to violate the basic maxims of our public administrative theory which has taken the reliability of a system to depend upon the perfectability of its parts. This belief underwrites our notions of effective and efficient performance (it has about reached the status of an axiom of right) and accounts for our tendencies to regard such redundancies as duplication of function and overlapping jurisdictions as waste. When change agents operate in a domain of scarcity, negative appraisal of such redundancy heightens and a much greater effort is expended on perfecting parts and linkages. In the hard technologies, redundancy is a recognized feature of design—we know it, certainly since the last moon flight; but in social technologies it is invariably frowned upon, treated as contrary to common sense, and removed as soon as circumstances permit.

But the point of the theory of redundancy is to take nothing as given—especially as regards the risk of failure and error. In this respect, it is rather pessimistic, operating on the assumption that if anything can go wrong, it will go wrong. Accordingly, it sets aside doctrines that tie the reliability of a system to the perfectability of its parts. That is, it accepts the inherent limitations of any organization by treating all parts, regardless of their degree of perfection, as risky actors. It, therefore, approaches the actual functioning of a system more realistically than any of its competitors.

The practical implication of this position is immediate for the underdeveloped area and is to be seen when one asks the question, "Is it possible to construct an organizational arrangement, an institutional form, that is more reliable, more adaptable, than any of its parts?" If this defies our commonsense notions, the answer is, nevertheless, yes. And it was Von Neumann who originally demonstrated that such could be done by the simple addition of sufficient redundancy—i.e., by an appropriate duplication of parts and linkages. In the latter case, this calls for a network of parallel linkages which provide a duplication of channels so that if transfer is not effected at one point, it can still be had at others. A redundancy of code and linkage is crucial to institutional development and, when reinforced by duplicate or overlapping intermediate agencies, the possibilities of success are increased. There is, therefore, a sound basis for John Montgomery's suggestion that one way to effect administrative reform in underdeveloped countries "is to duplicate functions."[28]

The theory of redundancy is a rather complicated affair and it serves no purpose to dwell upon it here. Suffice it to mention that its application rests upon an important theorem which states that the probability of failure decreases exponentially as redundancy factors are increased. This, in turn, rests upon the product rule of probability which, when translated practically, means that duplicate parts must be arranged separately so that one failure cannot and will not damage its duplicates—as, for example, in a dual braking system. While this is of considerable interest in designing the institutional features of any development plan, the point which I want to stress is the value, the immediate value, of overlapping operations.

Earlier, in outlining an energy-transfer system, I made reference to its self-regulating properties. As in the case of intermediacy, the principle of self-regulation has also been extended to cover a wide range of phenomena. Here, too, we can note that hard technologies make ever increasing use of its powers. It should suffice to point to the popularity of feedback devices, automated and self-correcting systems, servo-mechanisms and cybernetics in general. But it is more interesting that self-organizing systems, as they are frequently called, receive their fullest expression in terms of biological organisms. These exhibit a degree of reliability that is so far superior to anything that has yet been designed as to prompt redundancy theorists to suggest that their richly redundant networks demonstrate capabilities beyond anything we can yet explain. They can, e.g., readjust so as to minimize failure, block off faulty or damaged components, and they are even able to improve their reliability when malfunction sets in.

Now it seems that such systems possess a fantastic number of parallel arrangements of many different types (complexity). W. S. McCulloch, in commenting on the reliability of biological systems, speaks of redundancy of command, of code, of channels (linkages)—noting that each serves differently. To these we can add the property of "equipotentiality" which provides a system with its most fundamental corrective—adaptability.

Equipotentiality is often referred to in redundancy theory as "overlapping." It denotes the tendency of open systems to resist the kind of precise differentiation of function which is mutually exclusive. Even in the case of highly specialized subsystems, there is often sufficient overlap to enable other parts to take over, at least partially, the functions of those which have been damaged. It is this overlap which permits the organism to exhibit a high degree of adaptability—i.e., to change its behavior in accordance with changes in environment. We can hypothesize that it is precisely these redundancies—parallel linkages and equipotentiality—that allow for the delicate processes of mutual adjustment, of self-regulation, by means of which the whole system can sustain severe local injury and still function creditably. The intermediate organization described here is precisely of this order: it possesses sufficient ambiguity (overlapping) as to permit redundancies of code, channel, and control. The presence of such organizations enhances the ability of an open system to achieve reliability of performance and a considerable adaptability. Marked by a redundancy of law, of power and authority, of structure and function, of codes and channels—and by an extraordinary equipotentiality—the whole may operate more effectively than any of its parts. Where one part fails, the "uncertain" jurisdiction which obtains permits another to take over, however imperfectly. And it is this process, which we are prone to refer to as "latency," that enables a system to suffer severe injury without doing critical damage to the whole.

In the third world, such a strategy is mandated by the enormous risks which attend development. For the theory of redundancy is a theory of system reliability.

NOTES

1. Milton J. Esman, "The Institution Building Concepts—An Interim Appraisal," Pittsburgh: University of Pittsburgh, GSPIA, 1969, (mimeo). And see Milton J. Esman and Hans C. Blaise, "Institution Building Research—Guiding Concepts," Pittsburgh: University of Pittsburgh, GSPIA, 1966 (mimeo).

2. William J. Siffin, "The Institution Building Perspective," Indiana University, 1969 (unpublished manuscript), p. 2.

3. Esman, op. cit., p. 2.

4. Morton G. White, *Social Thought in America: The Revolt Against Formalism,* New York: Viking, 1950.

5. See Martin Landau, "On the Use of Functional Analysis in American Political Science," Social Research, Vol. 25, 1968.

6. The literature of development and modernization, almost without exception, exhibits this. Invariably these concepts are defined in terms of differentiation and specialization. The reader *Political Modernization,* edited by P. Welch (Belmont, 1967), is typical in this respect. And Welch, summarizing a rather full bibliography, states that the process of modernization turns on increased centralization, differentiation, and specialization. It is also of interest to note that the sociologist, Robert E. Park, postulated "complexity" as one of the primary criteria of difference between modern society and primitive or preliterate society. See R. E. Park, "Modern Society" in Robert Redfield, editor, *Levels of Integration in Biological and Social Systems,* New York: J. Cattell Press, 1942, pp. 223-226. In more recent vein, see David Apter, *Some Conceptual Approaches to the Study of Modernization,* Prentice-Hall, 1968, p. 330.

7. T. Parsons, *Essay in Sociological Theory,* New York: Free Press, 1949.

8. Esman, op. cit., p.l. Samuel Huntington uses a concept of "institutionalization" which is rather similar to (c). It "is the process by which organizations and procedures acquire values and stability." "Political Development and Political Decay" in World Politics, Vol. 17, April 1965.

9. "Decision Theory and Development Administrations," in E. W. Weidner, editor, *Development Administration in Asia,* Durham, N.C.: Duke, 1970.

10. Hence it is that science, secularization, choice, professional matter-of-factness, rational control, world culture (meaning the spirit of science) the empirical mode, and so on—are variously employed to define modernization. Needless to say, the very concept of change rests on empirical foundations as do the twin pillars of differentiation and functional specificity. To be sure, the prime requisite of modernization, as Huntington puts it, "is the belief that men can act purposefully and effect change." This is mandated by definition: i.e., Huntington's statement is a tautology. It does, however, point to the crucial character of "independent variable" in this process.

11. C. E. Black, *The Dynamics of Modernization,* New York: Harper, 1967, p. 27.

12. John Dewey, "Theory of Valuation," *International Encyclopedia of Unified Science,* Chicago: 1939.

13. This point draws greater emphasis from Ward Goodenough's definition of culture: "Culture . . . does not consist of things, people, behavior, or emotions. It is rather an *organization* of these things. It is the *form* of things that people have in mind, their *models* fro perceiving, relating, and otherwise interpreting them." "Cultural Anthropology and Linguistics," in D. H. Hymes, editor, *Language in Culture and Society,* New York: Harper, 1964, p. 36. Emphasis added.

14. *From Max Weber,* edited by H. H. Gerth and C. W. Mills, New York: Oxford, 1958, pp. 214-216, 228. And see M. Landau, "Sociology and the Study of Formal Organization" in *The Study of Organizational Behavior,* American Society for Public Administration, Special Series No. 8, 1966.

15. They are much more natural languages than they are ad hoc. Ad hoc languages exhibit dictionaries of more precisely, more delimited terms. We should note too that delimitation and predictability are directly proportional. Hence, the less exact the meanings, the less the degree of predictability.

16. E. Staley, "The Role of the State in Economic Development" in M. Weiner, editor, *Modernization,* New York: Basic Books, 1966, p. 299.

17. Herbert Simon, "The Architecture of Complexity," Proceedings of the American Philosophical Society, Vol. 106, April 1970.

18. V. Jones, "Representative Local Government: From Neighborhood to Region," Public Affairs Report, Vol. 11, April 1970. Bulletin of the Institute of Governmental Studies, University of California, Berkeley.

19. For the concept of "mazeway," see Anthony F. C. Wallace, "The Psychic Unity of Human Groups" in Bert Kaplan, editor, *Studying personality Cross-Culturally,* Row, Peterson, 1961; and see Wallace, *Culture and Personality,* Random House, 1961. See also Landau, "Decision Theory," op. cit.

20. This is Arthur Stinchcombe's phrase. See "Social Structure and Organization" in J. M. March, editor, *Handbook of Organizations* Chicago: Rand McNally, 1965.

21. Ibid., p. 149. E. Banfield, *The Moral Basis of a Backward Society,* New York: Free Press, 1958, is cited by Stinchcombe in this manner.

22. Alfred Schutz, "The Stranger" in *Collected Papers,* edited by Arvid Brodersen, The Hague: Nijhoff, 1964.

23. R. O. Tilman, "Emergence of Black-Market Bureaucracy," Public Administration Review, Vol. 28, 1968: 443. This quotation expresses David Bayley's formulation in "The Effects of Corruption in a Developing Nation," Western Political Quarterly, Vol. 19, 1966; cited in Tilman.

24. D. E. Apter, "The Role of Traditionalism in the Political Modernization of Ghana and Uganda" in C. E. Welch, Jr., *Political Modernization,* Wadsworth, 1967, pp. 65-66; emphasis added. Robert E. Ward observes "the rapid development of Japan . . . rested ultimately on the effective enlistment of traditional institutions . . . in the service of the modernizing process." Or "Communal solidarity eased modernization by providing a stable social framework within which change could occur." See Ward, "Political Modernization and Political Culture in Japan," in Welch, ibid., p. 13.

25. Stinchcombe, op. cit., p. 153. Emphasis added.

26. Simon, op. cit.

27. What follows is derived from Martin Landau, "Redundancy, Rationality and the Problem of Duplication and Overlap," Public Administration Review, Vol. 29, July/August 1969.

28. John D. Montgomery, "Sources of Administrative Reform: Problems of Power, Purpose and Politics" Comparative Administration Group, Occasional Paper, 1967 (mimeo), p. 63.

THE TIME DIMENSION IN INSTITUTION BUILDING

NORMAN T. UPHOFF

Cornell University

WARREN F. ILCHMAN

University of California, Berkeley

NORMAN T. UPHOFF is Assistant Professor of Government and a Fellow in the Center for International Studies at Cornell University. He is co-author with Warren F. Ilchman of the *Political Economy of Change*. He has done research for the Institute for International Studies at the University of California at Berkeley during 1967-1969 on the use of foreign aid for the development of Ghana under the Nkrumah regime. He also worked with the External Aid Division of the Ghanaian Ministry of Economic Affairs. Earlier he served as a consultant for Education and World Affairs on a project working with the National Manpower Board in Lagos, Nigeria. He recently presented a paper on Institution Building and Development at the Centre for Economic Development and Administration in Katmandu, Nepal.

WARREN F. ILCHMAN is Professor of Political Science, Chairman of the Center for South and Southeast Asian Studies, and Assistant Dean, University of California, Berkeley. He previously has been a fellow at Cambridge University, where he completed his doctorate, and at the Center for Development Economics, Williams College. His research and teaching have been in the fields of political economy and comparative organizations, and he has conducted empirical research over many years in South Asia and the Middle East. His most recent works are *Agents of Change: Professionals in Developing Countries* (1969), *Optimal Ignorance and Educational Planning in India* (1971), and *The Political Economy of Development* (with Norman T. Uphoff, 1972). In 1968 he received the Harbison Award from the Danforth Foundation for distinguished teaching. Professor Ilchman has participated in training programs for overseas professionals in AID and the Peace Corps and has served as a consultant for the United Nations and for AID.

THE TIME DIMENSION IN INSTITUTION BUILDING

NORMAN T. UPHOFF

Cornell University

WARREN F. ILCHMAN

University of California, Berkeley

Time is of the essence in institution building. An understanding of induced social change depends very much on an analysis of time with respect to the various elements involved in such change. Indeed, time is the salient link among these elements. The contributions of leadership, doctrine, program, resources, and internal structure cannot be understood without conceptualization and analysis of the time dimension. Aspirations, productivity, planning, even institutional coherence and interdependence—all have variable time dimensions.

In this chapter we will attempt to make explicit how time conditions the efforts of institution builders. Their goal is not simply social change. Unplanned changes in social, economic, and political relationships are likely to occur over time with or without their efforts. Institution builders aim at purposive social control. By establishing efficacious institutions, they seek to control the course of change and to achieve preferred objectives within a shorter period of time than would otherwise be possible. Once established, institutions commonly permit persons to control, at least for a while, the demands for further change which are likely to arise. Thus, institutions may be seen as giving persons some control over time itself. In the absence of institutional development, the effects of time's passage will elude men's control.

Organization Theory and Time

The acknowledged bias of the institution-building approach toward social engineering is appropriate. Appropriate too is the presupposition that formal

[113]

organizations are the key instruments in and through which significant social changes are to be introduced in developing countries. However, organization theory is hardly prepared at present to contribute much to this enterprise because it has given so little explicit consideration to the use or effects of time.[1] Neither the structural nor behavioral frameworks of analysis which characterize most organization theorizing encompass adequate time dimensions.

By and large, structural analysis has sought to describe conditions of equilibrium in established organizations. Equlibrium, of course, is a state in which time or change will have no effect. When the macro-environment of an organization has been included in structural analysis, the dependence of the organization on its environment has usually been stressed. Institution building, however, is premised on the consideration that institutions being built are not wholly dependent on their total environment for resources. The problem facing institution builders is how resources received from any part of the environment can be used over time to effect desired social change within the larger environment and to make this environment support and serve the goals of the institution.

A similar shortcoming is present in most behavioral analysis of organizations. The behavior of participants in an organization is observed and described, but often it is attributed to virtually immutable laws of "human nature." Too little attention, especially in cross-cultural contexts, has been paid to the orientation of organization theory which Chester Barnard proposed. Compliance as a function of inducements or incentives is as relevant to organizational change as it is to the maintenance of organizational patterns.[2] The purpose of institution building is to change behavior through changes in inducements and/or norms. Institution building also provides that for some period of time, personnel from outside the organization's immediate environment, that is, expatriates or nationals trained abroad with "non-indigenous" behavior patterns, will participate in the institution. Changes in personnel and in organization structure are made delibertately to effect changes in behavior. Most conventional explanations of observed behavior within organizations unfortunately impute "necessary" causes of such behavior without examining adequately the effects of changes in organizational structure, personnel, norms, or inducements.

The criticisms of organization theory implied above extend beyond it to political science and sociology. There are many criticisms which could be made of economics, but among the social sciences, it offers the most sophisticated analysis of time.[3] To be sure, its concern with productivity has required it to develop more dynamic theories and to consider the value of time. But it is this concern with productivity which makes economic conceptions of organizational reations rather appropriate in the analysis of institution building, which has a central concern with productivity, however broadly conceived or defined. No wholesale adoption of economic theory is possible or desirable for our purposes of developing models for the guidance of institution builders. But we will find its perspective fruitful in a number of ways as we consider the implications of time for the five institution variables dealt with in the institution-building approach.

A. INSTITUTION VARIABLES

1. Resources. Of the different institution variables, it is best to consider resources first because of the ambiguity and frequent confusion as to whether time is a resource. Wilbert Moore, who has made an extensive and thoughtful study of time in relation to social interaction, suggests that it is.[4] But we do not agree. Time has many of the properties of a resource: it is scarce, productive, and valuable. But this does not necessarily make it a resource. Time itself produces nothing, and it is not "combined" with resources as a "factor of production" in the usual economic sense. We suggest, without venturing into the philosophic controversies about the nature of time, that for the purposes of understanding institution building, time may be seen as a dimension of resources.

Time permits the productive use of resources. Resources may change within or over time, but they do not change time. There is no symmetrical convertibility. Time represents periods whereby one can measure the possession and use of resources.[5] In other words, time represents an interval—or a space, if one prefers a more archaic metaphor[6]—within which activities may be undertaken which yield or utilize resources, such as goods and services.

If time is not a resource, then to understand its role and value in institution building we need to elaborate what the resources involved are. Elsewhere, they have been defined as "the financial, physical, human, technological (and informational) inputs of the institution."[7] We believe it is possible and useful to specify organizational resources, that is, to identify the factors of organizational production.[8]

(a) Economic resources include goods and services. These can be secured with the currency of money, though under various circumstances they may be contributed without money payment. Skills, ofter considered as a resource, are more appropriately thought of as a qualitative aspect of human resources which makes services more productive and valuable. Similarly, technology is not a resource so much as an improvement in the quality or combination of factors of production. By and large, the resources defined in the institution-building approach have been primarily economic ones. In thinking about factors of organizational production, however, other resources deserve equal consideration.

(b) Information is an obvious resource with important productive characteristics in the institution-building process. It is both an input and an output of organizations. Unlike some other resources, information is not "consumed" or exhausted when used as a factor of production. Information can be shared without diminishing its initial amount. As a factor, its contribution to the production process is to make more productive the use of other resources.

(c) Status is less obvious but just as important, if one is not to overlook much of the incentive for human activity and one of the major factors in compliance relationships. Esteem and deference, the analogues in social relations of goods and services in economic relations, are desired by organizations and their participants because of the satisfaction these social goods bring (consumption) or the other benefits which these goods can help procure (production). Organizations and individuals can produce esteem and deference for others, these goods being valued according to the amount of status which the organization or individual has. As will be discussed below, the status of organizations is one of the factors which helps to establish them as institutions.

(d) Force must be included as a resource for getting compliance with an organization's decisions. Coercion or violence can be expended or received, but since these are negatively valued—persons wish to avoid the use of force against themselves—exchanges of resources involving force are not mutually beneficial. One person's gain is another's loss. An organization using force must reckon with the possibility of retaliation. But unless net losses are imposed by retaliation, coercion or violence can be productive for the organization using it.

(e) Authority is a tangible but often ambiguously delimited resource. It needs to be distinguished from *power* and *legitimacy,* two terms which are often treated, mistakenly, as synonymous with authority. In any organization, there is some division of political labor which provides for authority roles, whether by convention or by constitution. Persons occupying these roles are entitled to make allocations of the organization's resources on behalf of the organization. To be "in authority" is to be "in power" to the extent that other resources have been or are put at the disposal of persons possessing authority. Members can contribute economic resources, information, status, force, and/or legitimacy (discussed below) for promoting organizational objectives, or these resources can be received from outside the organization. In any case, a person who has authority has a resource because it enables him to make claims on the resources of organization members which no non-authoritative person can make.

(f) Legitimacy is, as suggested below, the most salient resource as far as institution building is concerned, though it is no more than primus inter pares. It is given to an organization in varying degrees (amounts) by members and non-members. To the extent that an institution is regarded as legitimate or its decisions are regarded as right and proper, compliance may be secured with fewer other inducements. This is to say that an organization possessing greater legitimacy is able to secure more resources or secure them more cheaply to the extent that favorable normative judgments are made about that institution.

The difference between an organization and an institution is one of degree rather than kind, but the main distinction is the degree to which the latter has acquired legitimacy in the eyes of those persons with whom it interacts. Legitimacy is seldom sufficient to get compliance with institutional decisions without some expenditure of other resources. A government is an institution but must still expend or threaten force to collect taxes. But to the extent that an individual accords the government legitimacy, proportionally less force must be threatened or expended to get compliance with tax laws.

(g) Support is viewed most usefully not as a resource but as a currency representing claims on organizational resources, just as money represents claims on economic assets. For members to give support to an organization is to pledge or commit their resources to it. Support is worth no more than the resources it can procure from individuals upon demand, their goods or services, their information, status, use of force, or their according of legitimacy. Thus, one of the problems for organizational leadership is the raising and maintenance of support, from members or from sources outside the organization. Another problem is the conversion of support into the desired or required resources at any particular time.

Legitimacy and support are related but are not synonymous. Support may be converted into legitimacy for decisions and therefore into compliance based on normative grounds. Persons according legitimacy to an organization will also give it support. But support can be acquired for relatively self-interested reasons—for example, as the result of financial or status rewards which are quite extrinsic to the maintenance of the organization (or institution) itself. An organization which has or can offer positive or negative inducements, money, status, or information, on the one hand, or force, on the other, can get compliance without much if any legitimacy. It can gain support by using positively valued resources or possibly through the use of force. But to the extent that an organization is intrinsically valued and its maintenance is regarded as legitimate, support and the resources it can make claim to will be forthcoming, at least from the persons according it legitimacy.

Because support has at least some aspect of self-interestedness, it is not an adequate criterion of institutionalization, though the maintenance of an organization over time usually contributes to its legitimation and its acquiring aspects of an institution. Institutions are marked by more routine and predictable flows of resources over time from their membership and, more important, from their larger environment. The time dimension of resources relates to the stability of their flow between an organization and its members and between the organization and its environment. The value or productivity of resources depends on the amount of time for which they are or can be used to achieve a person's purposes.

Time in itself is not productive and thus is not a resource. But it is directly associated with the resources discussed above, since we are concerned with flows and thus rates of flow, which amount to volumes over time. To possess resources without time in which to use them reduces their value to zero. Thus, the time dimension in institution building relates to the use of resources for building up organizations into institutions and to the general development of resource flows which characterize institutions as a more stable form of organization.

2. Leadership. All of the institution variables are related, but leadership appears to be central in any analysis of institution building. The essence of leadership is the mobilization and allocation of resources so as to achieve certain objectives. Leadership involves the formulation of doctrine and program by making normative and empirical choices about the optimum use of organizational resources. Both internal and external structure are shaped by leadership, which must direct the operation of an institution and pattern its relationships with the environment so as to secure the necessary or desired flow of resources from other organizations and individuals.

The central consideration for institution builders is that organizations are not simply redistributive. They produce a variety of resources or, in the final analysis, satisfactions. By establishing various channels for resource flows, organizations can increase the aggregate amount of resources available for achieving their purposes. There is no assurance that an organization must produce net benefits, that the value of outputs will exceed the value of inputs, though it cannot continue long unless some net benefits are produced. With skillful management of resources within an organization and in an organization's exchanges with others, leadership should be able to provide net benefits to contributors of resources, which is the ultimate test of leadership.

Institution-building man is not simply the counterpart of homo economicus, buying cheap and selling dear. An institution builder must be able to manage resources profitably, but he must also display qualities of entrepreneurship, combining factors of organizational production in such as way as to produce valued outputs. These in turn yield resources which can be used to further the process or organizational growth. An organizational entrepreneur who aspires to succeed as an institution builder needs a canny sense both of his market opportunities in the environment and of his own objectives. He finds new sources of support, new combinations of resources, which are more productive or new uses for resources which yield greater value of output.[9]

To be effective, an organizational leader needs to know not only the advantageous use of resources, but how they can be most advantageously used over time to achieve the greatest value. Not all individuals or groups which contribute to his success need endorse or approve his ends. But he needs to get them to believe that, thanks to the productivity of his organization, greater benefits will accrue to them than the costs they incur by contributing. Those groups which value the organization's output most are likely, of course, to be the most beneficent contributors to its success. Organizational strategy involves the use of resources over time to obtain or maintain control over sufficient resources to achieve organizational objectives, among which ary organizational maintenance and growth, or institutionalization.

One of the characteristics of leadership which can distinguish it with success, then, is an acute faculty for strategy, which is the planned use of resources over time. A person occupying a position of authority who lacks a sense of the time dimension in institutional development may well squander or dissipate the resources which accrue to his position. As a rule, persons in positions of authority have resources at their disposal, obtained from members of the group or from persons outside through exchange. Yet often by neither seizing nor making opportunities for organizational growth, they forfeit the possibility of strengthening the organization by increasing its inputs or its outputs, thereby making institutionalization less possible.

The situation of the institution builder is pervaded by the ubiquity of *scarcity;* and scarcity is measured, actually and metaphorically, by time. An insufficiency of resources and a plenitude of purposes in too brief a time is the essence of scarcity. The institution builder cannot achieve all of the goals he has or satisfy all the demands made on his organization by others. The insufficiency of resources produced by the organization by others. The insufficiency of resources produced by the organization or received from other organizations in the environment makes critical the formulation and implementation of *priorities.* Various alternative patterns of resource allocation (i.e., policies) have different productive consequences. To do X before Y yields more resources for achieving Y or some other goal, than to do Y first and not even have enough resources for X. If there were no scarcity constraint, strategy would be irrelevant. [10]

The importance of leadership is related inversely to the availability of resources. The more plentiful they are, the less important is leadership for achieving a given goal. A corollary is that with a given amount of resources, the more quickly a goal is to be achieved, the more important is the contribution of leadership in formulating productive strategies. Scarcity is temporally defined, being an insufficiency of resources at a particular time, while priorities are similarly delineated as the means for scheduling resource uses over time. The omnipresent constraint of scarcity makes critically important the leadership functions of priority setting.

3. Doctrine. We accept Esman's definition of doctrine as "the specification of values, objectives and operational methods underlying social action," suggesting at the same time that it can be understood best when institution builders and their advisors understand the range and significance of organizational resources. Doctrine states both the value of organizational outputs and the productivity of different combinations of inputs. Such productivity, of course, can only be judged with reference to the values assigned to outputs, but these values are also associated with doctrine, a term more neutral than ideology but otherwise much the same.

One of the basic elements of doctrine is the *time horizon* (or time horizons) adopted. The value of outputs and the value and combination of inputs are both determined in part by the time horizon adopted by leadership on behalf of the organization. As achievement of certain ends in the near future is judged more important, so are the resources needed to achieve those ends valued more highly. If distant goals are more exalted, the future value of resources is less heavily discounted than when present goals loom large. Insofar as quick achievement of goals usually requires greater present volume of resources, doctrine stressing this raises the value of present resources and/or the importance of leadership to achieve these goals.

The role of doctrine in specifying valued ends is usually, and unfortunately, emphasized more than its function of identifying preferred means. True, the productivity of certain means cannot be separated from the valuation of ends. But to the extent that objectively less productive means for achieving valued ends are chosen and fixed in doctrine, the organization will be less able to accomplish its preferred ends.

The productivity of certain means can only be judged with reference to time. Some means may appear quite productive vis-a-vis the valued ends in the short run, but may well reduce the achievement of these ends in the long run. Leadership through its doctrine places some value on the present or near future vis-a-vis the more distant future. This is a matter of preference, not scientific calculation. But if organizational objectives can be specified and projected over time, with the relative importance of different time horizons weighted, then the most appropriate and productive means can be more aptly chosen.[11]

This comparison of resource value in the present and future applies also to the choice between consuming or expending resources in the present and saving or investing them for the future. Any organization, to maintain itself over time and achieve new or more objectives in the future, will need to make certain capital investments which have no immediate return. These will improve an organization's productive capacity and/or its linkages with other organizations, thereby providing benefits in the future which are greater than if no investment had been made.

The productivity of investment, of course, is never self-evident or guaranteed. Doctrine can make the process of institutionalization more efficient or effective by clearly specifying ends and justifying appropriate and productive means. When resources are scarce or time short, then the more ambiguous are doctrine's ends and the less reliable its means, and the less can it contribute to institution building.

4. Program. An organization's program consists of the allocation of resources over time, balanced more or less by its receipt of resources during approximately the same period of time. Thus, this institution variable is perhaps most closely and consistently associated with the time dimension in institution building. To analyze a program, we need to consider the three dimensions of timing which Moore has so clearly distinguished: synchronization, sequence, and rate.[12] The idea of program implies *coordination,* a concept intrinsically bound to time. The desired resources are to be in the right place at the right time in the right amount and at the right cost (i.e., not exceeding the benefit received). Coordination also requires some maintenance of balance between resource income and expenditure. Budgeting of various sorts is usually critical to preserving what may be thought of as organizational solvency.

The strategy of institution building requires that the program increase the resource position of the organization either by raising productivity or by making more favorable or extensive its exchanges with other organizations. Timing inputs and exchanges in such a way as to achieve organizational objectives efficaciously is the aim of a program. Contributing to societal needs is not in itself sufficient for institutionalization. Leadership needs to know how to satisfy these needs in a *timely* manner. To satisfy them freely and quickly may waste resources and build no consciousness of interdependence. To satisfy them only in a costly way and late may be to encourage other organizations or persons to seek linkages with organizations other than one's own.

Program designates the translation of doctrine into practical activities of organization. Given the scarcity of resources, a program also represents a statement of priorities or a sequence of resource allocations judged to be most productive for attaining organizational goals. The time element is central. Most institutional programs will compromise their change objectives to avoid jeopardizing long-term linkages with relevant organizations in their environment. To the extent possible, demands for new services or improved traditional ones will be satisfied, but seldom at the expense of other widely accepted goals.

The conventional thesis of organization theory is that resources must be earned from the environment through organizational performance, i.e., as a consequence of an organization's program. The case studies provided for the institution-building program suggest that this thesis is not necessarily true. It is possible for institutions to survive on the basis of factors other than performance. Economic resources can readily be obtained from abroad. International prestige is another factor helping some institutions survive. The willingness of sponsors to wait a long time for measurable results also helps.

Institution building thus is in large part a function of time. The more rapid the results desired, just as the less the organization's outputs are initially valued by others, the more critical is the content and implementation of program. Further, the fewer resources available to an organization's leadership, the more important is their efficient allocation through program strategy. Thus, we see again how these different institution variables may be linked through the consideration of time.

5. Internal Structure. Many of the things said about program as the allocation of resources vis-a-vis the environment apply similarly to internal structure as the allocation of resources within an organization. Structure represents the pattern of internal resource flows of economic resources, information, status, authority, legitimacy, and force or other sanctions. As soon as we think of internal structure in terms of allocations and flows, the elements of time and timing reappear. Efficiency and productivity of an organization depend on the synchronization, sequence, and rate of resource flows.

The institution-building approach appropriately considers the internal structure and dynamics of an organization concomitantly. Most structural analysis has attempted to deal with interrelated functions seen within a given and static time period. Structure, on the other hand, seen in the perspective proposed here, is intrinsically dynamic, resembling more the Leontief conception of economic structure than an architectural notion of material and fixed structure.

We can say that the more ambitious the change goals of the institution builder and/or the less time in which he desires to achieve these goals, the more critical will be internal structure to him. Efficiency (the ability to achieve given goals with fewer inputs) and productivity (the ability to raise the ratio of benefits to costs) are twin aims of internal structure. The first is more important when organizational success is constrained most by the scarcity of means; the latter, when it is dependent most on the achievement of goals. Both invariably figure in the institution builder's considerations at some point.

Just as program represented a set of inducements to organizations in the environment to contribute to the maintenance and growth of an institution, so has internal structure the same consequences for participants. The distribution of rewards and penalties is a means by which leadership gets participants to contribute and use some of their resources in the manner most productive for achieving organization goals. For maximum effectiveness, timing is critical in such distribution, since it represents exchanges with participants in much the same way that program, carried out through internal structure, represents exchanges with the environment.

Many organizational devices have been developed to order time, conserve it, or allocate it productively. Budget bureaus, planning organs, coordinating committees, working parties, linear programming, operations research, and the like, assist in time management. So do fiscal arrangements which save time, and training schemes which enable functionaries to budget and plan more effectively. O&M, PERT, and now PPBS treat not so much with resources per se as with use of resources through time.[13] Delay or lack of synchronization can be costly in terms of the efficient use of resources and the attainment of objectives. Thus institutions seek to overcome dissynchronization, ill-sequencing and slow rates through budgeting and planning.

B. ACTION STRATEGIES

The very concept of strategy implies the use of time or timing. Given the constraints of resource scarcity and chosen time horizons, priorities are given to certain actions, or allocations of resources, which are judged to be most productive for attaining given ends. In this case, the ends are associated with the goal of *institutionalization*. "Planning, structuring, and guidance" all imply the use of resources over time and are only means to certain ends. We would reformulate these ends in terms of developing an organization which (a) achieves changes in values and structure within and outside of itself through strategic and tactical allocations, these changes bringing about changes in behavior; (b) establishes, fosters and protects desired normative relationships and action patterns through leadership and advocacy of doctrine, again, reinforced by strategic and tactical allocations; and (c) attains support and flows of resources from organizations and sectors in its environment.

Formulation of action strategies requires a discerning analysis of the organization's environment. We approve of Esman's description of environment not "as a generalized mass, but rather as a set of discrete structures with which the subject institution must interact. The institution must maintain a network of exchange relationships with a limited number of organizations and engage in transactions for the purposes of gaining support, overcoming resistance, exchanging resources, structuring the environment, and transferring norms and values. Particularly significant are the strategies and tactics by which institutional leadership attempts to manipulate or accommodate to these linkage relationships."[15]

This appears to us as a productive way of thinking about the environment of an organization striving to become institutionalized. It directs attention to the elements of an organization's environment which may resist, i.e., prevent or make more costly, the desired changes. The idea of structural linkages may still be too abstract, however. What is implied in the description is *exchange relationships*—acquiring resources, bestowing rewards, gaining support, establishing legitimacy, and so forth. This conceptualization points up the structural consideration affecting institutionalization—the establishment and maintenance of "interdependencies which exist between an institution and other relevant parts of the society."[16] It makes clearly, on the one hand, the importance of reciprocity, and, on the other hand, of asymmetry in relationships which characterize institutions. The notion of "enabling linkages" cloaks both distinctions.

An institution provides something in return for the inputs it receives from individuals and groups, whether or not these are tangible and immediate. The exchange relationships, however, are not simply a matter of quid pro quo bargaining if an institution is involved. In one respect, an institution involves increased dependence on the organization, so that action strategies aiming at institutionalization seek to increase over time the dependence of others on the outputs of the organization. This may be because it supplies resources previously supplied by others (displacement), because it creates new demands for its outputs, because it gets others to value its output more highly, or because through efficiency or new technologies it can offer its outputs at a lower price than before.[17]

In another respect, an institution receives greater legitimacy from those with whom it maintains exchange relationships. Possession of legitimacy enables an institution to make claims on other's resources without making as full or tangible compensation as it would if that legitimacy were lacking. The contributors receive benefits from the institution, but they may be more normative and less material and they may be quite deferred. (An institution's "credit" is good, and it can get resources more or less as needed from individuals.) A second focus of action strategies for institution building thus would relate to legitimation of an organization, its aims, operations, and outputs.

One important aspect of institutionality is the element of uniqueness. To be able to speak of this in terms of degree, we need to (and appropriately can) speak of it in terms of monopoly or monopsony position. This is to say that to the extent an organization is the only supplier or the only buyer of a resource which is desired or made available by persons, the organization has greater power to secure for itself necessary and desired resources from others. This is another aspect of creating greater dependence which raises, so to speak, an institution's "terms of trade" with other organizations. At the same time, organizations commonly claim, where possible, a monopoly on legitimacy in a certain field, be it higher education, social services, or economic forecasting. The traits of institutions proposed by the institution-building approach, survival, intrinsic value, autonomy, and pervasiveness, are all enhanced by uniqueness or what could be considered a monopoly position.[18]

If we relate the various institution variables to institution-building action strategies in the context of time and timing, we can clarify further the connections among them.

1. In understanding or formulating action strategies, it is important that *leadership* neither become an abstraction nor be reified as a concept. The leadership of an organization are those persons who have responsibility for formulating strategies, whether they in fact do so or not. We can comprehend their strategies best in terms of how the other institution variables—doctrine, program, resources, and internal structure—are utilized. If these are utilized effectively, then almost by definition, leadership is judged good. If these are not so used, leadership is considered incompetent or uncommitted, according to some of the institution-building analyses.[19]

Rather than look at commitment and competence, we would suggest looking at the costs and benefits of affecting different sectors of the environment, not just in terms of economic resources but in terms of the full range of a program's outputs. It is the task of leadership both to mobilize and manage resources so as to sustain strategies of institutional change and development. This requires sufficient comprehension of the needs and resources found in the leader's human and physical environment. The specific strategy most productive in a given situation will vary according to the ends and means at hand; but to the extent that leadership grasps the institution variables and turns them to the requirement of establishing stable and/or expanding resource flows producing net benefits to contributors, institution building will be advanced.

2. The role of *doctrine* in institution-building action strategies is primarily one of influencing the process of resource allocation over time. There is nothing

necessarily magical or mystical about doctrine or ideology. What is involved is some normative judgment about the value of alternative distributions of resources, now or at some future time. Also involved is some judgment about the efficacy of means for achieving or maintaining a preferred distribution of resources. The benefits claimed by a doctrine may lie in the future, but they can still be real in terms of motivating effect. Future benefits must, to be sure, be discounted by some margin, according to intervening benefits foregone and the degree of uncertainty that they will be achieved. But this conditions, rather than disallows, the contribution of future-oriented doctrine.

In formulating action strategies, the time dimension bears heavily on the contribution of doctrine. Considerations of the long run and the short run compound calculations about the desired ambiguity or specificity of doctrine. In the short run, ambiguity can give leaders desired flexibility, enabling them to mobilize resources from many sources to support achievement of their program. If, however, the contributors understand doctrine to promise them short-run benefits, the program must yield them these benefits or contributions will slacken. Ambiguity may lead many more persons to expect benefits than can be satisfied with the outputs of a program. Specificity would limit both the number of persons expecting rewards but also the number making contributions. If doctrine persuades persons to adopt longer time horizons, the degree of ambiguity which will be tolerated is correspondingly increased.[20]

3. Actions strategies are in a real sense *programs* given a time dimension. A strategy establishes priorities for the expenditure of resources and sets the rate, sequence, and synchronization for activity. The *rate* of change which is possible depends on resource availability, but this is not necessarily fixed if resources can be acquired from outside the organization or its immediate environment, as discussed below. Organizational performance is not the only factor determining resource availability, contrary to most conventional models of organization theory, which are closed models.

In economic theory, one of the leading issues of development strategy has been the respective merits of "balanced" versus "unbalanced" growth. Institution builders have to make some judgment about their strategy (and program) with respect to this issue.[21] Balanced institutional growth assumes that resources will be most productive over time; that is, will bring forth a greater volume in successive periods, if allocated with regard to coordinated investment, or *synchronization.* Advocates of unbalanced growth argue that more resources will be elicited for the same or less volume of investment if investment resources are allocated in *sequence.* Forward and backward linkages are presumed to lead to complementary (if successive) investments by others.[22]

In principle, assuming that institution builders have near-perfect knowledge—a tenuous assumption—the balanced growth strategy is likely to accomplish goals in the shortest period of time. It does not rule out sequencing of investment, but only stipulates that all complementary investments be coordinated to maximize the gains from external economies. This strategy is most easily rejected on the grounds that no organization has sufficient resources to carry off balanced growth. The costs and requirements of such a strategy go far beyond, if one tries to follow the strategy through to its logical completion, the direct investments.

To the extent that institution builders can ascertain the net productivity of establishing successive linkages in sequence, unbalanced growth will be preferred. Efforts should be made to estimate the benefits of alternative sequences of activity and investment, since scarce resources are bound to be wasted if dispersed over a wide range. Institution-building strategy, like military strategy, requires the intelligent concentration of resources, to win strings of victories which culminate in a successful campaign. The opposition is engaged at its weakest points, with one's own resources distributed so as to have a margin of strength at the various points when contact is made.

Given the scarcity of means to achieve an organization's ends, some calculation of sequence, expenditure, and investment is required. Indeed, this is the essence of strategy. This does not mean that synchronization and rate are not important or considered, but that sequence is the dominant concern. Certain expenditures within a sequential strategy must be synchronized, and rates of expenditure must be controlled so as not to exceed the rates of incoming resources. But it is the sequence of efforts which sets the requirements for synchronization and basically determines the rates of income for an organization.

One of the analytical devices developed by social scientists to deal with sequences in development has been that of developmental "stages."[23] Many critical refutations of this mode of thinking have been offered. We accept the findings of institution-building studies that there seem to be no necessary successive stages of development toward institutionalization. That there are differences among various levels of development may be true, but a particular level does not indicate deterministic progress in the future or necessarily constrained progress, either. We think that social scientists will contribute more to understanding and aiding the solution of institution-building problems, and many others as well, if they focus on the productive consequences of alternative sequences of activity among which leadership may choose than on the presumed necessity of certain sequences observed in historical circumstances.

4. The difference between strategy and tactics is in part one of differences in time horizons. Strategies have longer time horizons than have tactics. The payoff for a strategy is reckoned over a longer period of time than for a tactic.[24] A strategy represents a major commitment of resources to the attainment of a goal or set of goals, while a tactic involves a minor commitment of resources, often aiming not so much at achieving a goal per se as at improving an organization's resource position in order to be better able to achieve a certain goal. Obviously various tactics must be formulated to support and advance a strategy. Also insofar as the goal is that of institution building, tactics which preserve the viability of the organization are important and essential.

5. The critical importance of *environment* in conditioning change tactics is recognized in the institution-building approach, as seen, for example, in Esman's statement that the environment "is not an inert substance waiting to be manipulated."[25] There will be quite varied interests in that environment, having quite varied contributions to make or withhold from the organization. To achieve short-run cooperation, leadership needs to persuade those on which it depends for resources and support that it can provide them with significant net benefits in return for contributions, perhaps to convince them to redefine what constitutes their real interest, or to expend the resources necessary to get compliance with organizational aims. With change tactics as with strategy, leadership and resources are to some extent substitutable, though nothing can be achieved if the organization is endowed with leadership and no resources or vice versa.

C. TECHNICAL ASSISTANCE IN INSTITUTION BUILDING

Consideration of the time dimension in institution building points up the contribution which technical assistance can make to this effort. There are a number of ways in which a given change can be achieved more quickly. Improvements in leadership and internal structural reform can help in this, as can modifications in doctrine and program. Technical assistance can aid in upgrading any of these four institution variables, but the usual contribution is to resources.

With other variables held constant, it is nonetheless usually possible to accelerate change by increasing the availability of resources to be used in order to gain compliance with organizational decisions internally and externally. Economic resources, information, status, and force can all be "imported" from outside the organization's indigenous environment. Money, goods, and technical services can be provided by foreign donors, as can education and training, within or outside of the organization. Those attributes or possessions which confer status can be acquired from abroad, and the means of coercion (weapons, personnel, and/or logistical support) are often obtainable.

Resources, however, should not be considered quite separately from the other variables (leadership, doctrine, program, and internal structure). If there are no improvements made in the productivity of the other four variables, the increased output to be achieved with an additional input of resources is likely to be less than if other changes are made, simply because of the ubiquity of the law of diminishing marginal returns. Inputs of a given resource will add to total output, but, in the absence of other changes in the composition of inputs or the structure of production, will add increasingly smaller increments. This is not to advise against providing additional resources through external assistance, but to caution against overly optimistic expectations of results. Where the externally acquired resources "break bottlenecks" in production, the increase in outputs will be more than proportional to the inputs added. But over time, the increase will become less than proportional, and possibly it can decline to zero unless other organizational changes are made.

Giving additional resources to an organization is often an inefficient means of bringing about change, but it is frequently the only or most readily available means by which foreign agencies can seek to bring about change. Despite the fact of diminishing returns from simply augmenting resources, a foreign country, especially an affluent one, may choose this method. For one thing, it incurs fewer political costs because less interference in the organization is involved. It may also be used to stimulate or make possible innovation in organizational technology in order to meet domestic needs better and thereby create conditions for institutionalization.

There is another limitation on the use of resources externally derived for tasks of institution building. Institutionalization requires establishment of resource flows between the organization and its environment. External resources can be helpful for "pump priming" to get these flows started, but there is a danger that they will stunt flows from the indigenous environment. The leadership may become too satisfied with outside flows, too disinclined to make the effort to mobilize and engage resources in the immediate environment, too intent upon pleasing external donors, too unresponsive to the needs of persons who could become the institution's steady supporters if it would satisfy their needs and provide them net benefits for their contributions. Providing resources from abroad can alleviate resource scarcity for some period of time, but if they are not used to establish indigenous resource flows, the aim of institutionalization will be defeated.

The limitations encountered in using external resources for institution building are highlighted by considering the particular organizational resource of legitimacy. In some ways, legitimacy resembles the asset of "good will" in economic accounting, though it is a much more significant resource in the political economy of organizations. It represents the margin, when balancing accounts, between total liabilities and tangible assets which can be used to liquidate these liabilities. As noted already, the more legitimacy an organization has, the less it needs to expend in the way of tangible assets for getting compliance from an individual. An organization with high legitimacy is assured of a considerable and predictable flow of resources from those persons who accord it that legitimacy.

An organization may be viewed as legitimate by persons or other organizations outside its immediate environment, and on this basis (or by giving full tangible compensation for resources received) may procure resources for its operation. But the problem involved in institution building is that of building up legitimacy from the more immediate environment so that a regular and adequate flow of resources is assured to the organization. It is a fact that often the receipt of resources from abroad is viewed as illegitimate by local persons, and this may block institutionalization. Or it may simply be that, to the leadership, seeking legitimacy in the eyes of foreign donors (to procure external aid) serves their needs more than legitimacy in the eyes of local persons, and thus it fails to establish the organization's legitimacy on a local basis.

We would suggest that resources imported from outside can compensate for scarcity of time, to some extent. Change can be accomplished more quickly, other things being equal, if more resources are available to the leadership. However, resources are not freely substitutable for time. Let us accept, for the sake of analysis, the abstract distinction between environments that are more or less responsive to change. Where they are more ready for change, the "elasticity of substitution" of resources for time is greater. But where there is little responsiveness to change, it will be more difficult and less productive to try to compensate for time with resources. [26]

If resources appear to be the basic variable in institution building, and the one most easily treated through external assistance, leadership may still be the critical variable, mobilizing and expending resources according to the doctrines and programs it formulates. But leadership is probably the most difficult organization variable to import. In some situations, expatriates may occupy leadership positions for a short period of time and bring about changes in doctrine, program, and internal structure which leave the organization more productive than before and closer to institutionalization. But this is rare. Many is the case where gains made by expatriate leadership have been dissipated after their departure. [27]

Leadership training is a common form of technical assistance. In principle, it is a wise choice. Especially if a more productive time perspective can be imparted so that leaders will know how to use resources most effectively through time to achieve given goals, such training will be successful and worthwhile. How often, however, are the perspectives given through training in developed countries irrelevant or irreconcilable with the conditions of the developing countries. One of the perspectives—ideologies, perhaps—which has been often inculcated through Western or Westernized education is that of rational productivity. It guides the choices and styles of many indigenous leaders with responsibility for institution building, but with uncertain success. [28]

If training abroad has many shortcomings, a better case can be made for on-the-job training through technical assistance programs in the country itself. It is noted, however, that indigenous counterparts have a different sense of time and timing than their expatriate colleagues. Different methods and tactics of organizational operation are preferred. And, as Esman reports, counterparts have a keener sense of feasibility than their advisors. Unlike their advisors, they usually weigh costs as carefully as benefits. [29] We would not rule out the possibility that useful leadership training could be used to promote institution building, especially when reinforced by the input of resources. But to be useful, it requires much greater sensitivity to the conditions and needs of counterparts' environment and much less ethnocentrism than is usually displayed.

Doctrine is less readily imparted directly through technical assistance, though it can be affected by foreign agencies. The problem is that for doctrine to be effective in institution building, it must be fully accepted by leadership; and they may be less ready to receive doctrine than resources, generally feeling more in need of the latter than the former. However, insofar as leaders come to adopt the doctrines associated with science and technology or large-scale organization, these doctrines can be used to justify measures such as taxing or expropriating resources from the population. They can legitimate such measures on the grounds that greater welfare can be achieved at some future time if certain sacrifices of resources are made in the present and used for technological advancement. [30] Such doctrines are imparted primarily through Western or Westernized formal education, but they are perpetuated and proselytized through the school systems of developing countries as well as through the public statements of political leaders. [31]

Program is no easier to import through technical assistance. Outsiders have a difficult time in devising programs for institution building which will take effective advantage of the opportunities presented by the environment and overcome the obstacles there. Program formulation is usually a task for indigenous leadership, however much training and doctrine they may receive or have received from abroad.

There is one way in which program formulation can be externally assisted, and that is through social science development. The Research Program on Institution Building, for example, to the extent that it devises and tests action strategies for institution building and then makes them known to the leadership of organizations in developing countries, is aiding program formulation. To assist leaders in calculating costs and consequences over time of alternative choices for the use of scarce resources—allocated in the form of policies—is to help them formulate priorities and programs for bringing about the kind of institutional change which they judge most productive for their organizations and members. [32]

It is assumed that technical assistance can facilitate the tasks of institution building by helping to devise more productive internal structures of organizations. This assumption is, at least with our present state of knowledge, we believe, quite fallacious. We are struck that Western students of public administration and organization theory have accepted without testing the proposition that Western forms of organization and administration are more developed and more productive. They have assumed a connection between the wealth and productivity of Western countries and the organizational and administrative structures these have developed over time. Yet no real verification of this has been attempted. [33] We would suggest that technical assistance for institution building proceed very warily and humbly when considering internal structure.

Summary

The study of the time dimension in institution building requires, of course, considerable research in order to determine how action strategies can best be formulated under specific conditions taking into account the time factor. One thing should be evident from the foregoing discussion, however. The time dimension links the various institution variables and conditions their effect upon one another. On the basis of the analysis presented above, several propositions can be made about institution building and time.

(1) In trying to accomplish a given increment in institutionalization within a fixed period of time, the scarcer resources are, the more important will be leadership and the other institution variables; conversely, the more plentiful resources are, the more slack, ambiguity, or error can be tolerated in the other variables.

(2) With given leadership, doctrine, program, and internal structure, the more resources are available, the less time is required to accomplish a given increment in institutionalization.

(3) The greater the net benefits provided by program to an organization's contributors of resources, the more institutionalization can be accomplished within a given period of time.

(4) The longer the time horizon adopted and promulgated by doctrine, the fewer net benefits need to be provided to contributors of resources within a given period of time.

(5) With respect to foreign aid in institution building, the contribution of resources can reduce the time required for a given increment in institutionalization, other things being equal.

(6) Equally important, the contribution of resources through foreign aid channels can impede the process of institution building if continued over a long period of time or provided in such a way that indigenous flows of resources are deterred or discouraged.

(7) The development of legitimacy as a resource accorded to an organization by persons and groups in its environment is the most critical factor in institution building; and this change in attitudes and values invariably requires time in which the organization can establish its normatively beneficial relationship to those persons and groups with whom it interacts.

NOTES

1. Alfred Diamant, after surveying existing models of administration and organization, concludes that most either ignore the question of change or conceive of the nature of organizational change along the lines of an equilibrium concept; that is to say, change is either non-existent or is kept within narrow limits. "As a result there is little concern with time—surely a paradoxical condition for a body of literature dealing with complex

organizations which are, after all, the very epitome of sophisticated timing." "The Temporal Dimension in Models of Administration and Organization," Comparative Administration Group Occasional Papers, ASPA, pp. 11-12 passim.

2. It is unfortunate that one of the best recent works in organization theory, Etzioni's *A Comparative Analysis of Complex Organizations,* New York: Free Press, 1963, tries to translate behavioral relations into structural ones. Impressive as this typological analysis may be, it offers no guidance to an institution builder.

3. E.G., see William C. Hood, "Some Aspects of the Treatment of Time in Economic Theory," The Canadian Journal of Economics and Political Science, Vol. XIV, November 1948; also, Redvers Opie, "Marshall's Time Analysis," Economic Journal, Vol. XLI, 1931: 199-215.

4. See *Man, Time and Society* (1963), p. 9 and passim. Moore suggests that it is time which gives orderly qualities to human action. It acts as a boundary condition and as a measure of persistence or change. Only money, he says, rivals time in terms of the pervasiveness and awkwardness of its scarcity. It is in connection with this finity and scarcity that Moore refers to it as a resource. The old adage, "time is money," is more a metaphor than a simile. Moore draws this analogy, suggesting that time and treasure are somewhat interchangeable. Either is, he says, a potential instrument for increasing the other. But this overlooks differences between the two.

5. This statement is somewhat complicated by the fact that time represents amounts of possession and use of amounts of resources. This amplification is implicit in our discussion.

6. The historical and philosophical relation of time and space, in particular the traditional view of temporal ordering as subservient to the traditional concept of space, is discussed by Ilchman in "New Time in Old Clocks: Productivity, Development and Comparative Administration," in Dwight Waldo, editor, *Temporal Dimensions of Development Administration* (1970), 137-178.

7. Milton Esman's monograph, "The Institution Building Concepts—an Interim Appraisal" Pittsburgh: Inter-University Research Program on Institution Building, 1968, provided the framework from which we worked in our analysis, and our references are often to it rather than the formulations presented in the previous chapter, though there is little substantial difference between the two.

8. For an extended analysis of resources, see Chapter 3 of Warren F. Ilchman and Norman Thomas Uphoff, *The Political Economy of Change* (1969). In this present chapter, we have tried to link our policy-oriented approach for political science ("the new political economy") to the analytical framework for strategies of institution building proposed by Esman and others associated with the Inter-University Research Program. Obviously we cannot develop the full model of our "new political economy" within the limitations of a single chapter. Rather we have attempted to elaborate various elements of the institution-building framework. For a complete exposition of the model, we must refer readers to our book.

9. The conception of entrepreneurship employed owes much to Joseph Schumpeter, applying his formulation in *The Theory of Economic Development* (1934) to organizational analysis.

10. Exceptions to this rule of scarcity are organizations which are so inconsequential that they make few demands for resources or so indispensable that resources are invariably adequate. For the first kind of organization, strategy is irrelevant; for the second, it is unnecessary. Thus, leadership is irrelevant to the first and unnecessary for the second.

11. Alexander Eckstein has set forth some propositions which may be applied to institution building and the interaction of doctrine, resources, and time. He says that the greater the range of ends and the higher the level of attainment sought (i.e., the greater resources required as a function of doctrinal goals), the shorter the time horizon within which the ends are to be attained. That is, the more rapid the rate of economic growth desired, the more unfavorable the factor and resource endowments; the greater the

institutional barriers to economic change and industrialization (i.e., under normal conditions the greater time necessary to bring about change); and the more backward the economy in relative terms (also measured in temporal terms): the greater will tend to be the urge, push, and pressure for massive state intervention and initiative in the process of industrialization, and at the same time, the greater will be the need for such intervention if a breakthrough, rather than a breakdown, is to be attained. "Individualism and the Role of the State in Economic Growth," Economic Development and Cultural Change, Vol. 6, January 1958.

12. Moore, *Man, Time and Society,* op. cit., pp. 8-9. Simultaneous action by a number of persons or at least their presence at a particular time is synchronization; actions which follow one another in a prescribed order is sequence; and the frequency of actions or events some period of time is rate.

13. See Ilchman, "New Time in Old Clocks," op. cit., passim.

14. The emphasis on allocations of resources results not only from our own preference for thinking in these terms. We note Gabriel Almond's prognostication-qua-exhortation in his presidential address to the American Political Science Association, September 8, 1966: "And we are on the eve of a search for rational choice theories of political growth—an approach which may make political theory more relevant to public policy . . . contemporary political theorists are inescapably confronted with the problem of how resources may be economically allocated to affect political change in preferred directions. The justification for this quest for an allocation-of-resources theory of political development is not only its relevance to central concerns of public policy, but its uses as a test of the validity and power of our theories. It forces us to place our bets, set the odds, and confront straightforwardly the issue of the kind of prediction which is possible in political science." "Political Theory and Political Science," American Political Science Review, Vol. LX, December 1966: 877.

15. This formulation is from Esman's monograph, "The Institution Building Concepts—An Interim Appraisal, op. cit., p. 5.

16. One benefit of thinking in terms of exchange relationships rather than of linkages is that one has less need to squander intellectual effort and research time on typologies. Instead, one examines the amounts and kinds of resources actually exchanged. One would look at those exchange relationships which yield for an organization or institution the resources and support which are crucial for its operation. There is no need to label these "enabling linkages," since this says little either quantitatively or qualitatively and they may change over time anyway. Further, "normative linkages" are significant for an institution only if they yield legitimacy which can be used to gain resources of one kind or another. Purely "normative" linkages are probably irrelevant. There is need to consider what are described as "diffused linkages," but we prefer to describe an organization's environment in terms of "sectors." This term connotes productive characteristics, but it also does not require that there be any formal organization.

17. This is another way of describing the tests of institutionality: ability to survive, being viewed by its environment as having intrinsic value, and in turn having gained some degree of autonomy, exercising influence, and having a spread effect from its activities.

18. When uniqueness is only partial, we can still think in terms of the economist's firm engaging in "monopolistic competition." Any advantage stemming from product differentiation contributes to institutionalization, and this enhances the value of the output.

19. Actually, we find little analytical power or merit in the terms "competence" and "commitment," inasmuch as they verge on tautology. Effective leaders are judged competent and committed, and ineffective leaders are thought not to be.

20. Another aspect of the time dimension in this regard is suggested by Hirschman, who says "it is in the nature of most innovations that its beneficiaries are anonymous, inarticulate and unaware of the benefits to accrue (they include among others the consumers that are yet unborn), while those who stand to lose from the innovation are highly vocal vested interests." *The Strategy of Economic Development* (1958), p. 61. Another way of putting this, to make the time dimension stand out more clearly, is to note

that by and large, benefits accrue over time while costs are incurred more immediately. Short-term perceptions usually find costs exceeding benefits. When a change has immediate benefits with costs spread out over time, one may expect there to be little opposition, even if the costs and benefits are approximately equal, or even if costs are somewhat greater in the long run. In both situations, benefits or costs in the future are devalued in personal calculations. These considerations have important ramifications for change tactics and strategies.

21. The most succinct case for balanced economic growth is offered by P. N. Rosenstein-Rodan, "Problems of Industralization in Eastern and South-Eastern Europe" (1943), reprinted in A. N. Agarwala and S. P. Singh, *The Economics of Underdevelopment* (1963), pp. 245-256. The best statement of the case for unbalanced growth is by Hirschman, *The Strategy of Economic Development,* op. cit. For a critical discussion of these strategies, see Ilchman and Ravindra C. Bhargava "Balanced Thought and Economic Growth," Economic Development and Cultural Change, Vol. 13, July 1966: 385-399. The balanced-unbalanced growth distinction as it affects administrative reform is discussed by Ilchman, "Rising Expectations and the Revolution in Development Administration," Public Administration Review, Vol. 25, December 1965: 314-328.

22. Forward linkages are those where an organization's output is the input of another organization, so that increasing production of one is an incentive to the other to increase its production. Backward linkage has the same effect, only there another organization's output is one's own organization's inputs. Increasing one's production raises demand for the other's product.

23. The most elaborate statement of this kind of analysis is W. W. Rostow's *The Stages of Economic Growth* (1959). It is implicit or explicit in much of the writing on development administration, e.g., Fred Riggs, *Administration in Developing Countries* (1964).

24. Esman's discussion of tactics suggests a conception which we have found useful in our own work. He writes of *managing* environmental linkages and transactions, where we would write similarly of "resource management." We appreciate his commentary: "The determination of tactics for each significant linkage, the need to monitor and to adapt these tactics to feedback from experience and to new circumstances in the environment emphasizes the importance of timing, capacity to bargain, willingness to adjust to changing situations—the whole panoply of the political arts of management—these determine the ability of an innovative organization to make its way in an ambiguous environment while protecting its main programmatic objectives." "The Institution Building Concepts," op. cit., pp. 32-33.

25. "Each of these groups has its own perceived interest," he continues, "which it will attempt with varying degrees of skill and vigor, and through a variety of tactics, to protect in its relations with the new institution." Op. cit., pp. 31-32.

26. When the British colonial administration decided to undertake large-scale schemes to grow groundnuts (peanuts) in tropical Africa after World War II, they assumed that the ordinary time required to effect a revolution in production could be telescoped or collapsed by the input of sufficient capital. The East Africa Groundnut Scheme, located at Kongwa in Tanganyika, was a colossal failure. In her analysis of it, S. H. Frankel writes: "All that capital provides is what the past has created. It cannot buy future time in any other sense than that it will aid men and women in exploring the future." *The Economic Impact on Underdeveloped Societies* (1953), p. 149. The mechanistic bias of project planners, with its assumption that capital could overcome all obstacles, led them to view time as an enemy, not as an ally, she says. The inability of capital to substitute for time under given conditions is made graphically clear by K.D.S. Baldwin in his analysis of the groundnut project at Mokwa in Northern Nigeria; see *The Niger Agricultural Project* (1955).

27. This is often considered to be the case with colonial regimes. After they leave, so the argument goes, the administration and other institutions in the newly independent country "go downhill." Seldom is it considered how much of their productivity depended on the import of resources from outside, particularly economic resources, coercive force, and information. Indeed, colonial administrations may have been quite inefficient despite their ostensible productivity. Their successor indigenous administrations may well be more efficient with the meager resources at their disposal.

28. Ilchman, "Productivity, Administrative Reform, and Anti-Politics," in Ralph Braibanti, editor, *Political and Administrative Reform* (1969). The model of "rational-productivity" is presented in this essay as a variation on the Weberian ideal type of "legal-rationality." It is suggested that this outlook dominates the thinking of many public officials in low-income countries charged with responsibility for economic development and planning. It is not clear, however, that this outlook, despite its formal intention, is clearly related to substantive productivity.

29. Op. cit., p. 37.

30. Ilchman, "New Time in Old Clocks," op. cit., pp. 137ff.

31. See Paul E. Sigmund, *The Ideologies of Developing Nations* (1963).

32. This is the kind of political or social science which we propose in *The Political Economy of Change,* op. cit.

33. A survey of virtually all literature on comparative administration and bureaucracy was conducted by Ilchman and Todd LaPorte under the auspices of the Institute of International Studies, University of California, during the summer of 1967. Propositions pertaining to organizational power and productivity were to be found in or derived from the literature. Few emerged; those which did were unconfirmed or contradictory. The conclusion is that the social sciences at present can say little of relevance and reliability about the productivity of alternative organizational structures. A book by Ilchman and LaPorte analyzing and summarizing this literature is being written.

GUIDELINE TO DEVELOPMENT THEORY FORMULATIONS

JOSEPH W. EATON

University of Pittsburgh

JOSEPH W. EATON is Professor of Sociology in Public Health and of Social Work Research at the University of Pittsburgh. Until this new post, accepted in January 1970, he served as the Director of the Advanced Program of the Graduate School of Social Work. He also is administratively responsible for the Inter-University Institution Building Program, after serving briefly as a member of its Board of Directors. He has been engaged in extensive field research studies in social treatment programs, prisons, the sociology of professions, and mental health, including a study of the Hutterites in Canada and the United States. His most recent book (in collaboration with Michael Chen) reporting the findings of a research contract with the United States Office of Education is *Influencing the Youth Culture: A Study of Youth Organizations in Israel,* Beverly Hills: Sage, 1970.

GUIDELINE TO DEVELOPMENT THEORY FORMULATIONS

JOSEPH W. EATON

University of Pittsburgh

RESOURCE AND SYSTEM MODEL SUPPORT

Aid sent overseas to assist another country's development has two components. One of them has a dollar-and-cents value and therefore tends to be quite explicit. What is involved is the shipment of a tractor, the salary of a physician, or a gift of a thousand tons of wheat. Such monetary aid may be welcome, but will leave little lasting impact, unless it is associated with *systems model* transfer, *the adaptation in a new country of ideas that become institutionalized.* Foreign aid has a lasting impact when the gift of a tractor becomes the precipitant of more modernized agricultural practices, that lead farmers to earn enough to repair their machines and ultimately, to replace them from their earnings. Similarly, a foreign doctor will leave an impact only if he can introduce a different model of providing medical services, with local staff who will carry on, after his services are withdrawn.

A principal theorem of institution building is that new service programs are most likely to become adopted by the host country when they are part of an organized or patterned way of doing things, such as a hospital, a school of public administration, a local planning agency, a youth corps, or other economic and social agency.

This concept of development assistance represents a clear-cut break with the concept of charity which involves a quite different approach of help-giving. Charity was a strong element in the precursors of modern development administration—the missionaries. Many of them went abroad primarily to do

[139]

good deeds, while meeting their need to save the souls of persons whom they regarded as less fortunate and more primitive. Generally in return for acceptance of their religious creed, missionaries were willing to give gifts in resources, skills, know-how, and therapy. Modern foreign aid is no longer focused on merely helping such worthy individuals, no matter how defined. Aid is given to a social system. Assistance is more often rendered by means of development of new organizations which can perform innovative functions affecting many people.

One of the criteria of successful aid remains improving the opportunity structure of individuals. It does matter, in the end, if a blind beggar was helped or an orphan child provided with a home. But the strategy is not focused on microsystem interactions of the charity and missionary approach. Contemporary social and economic development more often emphasizes macrosystem interventions. Friendship and charity, the concepts of the missionary and of the private benefactor, are being superseded by community organization, planning, and institution building. It is a process of organizational innovation intended to have an impact on the prior and already well-established institutions of an emerging nation. Esman suggests that such new or reconstituted organizations should:

(a) embody changes in values, functions, physical, and/or social technologies;
(b) establish, foster, and protect new normative relationships and action patterns;
(c) attain support and complementarity in the environment.[1]

In summary, institution-building concepts provide guidelines for a systematic description of macrosystem interaction processes planned to facilitate development of innovative organizations. Their effectiveness will be measured by a variety of criteria, including their capacity to deliver goods and services to particular categories of persons and their capacity to survive as part of a network of complementary units that advance the rate of socioeconomic growth. Only through systems model transfer can a development program survive after the transfer of resources ends, as it always must. A new school of public administration ultimately must live on local budgets and use local teachers. Agricultural aid can survive if it leads to such innovative programs as a soil conservation service, a financially solvent machine cooperative, and modern marketing techniques.

If we accept the theory that social change must become institutionalized in order to acquire permanency, there must be more emphasis on the time dimension of development planning.[2] New ideas and programs must be supported long enough to develop normative relationships with already existing organizations. They must attain survival power through strong enabling and functional linkages with other parts of the social system.

From Organization to Institution

The new network of patterned practices, like rules and power hierarchies, within a single administrative unit to accomplish well defined functions is popularly referred to as an "organization." At times, it has been described in this book as an "institution." The two words have nearly synonymous dictionary meanings. Although there is as yet no uniformity in their usage, there is a tendency among social scientists to use these concepts to draw distinctions between several types of large scale social units.

The concept of institution has often been used to describe the more generalized or model aspect of an organization. Innovative organizations are viewed as becoming institutionalized to the extent that their functions acquire more than limited and local significance. In the words of Richard L. Duncan and William S. Pooler, organizations can be called institutions when they develop the capacity "to act as agents for the larger society by providing valued functions and services. More than this, they serve as models for defining legitimate normative and value patterns, conserving and protecting them for the larger society."[3]

A quite different distinction has been made by Philip Selznick, who equates institutionalization with *loss of innovative impact.* In the light of this proposed meaning, a given enterprise can be an organization as well as in the process of becoming an institution. While an extreme case may approach either an ideal organization or an ideal institution, most living associations resist so easy a classification. They are complex mixtures of both designed and responsive behavior.[4]

A more operational and, therefore, precise definition in the use of the concept in economic and social development is suggested by the following tests of institutionality proposed by Jiri Nehnevajsa: [5]

(1) An organization's ability to survive.
(2) Extent to which an innovative organization comes to be viewed by its environment to have intrinsic value, to be measured operationally by such indices as its degree of autonomy and its influence on other institutions.
(3) The extent to which an innovative pattern in the new organization becomes normative for other social units in the larger social system.

Planned administrative patterns—be they called organizations or institutions—can be studied in terms of their function to become instruments of change, by influencing other units of the larger social system. This is the link between theory—or the blueprint element of planning—and practice—the administered programs to implement the blueprint.

WHAT IS THE UTILITY OF CONCEPTS?

The literature on foreign aid includes a good deal of ad hominem and episodic description. There are accounts of how a particular program got started, who helped, who hindered, and what was accomplished. But such case studies make it difficult for the reader to transfer experience from one situation, which will never be entirely duplicated, to a new one, the details of which can never be fully anticipated.

Any observer of a segment of social reality is confronted with the methodological issue of how to transform unique events into data for comparative study. The experience of planning for dams in the TVA area is relevant to other dam projects, as in the Nile Valley; but in order to generalize from a unique event to a more generic variable, concepts are needed. Principles, be they tentative or somewhat confirmed by evidence, can be formulated only with the help of abstracted analytic variables. They can be quantified, compared, and contrasted to facilitate comparison of one event with other, though not identical phenomena.

This comparative research potential motivated the scholars associated with the Inter-University Research Program on Institution Building to adopt a common conceptual framework. From the start no implication was intended that it is complete. It was anticipated that in the process of research, the initial concepts would be refined. Others would be added to move in the direction of a profession-wide terminology that could lead to the formulation of systematic propositions and "guesstimates" about institution building. Missing variables, such as power, would be included by the addition of analytic concepts. Other original concepts would be replaced by different words, coined with greater specificity and less likelihood of confusion with related concepts.

Concepts are seen as "professional lingo" to those who do not use them or understand their value for designating subsets of a well-defined collection of objects and elements.[6] This is not the place to elaborate on the utility of applying the mathematical notion of a *set* to social science concepts,[7] except to note that both follow the same logical process: distillation of common elements or variables from a more complete set of circumstances, and their refinement into more precise subvariables that can be used in hypothesis formulation and hypothesis testing.

Conceptual analysis permits the use of experience in one case to understand another, in some ways quite different, situation. Concepts permit the analysis to combine the idealism of utopian youth movement members (manpower resource), with a subsidy from the Ministry of Education (budgetary resource) and the educational skill of trained youth leaders (academic resource) into a leadership training resource.[8] No such program could exist without money to finance it, teachers to provide instruction, and customers (students) who want to attend. A concept represents a common meaning which can be attached to otherwise very different entities. The attributes are often not apparent. They must be inferred analytically. They are logical abstractions which, as Arnold Rose points out, rarely occurs in a pure form.[9] The logical process is that which Florian Znaniecki described as "analytic induction."[10] This quality, for which Max Weber used the term "ideal type,"[11] takes the form of a logical sketch. Each concept is an accentuation of one or more qualities and a synthesis of a great many diffuse and discrete facts.

Refinement of Concepts

The present IB conceptual framework will become more precise as existing sociological and political science distinctions are utilized more extensively. For instance, the commonplace distinction between charismatic development leaders, like Kemal Ataturk and Abdul Nasser, and the more bureaucratic institution builder who tries his hand at executing concrete plans, comes to mind. Another attribute of leadership that could be differentiated is the distinction between revolutionaries and reformers, as proposed by Gerald A. Caiden.[12]

Precision in the use of concepts requires the specification of subcategories, as is provided, for instance, by the Esman-Blaise categorization of linkages into:

(a) enabling linkages
(b) functional linkages
(c) normative linkages[13]
(d) diffused linkages

This organizing scheme was further refined in the study by Donald A. Taylor on Brazil,[14] but his refinement did not call systematic attention to the fact that some linkages are hostile or dysfunctional. When a new organization is established, some of the relevant linkages are competitive and disabling. Old units may siphon money allocated for the innovative unit. Since concepts help to organize otherwise isolated facts, Willis P. Porter was induced by the IB concepts to search for all linkages that supported the development of the College of Education in Bangkok. Equally important resistances, from already established educational agencies, while occasionally mentioned, were not analyzed in a similar systematic fashion.[15]

The original IB conceptual scheme of linkages had positive bias. This fact conforms to the general preference of action-oriented personnel to look at the positive possibilities of a situation. Negative forces are seen as an emergency or crisis. They are less often planned for.

Comparative analysis of field study data can lead to refinement of concepts through deduction, as for instance between leadership that is entrenched— because a person serves for a long time—or changing. Either type can be an absentee or a resident leader. Several IB studies have indicated that when organizational leadership is performed by a nonresident official, be he entrenched or changing, he can at best take only a spasmodic interest.

Concept	Observations
Absentee and Changing Leadership	"Up to 1959, the United Nations sent twenty 'experts' to the Institute for a total of twenty-nine-and-a-half man-years of consultantship. During these years, Turkey provided no full-time senior person for the staff, although six or seven

junior employees were gradually attaining experience and status, including for several of them a year of education abroad."[16]

Resident
and
Entrenched
Leadership

"... the school was placed within the Brazilian Institute of Administration under the leadership of Prof. Luiz Alves de Mattos. Two years previously, Prof. Mattos had conducted the initial study which formed the basis for the establishment of the Brazilian School of Public Administration in Rio de Janeiro (EBAP). He had recent experience with the numerous problems connected with creating a new educational institution. Throughout the twelve years of the EBAP's existence, Prof. Mattos has nurtured its growth."[17]

Resident
and
Entrenched
Leadership

"... The Dean of the Thai Institute of Administration manifested many of the normative qualities of the established bureaucracy. He was kindly and considerate towards the staff; he sought their loyalty; he was pleased to respond to their requests and reluctant to impose sanctions. In return he expected and desired loyalty, and he saw little real need for an endless abiding emphasis on program development and functional specificity."[18]

Each of these situations is different. One refers to a situation in Turkey, the other in Brazil, and the third in Thailand. Each deals with a university-level school designed to train administrators. In all the three situations, the concept of leadership is relevant, each with somewhat different subcategories because of the way they perform their leadership roles.

INFERENCE FORMULATION

The IB consortium financed studies went beyond a description of how a particular organization developed. Each reported analytic and explanatory inferences by relating two or more concepts to formulate hypotheses such as the following:

Resident and entrenched leadership can more easily command resources for a new program and develop strong enabling linkages with other institutions in the society than absentee and changing leadership.

Another inference about institution building was identified by Milton Esman on the basis of his comparative analysis of four case studies: "There is an inherent dilemma between (a) institutionalizing and organization and (b) insuring its capacity to continue to innovate—its innovative thrust."[19]

In noting this tendency, Esman was in accord with a similar inference made by Selznick, who had not cited the evidence he used to derive it:

"When an enterprise begins to be more profoundly aware of dependency on outside forces, its very conception of itself may change, with consequences for recruitment, policy and administrative organization at many levels. As a business, a college, or a government agency develops a distinctive clientele, the enterprise gains in stability that comes with secure sources of support, an easy channel of communication. At the same time it loses flexibility. The process of institutionalization has set in."[20]

In quite a few studies sponsored by the IB consortium, the new organization showed this "sell-out" syndrome. Its leaders purchased support from existing organizations by reducing their innovative thrust to protect, as Esman noted, "their longer term relations with other linked organizations and groups."[21] They certainly shied away from revolutionary tactics; reformist techniques were preferred.

Another widely reported inference is what might be called the *multiple interest syndrome.* It was made particularly explicit in the study of the Thai Institute of Public Administration, which documented the incongruity between the "resource requirements for the building and maintenance of an institute whose doctrine depends on scholarly and other professional commitment and competence," and the pressure on its leadership personnel to engage in "a variety of non-professional activities in the quest for income, status and identity."[22] The multiple interest syndrome was also a finding in the other studies of academic institutes:

"Key professional personnel failed to perform their designated roles because their commitment to the new program conflicted with a pre-existing network of linkages to other institutions in the system who were already providing them with income, status and identity."

HYPOTHESIS-TESTING

The above-mentioned hypotheses about the superiority of resident and entrenched leadership over absentee and changing leadership, the sell-out phenomenon and the multiple interest syndrome are highly plausible. But these inferences remain to be tested under more rigorous field study conditions to identify their limits. What could be done, but has not yet been attempted in any IB study, is a prospective field experiment. Experimental controls would be introduced within certain limits, since every institution has compelling functions which cannot always be controlled in accordance with a detailed research design, no matter how meritorious the research may be, to test one or a few major hypotheses. What new country would be willing to go to the expense and effort to set up a school of public administration just to serve as a research laboratory of institution-building processes? But in a society open enough to tolerate field research, experimental conditions can be approximated before a new organization is planned. A detailed monitoring of key variables can then be undertaken as the planned development occurs. Such a process of inquiry can meet some, but never all, of the conditions of a controlled experiment:

Prior hypotheses formulation: identification of propositions to be tested before the institutionalization process begins.
Prediction of outcome: anticipation of alternate outcomes, on the basis of various types of assumptions of what is likely to occur in view of known facts regarding

the present leadership, the impact of doctrine on social action, the nature of the linkage to the larger social system, and other types of information available in advance to those planning an innovative organization.

Process monitoring: periodic data collection during the process of institutionalization to examine what occurs and how it is related to what had been predicted.

Follow-up study: examination of outcomes at end of the natural experiment to evaluate the validity of different hypotheses that were being tested, with full allowance for the limitations imposed by the fact that, during the actual institutionalization process, the experimental model was modified by certain unanticipated events.

The recommendation favoring such hypothesis-testing was made by every research director of the IB program during its seven-year history.[23] If such research was not done, this may be because of the difficulty of finding a suitable laboratory that met a number of difficult conditions:

(1) A new organization, which intends to become institutionalized, must be identified before the planning process proceeds very far.

(2) Those responsible for the organization must be interested in serving as an experimental setting for testing hypotheses or include a researcher who has such an interest in the group responsible for the conduct of institutionalization process.

(3) Planning must include written specification of alternate outcomes or blueprint mapping.[24] Included are operationally expressed descriptions of what the organization ought to be doing once it has been set up.

(4) There must be a follow-up study. The process of institutionalization must be monitored by participant observers (insiders as well as outside researchers) without any responsibilities for operations. Plans or blueprint must then be focused on fairly specific predicted outcomes so that relevant information can be collected over a period of time in terms of a systematic data collection process.

CONCLUSION

Modern men have moved far from the "evil eye" theory, which ascribed problems to the malevolent intent of particular persons. Personal problems will confront every man at some time, but most social problems involve the malfunctioning of organizations and their programs, far more than the inappropriate role performance by a single or a few individuals. Nevertheless, it is the rare official who can separate what is done by his organization from how adequate he feels or how others regard him.

Institution-building research must take note of this personalizing quality, especially when a not-yet-developed organization is to be subjected to systematic study in order to test a number of institution-building theorems. Such research is most likely to occur when it can be built into the original blueprint and when planners are given recognition for risk-taking by a willingness to open up their operation to scientific scrutiny.

In institution-building research, much like in a teaching hospital of a medical center, the focus of inquiry must be the problem rather than the people handling the problem. When this occurs, it becomes possible to test propositions with greater precision than is possible when institution building is investigated primarily through a "whodunnit" episodic description or through uncontrolled retrospective case studies.

NOTES

1. Milton J. Esman, "Institution Building Concepts—An Interim Appraisal," Pittsburgh: Inter-University Research Program in Institution Building, 1967, p. 1.

2. Norman T. Uphoff and Warren Ilchman, chapter 5, above.

3. Richard L. Duncan and William S. Pooler, "Technical Assistance and Institution Building," Pittsburgh: Inter-University Research Program in Institution Building, 1967, p. 1. Their view is similar to that of Peter Nokes: "The structure of society, then, and of segments of society operates to maintain a humane institution in existence once it is established . . . social institutions that are intended to supply recurrent human needs have a peculiar toughness that appears to defy dissolution. For them to be viable it is not, in fact, necessary for them to be efficient . . . at this point it is sufficient to note that it is not merely unnecessary for a humane institution to be efficient for it to remain in existence. It is not even necessary for its personnel to have a clear idea what it is for." "Purpose and Efficiency in Humane Social Institutions," Human Relations, XIII, No. 2, May 1960: 144-145.

4. Philip Selznick, *Leadership in Administration*, Evanston: Row, Peterson, 1962, p. 6. Selznick also differentiates organization from institution, as do Duncan and Pooler, on the basis of the relevancy of the activities of a social unit to the social system as a whole: "organization . . . is a technical instrument for mobilizing human energies and directing them toward set aims. We allocate tasks, delegate authority, channel communication, and find some way of coordinating all that has been divided up and parcelled out. All this is conceived as an exercise in engineering; it is governed by the related ideals of rationality and a lean, no-nonsense system of consciously co-ordinated activities. It refers to an expendable tool, a rational instrument engineered to do a job. An institution on the other hand, is more nearly a natural product of social needs and pressures—a responsive adaptive organism." (p. 5)

5. Jiri Nehnevajsa, personal communication.

6. J. Kemeny, J. Snell and G. Thompson, *Introduction to Finite Mathematics*, Englewood Cliffs: Prentice-Hall, 1956, p. 54.

7. See, for instance, Fred N. Kerlinger, *Foundation of Behavioral Research*, New York: Holt, Rinehart & Winston, 1965, pp. 67-79.

8. Joseph W. Eaton in collaboration with Michael Chen, *Influencing the Youth Culture: A Study of Youth Organizations in Israel*, Beverly Hills: Sage, 1970, pp. 208-214.

9. "A Deductive Ideal-Type Method," in Arnold Rose, editor, *Theory and Methods in the Social Sciences*, Minneapolis: University of Minnesota Press, 1954, pp. 327-343.

10. Florian Znaniecki, *The Method of Sociology*, New York: Farrar & Rinehart, 1934, pp. 249-331.

11. Max Weber, *The Methodology of the Social Sciences*, translated and edited by Edward A. Shils and Henry A. Finch, New York: Free Press, 1949, p. 90. For an illustration of this method of obtaining social science knowledge, see also: Howard Becker, "Constructive Typology in the Social Sciences," American Sociological Review, Vol. V, No. 1, February 1940: 40-55.

12. Gerald Caiden, *Administrative Reform*, Chicago: Aldine, 1969, p. 5.

13. Milton J. Esman, Chapter 1, above.

14. Donald A. Taylor, *Institution Building and Business Administration: Brazilian Experience,* East Lansing: Michigan State University Press, 1968, pp. 3-4.

15. For instance, the Governing Board of the College in Bangkok included the Minister of Education, who also was responsible for the development of secondary education in Thailand. At one point, he decided to use funds allocated for a college classroom building to build a secondary school building. This disabling (to the college) decision was reversed only after intervention of the project's American staff. He "diplomatically" warned the Minister: "If the classroom building is not constructed, the student enrollment cannot increase. We will not have enough students or staff (at the college) to justify our contract personnel being in Thailand." Enabling and competing linkages were clearly at work. Willis P. Porter, "College of Education, Bangkok, Thailand: A Case Study in Institution Building," Pittsburgh: Inter-University Research Program in Institution Building, 1967, pp. 103-105.

16. Guthrie S. Birkhead, "Institutionalization at a Modest Level: Public Administration Institute for Turkey and the Middle East," Pittsburgh: University of Pittsburgh, Graduate School of Public and International Affairs, 1967, p. 2.

17. Donald A. Taylor, op. cit., p. 40.

18. William J. Siffin, "The Thai Institute of Public Administration: A Case Study of Institution Building," Pittsburgh: Inter-University Research Program in Institution Building, 1967, p. 84.

19. "The Institution Building Concepts—An Interim Appraisal," op. cit., p. 63.

20. *Leadership in Administration,* op. cit., p. 7.

21. "The Institution Building Concepts—An Interim Appraisal," op cit., p. 64.

22. William Siffin, op. cit., p. 258.

23. Jiri Nehnevajsa, "Methodological Issues in Institution Building Research," Pittsburgh: Inter-University Research Program in Institution Building, 1964, especially pp. 6, 7, 20-21; and Milton Esman, "The Institution Building Concepts—An Interim Appraisal," op. cit., pp. 51-52.

24. See Chapter 3, p. 78.

Part II

APPLICATIONS

THE INSTITUTION-BUILDING MODEL:
A SYSTEMS VIEW

SAUL M. KATZ

University of Pittsburgh

SAUL M. KATZ is Professor and Chairman of the Department of Economics and Social Development in the University of Pittsburgh's Graduate School of Public and International Affairs. During a just-completed sabbatical he served as head of a United Nations mission to Venezuela, advising a Venezuelan Presidential Commission studying ways of modernizing public administration in that country. He is one of the founding members of the Institution-Building Consortium. Prior to joining the University of Pittsburgh faculty, he held a number of U.S. government positions including membership on the Central Program Planning Staff of the U.S. Agency for International Development. He also served on the U.S. delegation to the International Meeting on the Application of Science and Technology to the Problems of Less Developed Countries. Among the more important of his many publications is *A Systems Approach to Development Administration: A Framework for Analyzing Capability of Action for National Development,* Washington, D.C. American Society for Public Administration, 1965.

THE INSTITUTION-BUILDING MODEL: A SYSTEMS VIEW

SAUL M. KATZ

University of Pittsburgh

Economic and social development, unlike spontaneous historical change, is a deliberate process of systematically guiding and accelerating societal change. The planning process is based on a model of action—implicit or explicit—that can encompass the many elements and the complex interrelationships. Institution building is one such model. It focuses on the role of organizations that formulate and implement programs propagating innovations that contribute to developmental purposes.

We begin by noting four starting premises of the model. We then discuss the concepts in term of a systems framework encompassing purposes, functions, and linkages. Since the systems view of institution building differs from earlier views, we compare the systems view with the early guiding concepts. We conclude with some comments on the utility of an institution-building model.

FOUR PREMISES

As an approach to the complex problems of deliberately inducing societal change, institution building involves, among others, three starting premises. To these we add a helpful fourth, a systems view of the approach.

The first premise is that the guided societal change known as "development" is generally induced by the deliberate introduction of physical and social innovations. The famous economist Joseph Schumpeter considered innovation—

[153]

the application of new techniques to production and distribution—to be the source of economic development. [1] A similar view may be identified in other social sciences. In fact, the cumulation of innovations may be seen as the core of societal change. [2]

The second premise is that innovations, no matter how technical, affect and are affected by values, norms, and attitudes, as well as explicit behavior. These are not random occurrences. They have planned and anticipated interrelationships that can be expected. Any strategy of development must take this into account. [3]

The third starting premise is that the deliberate propagation of innovations, by and large, takes place through formal organizations. Modern economic life puts particular emphasis on formal organizations that make possible specialization of tasks and exchange of goods and services. They make it feasible for large numbers of people to carry out complex tasks related to each other and to the deliberate establishing and achieving of common purposes. For example, large numbers of such organizations are required to carry out the many activities of agricultural development. Thus, there are organizations concerned with providing factor inputs such as: improved seed multiplication stations; fertilizer, pesticides, and equipment-distribution agencies; and agricultural credit cooperatives. Organizations directly involved in crop and livestock production include groups of private farmers, producer cooperatives and agricultural collectives; as well as research and education organizations such as experiment stations, farmer advisory agencies, and vocational agriculture schools. A recent study describes 45 different governmental and quasi-governmental organizations as being of major importance in Venezuelan agriculture. [4]

The fourth premise is that a systems view of organizations is a useful frame for description and prescription. The use of "system" here, as an assemblage of elements that have ordered and recurrent patterns of interrelationships built around definable objectives or purposes, is not dissimilar to its usage by economists and sociologists. [5] Systems are intellectual constructs that provide methods for categorizing, abstracting, and organizing data on human behavior and studying their interrelationships. The systems view may be used at different levels of aggregation and for various purposes. Organizations, and often, groups of organizations, interact as systems. Their analysis will, therefore, be helped through a study of them as individual and multi-organizational systems. [6]

A systems view suggests three dimensions of analysis: identifiable purposes; subsystems for carrying on essential organizational functions; and linkages between the organization and its environment.

THE PURPOSES DIMENSION

Systems, of the kind we are considering, are constructed around purposes or objectives. These may be substantive or instrumental, or both.

Substantive purpose concerns the organization's anticipated contributions to developmental objectives—that is, its contributions of outputs and innovations to the society. These are complex; some are manifest and others are latent. An agricultural bank's avowed objective of providing credit to farmers is usually only a part of its purpose. There may be many other, more or less hidden, objectives such as fostering particular kinds of crop production, or helping particular types of farmers, say small holders, or contributing to the power of the organization's political sponsors.

Organizational systems generally have, in addition, what might be called instrumental purposes. These usually relate to the survival, growth, and change of the organizations. The instrumental purpose identified in the institution-building model is that of institutionality. This concept denotes that "at least certain relationships and action patterns incorporated in the organizations are normative both within the organizations and for other social units, and that some support and complementarity in the environment have been attained." Institutionality is a major evaluative concept in the institution-building model, and three indicators of it are given. First is the organization's ability to survive. Associated with this, but perhaps more important, is the degree to which its innovational purposes survive, although the two purposes are not synonymous and actually may be in conflict. Second, is the extent to which the organization is perceived by its environment as having intrinsic value. This may be indicated by the degree of its autonomy and influence. Finally, the third indicator is its spread effect, the degree to which specific relationships and action patterns embodied in the organization have become normative for other social units.[7]

Organizational purposes, in the early guiding concepts, were identified in doctrine. This is defined as " 'the specification of values, objectives, and operational methods underlying social action.' Doctrine is regarded as a series of themes which project, both within the organization itself and in its external environment, a set of images and expectations of institutional goals and styles of action."[8] This may be seen as including both the detailed development programs fostered by the organization and the underlying set of value preferences, since it is extremely difficult to identify the latter except by studying program objectives and methods. The early IB concept of program, thus, seems somewhat ambiguous and we shall discuss it later.

FUNCTIONAL SUBSYSTEMS DIMENSIONS

Contemporary knowledge suggests that every organizational system must carry on, at a minimum, four functions if it is to be able to establish and achieve its purposes. These functions and the organization's internal entities and relationships that accomplish them may be called its four functional sub-systems.[9]

First is the *transformation subsystem* which is concerned with transforming inputs into the organization's outputs or payoffs. This subsystem, sometimes called the production, conversion, or technical system, is a major and central part of any organization. In an extension organization it would involve converting the service of skilled people, financial resources, and physical facilities into educational output such as advice to farmers. The transformation subsystem is equally identifiable in a financial organization, or a school, or an experiment station. It is also present, although harder to identify, in an organization whose purpose is to obtain support for agrarian reform. It is technical in the sense that it involves rationally determinable sets of input-output relationships. For example, to educate a given number of agricultural extension agents to a defined level of ability requires determinable amounts of money, staff, and other inputs. The time required can be estimated reasonably accurately. This subsystem is the most evident one in any organizational system and is often used for characterizing the entire organization such as schools, banks, and grain elevators.

Second is the *maintenance subsystem* which, as the name implies, is concerned with maintaining the patterned behavior necessary to carry out the transformation activities. This subsystem has both internal and external aspects. Internally, it is concerned with maintaining the stability and continuity of the organization. This involves the intra-organizational allocation of resources, such as finances, by a budgeting office and supplies by the procurement office in a way that will preserve the existing patterns of relationships. It also includes stabilizing behavior by the selective recruitment and indoctrination of staff through personnel practices. Externally, the maintenance subsystem is a part of the organization that deals with the environment. It is concerned with obtaining the necessary inputs of supporting resources such as personnel, budget, and operating authority through enabling legislation. It is also concerned with the disposal of outputs and the linking of the organization to other organizations or groups.

Third is the *adaptation subsystem,* which is concerned with the survival of the organization and its mission in the face of what may be a difficult or changing environment. While the maintenance subsystem has as its major emphasis the internal stability and survival of the system as it is, the adaptation subsystem is primarily concerned with external continuity and the innovations necessary to insure this survival. It includes planning and evaluation, and research and development staffs, and public relations offices, all to help cope with the environment.

Finally, every organizational system requires a *guidance subsystem* to direct and coordinate all the activities of the organization. People in each of the three preceding subsystems tend to view their organization in different ways. Staffs of the transformation subsystem tend to see the whole organization as a production enterprise primarily concerned with the technical relationships of processing inputs and producing outputs. Bureaucrats in the maintenance subsystem view the organization as concerned with internal stability, continuity, and survival. The people in the adaptation subsystem may stress the organization's concern with its contribution and adjustment to a changing external environment. This kind of conflict is common in organizations. It is in the guidance subsystem that they are supposedly managed and overall organization decisions are made and legitimated. Priorities, subtargets, timing, unit responsibilities, resource allocations, and other details are specified, hopefully in a consistent manner, by those who operate the guidance subsystem. Communication of common understandings between decision makers and action centers are insured there. The subsystem is also concerned that organizational performance is, to some specified degree, in conformity with the decisions and detailed specifications. The guidance activities may all be carried by one unit within an organization or, as is more often the situation, there may be a number of specialized guidance units in the subsystem. In any case, these activities must be carried on consistently and continuously if the organizational system is to achieve its purposes.[10]

This view of functional subsystems is reflected in the institution-building concept of internal structures which is defined as " 'the structure and processes established for the operation of the institution and for its maintenance.' The distribution of roles within the organization, its internal authority patterns and communication systems, the commitment of personnel to the doctrine and program of the organization. . . ."[11] There is some relation to two of the other concepts—namely, program and leadership; but in view of some apparent ambiguities, we will discuss them after we have considered environmental linkages.

ENVIRONMENTAL LINKAGES

All organizational elements function in an environment of other organizations, groups, and individuals. They are linked to this environment by exchanges or transfers of people's services, commodities, and information and psychological states. Four generic types of such linkages, or continuing transactions, are identified in the institution-building approach.[12]

(1) Enabling linkages are those that relate the organizational system to authoritative organizations, groups, and individuals. Such linkages authorize the establishment of the subject system and enable it to continue to operate. They may be evidenced by what, in Latin America, is called its "organic law" and by the formal approval of influentials such as by coffee growers for coffee research stations.

(2) Functional linkages encompass the flows of resources and products necessary for carrying on the system's activities. Thus the functional linkages for an extension service may include relationships with universities to obtain skilled people and with budget offices to obtain the financial resources. They may also

include relationships with complementary organizations, for example, between an extension service and agricultural credit organizations, where there are exchanges of services and coordination of activities. Functional linkages can be divided into two types: those related to inputs and those related to outputs, although functional relationships to other social units often include both types. The institution-building concept of "resources" is defined as "the physical, human and technological inputs of the institution." Two of the subvariables in evaluating resources are their availability and sources.[13] No specific concept is identified for outputs, although here too "program" might be fitted in.

(3) There also are normative linkages that involve relationships of acceptability and influence associated with societal values and norms. These are generally with groups such as political parties, religious organizations and special interest associations which help set ideological norms for the society. Unless a land tenure reform agency is acceptable to important value-setting groups in the society, it is unlikely to be able to carry on its activities for any length of time.

(4) Finally, there are diffuse linkages that are hard to pin down and classify. For example, there usually are amorphous attitudes of generalized support or opposition to an organizational system and its activities that say "an extension system is good" or that credit bank directors "only feather their own nests."

Institution building has another concept concerned with environmental relationships called "transactions." This is defined as the exchange of goods and services, and the exchange of power and influence. Four groups of transactions are identified in terms of their purposes: (1) gaining support and overcoming resistance; (2) resource exchanges; (3) achieving complementarities in the environment; (4) transfer of norms and values.[14] The transactions concept underlies linkages which are continuing patterns of transactions, but classifies them in terms of purposes rather than in the content types noted earlier. Since purpose determination of transactions raises some interesting methodological problems, the earlier typology seems preferable. Although this, too, in its present state is not satisfactory in view of the variety and complexity of linkages, clearly, the ordering and analysis of environmental linkages needs further development.

THE GUIDING CONCEPTS

In the Pittsburgh institution-building model there were eleven concept categories. One, institutionality, is identified as an end-state. Five are "institution variables": leadership, doctrine, program, resources, and internal structure. These are presumed to be the categories of variables "necessary and sufficient to explain" the behavior of the institution. Four are grouped as linkages: enabling, functional, normative, and diffused. The linkages "specify the interdependencies which exist between an institution and other relevant parts of the society." The transactions concept is listed separately and is portrayed in a chart as connecting the institution variables and the linkages.[15]

In our preceding discussions, we have included nine of the concepts but grouped them differently. Under purpose we considered doctrine and institutionality. In the discussion of functional subsystems we considered internal structure. Under environmental linkages we included six: enabling; functional (to which we added resources); normative; diffuse; and we also discussed transactions. Two concepts—leadership and program—were not included because they seem ambiguous and redundant for our purposes, and remain for discussion.

Leadership is an important and much-used term that has many meanings and concerns a wide variety of phenomena. It is an elusive concept whose description in objective terms involves the whole range of institution-building analysis. Leadership is defined in the guiding concepts as "the group of persons who are actively engaged in the formulation of the doctrine and program of the institution and who direct its operations and relationships with the environment." Some of the leadership properties that are expected to correlate positively with "success" are identified as "political viability, professional status, technical competence, organizational competence and continuity."[16] We are talking about a group of persons here, but we are really concerned with their organizational behavior and, particularly, their effects on the behavior of others within and outside the organization. Even from a psychologist's point of view, leadership "is probably best conceived as a set of functions which must be carried out in the group."[17] In sum, leadership is expressed in and evidenced by all three dimensions of purpose, functional subsystems, and environmental linkages.

Program is also clearly important but, as presented in the guiding concepts, it, too, seems ambiguous. It is defined as "those actions which are related to the performance of functions and services constituting the output of the institution." It is described as "the program of output function." Some of the subvariables identified are "consistency, stability and contribution to societal needs."[12] If program, as commonly used elsewhere, refers to detailed working plans of objectives and operational methods, specifying resource allocations and prescribing priorities, it seems to overlap with the concept of doctrine, as "the specification of —operational methods." In such case we include it under purpose as part of doctrine. If it refers to the concrete patterns of action, it overlaps with internal structure—"the processes of operation of the institution"—and we have included it in our functional subsystems. If it refers to the outputs of the institution, it overlaps with the concept of functional linkages, particularly the functional output linkages. With so many references, program is clearly important; but as used in the guiding concepts it, like leadership, is expressed in and evidenced by all parts of the institution-building analysis.

UTILITY OF THE INSTITUTION-BUILDING MODEL

The institution-building model is in the process of development. As indicated earlier, a considerable number of field studies have been sponsored by IB and others. A number of analytic reviews have been undertaken. However, comparative analysis in depth is still in an early stage. Much remains to be done. Nevertheless, the model shows promise in three ways. If it can contribute to our understanding of the development process by generalizing from a variety of cases using a set of similar analytic concepts, it facilitates comparative study. Based on efforts at normative analysis, it assists in developing a framework for evaluation.[19] Finally, it contributes to guides for developmental action.[20]

NOTES

1. Joseph Schumpeter, *The Theory of Economic Development,* Cambridge: Harvard University Press, 1949.

2. See, for example, Wilbert E. Moore, *Social Change,* Englewood Cliffs: Prentice-Hall, 1963.

3. See the interesting essays in Ralph Braibanti and Joseph Spengler, editors, *Traditions, Values and Socioeconomic Development,* Durham: Duke University Press, 1961.

4. See *Organizacion y Administracion del Sector Agropecuario de Venezuela,* Caracas: Ministerio de Agricultura y Cria y Instituto Interamericano de Ciencias Agricolas, 1969.

5. Walter Buckley describes a system as "a complex of elements or components directly or indirectly related in a casual network such that each component is related to at least some others in a more or less stable way within any particular period of time." In *Sociology and Modern Systems Theory,* Englewood Cliffs: Prentice-Hall, 1967.

6. See Saul M. Katz, "A Systems Approach to Development Administration," Washington: Comparative Administration Group Special Series No. 6, American Society for Public Administration, May 1965.

7. Milton J. Esman and Hans C. Blaise, "Institution Building Research—The Guiding Concepts," Pittsburgh: Inter-University Research Program in Institution Building, February 1966, pp. 5-7.

8. Ibid.

9. Adapted from the generic types of organizational subsystems discussed in Daniel Katz and Robert Kahn, *The Social Psychology of Organizations,* New York: Wiley, 1966.

10. For a more detailed discussion of guidance activities, see Saul M. Katz, "A Systems Approach to Development Administration," op. cit., and "Exploring a Systems Approach to Development Action" in F. Riggs, editor, *Frontiers of Development Administration,* Durham: Duke University Press, forthcoming.

11. M. J. Esman, "The Institution Building Concepts—An Interim Appraisal," Pittsburgh: Research Program in Institution Building, 1967, p. 4.

12. See Jiri Nehnevajsa, "Methodological Issues in Institution Building Research," Pittsburgh: Research Program in Institution Building, 1964 (mimeo), pp. 27-29.

13. Esman and Blaise, op. cit., pp. 11-12.

14. Ibid., pp. 15-17.

15. Ibid., p. 9.

16. Esman, op. cit., p. 3.

17. Cecil Gibbs, "Leadership" in Gardner Lindsey, editor, *Handbook of Social Psychology,* Vol. 2, Cambridge: Addison-Wesley, 1954, pp. 877-920.

18. Esman, op. cit., p. 4.

19. See Saul M. Katz, "Additional Note 4, A Methodological Note on Appraising Administrative Capability for Development" in *Appraising Administrative Capability for Development,* United Nations Publication, ST/TAO/M/46, 1969.

20. Saul M. Katz, *Guide to Modernizing Administration for National Development.* Pittsburgh: University of Pittsburgh, GSPIA, 1965. See especially chapter IV.

THE INSTITUTION-BUILDING MODEL
IN PROGRAM OPERATION AND REVIEW

THOMAS W. THORSEN

Assistant Director for Public Administration
AID Saigon

THOMAS W. THORSEN is the Assistant Director of the U.S. Aid for International Development Program of the U.S. Aid Mission to Vietnam. Before this he held foreign service posts in Turkey, Liberia, Yugoslavia, and Iran, plus assignments in Washington. He has his Master's and Ph.D. degrees in Economics and Public Administration, with a minor in economics. During 1949-1950 he was a Fulbright scholar in Norway.

THE INSTITUTION-BUILDING MODEL
IN PROGRAM OPERATION AND REVIEW

T H O M A S W. T H O R S E N

Assistant Director for Public Administration
AID Saigon

THE NATURE OF INSTITUTIONAL GROWTH

Effective institution building is critical to modernization and nation building. A better understanding of the nature of institutional growth and maturity, both on the part of the host government leaders as well as donor technicians, is necessary for sustained national development. It should be recognized at the outset that institutional growth is an unstable or flucturating process in which institutions experience both highs and lows or mountains of success and valleys of despair. Institution building is crisis-ridden: plan for it. Most aid donors involved in institution building in developing countries would like to think that the developmental process is a steady upward growth curve (Figure 1). Actually, most institutions experience a cyclical short-run growth pattern such as Figure 2, but usually within an upward long-run growth trend.

An institution which experiences a steady upward growth trend without fluctuations is probably experiencing hothouse growth and survives well because it is under the protection of an aid donor or some other umbrella and has not been really subject to the rigors of growth in the real world. The chances for survival of this type of hothouse institution are not too good. Sustained institutional growth requires exposure to the real environment. Aid donors and technicians like to spare new institutions in developing countries the agonies of growth. Aid donors must be careful not to deny these institutions this significant

[165]

Figure 1   Figure 2

growth experience. When the institution reaches the critical low point, it usually goes through a period of serious institutional reassessment. Major goals, organization structure, resource shortcoming, manpower, management weakness, usefulness or contribution, duplication of other activities, consistency with other institutions, are usually reexamined. Such an examination usually leads to improved institutional strategies and programs, improved organization to carry out objectives, better resources, stronger linkages with other supporting organizations, and improved management techniques. This type of periodic reassessment is critical but, unfortunately, it usually takes an adverse situation to trigger such a review.

Most aid donors are delighted to be associated with institutions when they are moving to the top of the cycle. Unfortunately, most aid donors also are disposed to phase out their involvement when the institution is on the down swing—actually at a time when technical assistance is most needed and perhaps critical in the life of the institution. It goes without saying that institutional development should be given a much longer time horizon; and aid donors should be more tolerant and understanding of the institution developing process and more perceptive in the use of the aid resources at critical points in the growth pattern of the institution.

THE INSTITUTION-BUILDING MATRIX

I believe that there is a general consensus that institution building is critical to national modernization, sustained growth, and development. I also believe that there is a general consensus that the analytical and evaluative tools presently used for programming are inadequate to permit me to chart, with confidence, the critical path of institutional development. I believe that a great deal more applied research into the process of institutional development is required if continuous and rapid national development is to take place.

For several years I have experimented with a variety of analytical and evaluative techniques in order to determine whether or not the Esman institution-building model could be made operational. I found that translating ideas and concepts into meaningful, operational, and evaluative processes was extremely difficult as well as hazardous because of the high risk of oversimplification and the possibility of becoming dangerously mechanistic. Despite this risk, I have attempted during the past three years to translate these concepts into processes. I am satisfied with the preliminary results. I am delighted to share my experiences and methodology with you, with full recognition that the process is indeed incipient, purely in the experimental stage, and in need of additional refinement and experimentation.

Effective institution development analysis requires careful rationalization of the entire process of institution building, identifying significant institutional characteristics and putting these into an analytical framework that can be understood and operationally applied. The institution-building matrix (Figure 3) is the end product of this process. The Esman institution-building model became the core of the matrix. I have considerably expanded the model in developing the matrix because I felt the institution-building model was not operationally complete. The matrix is a synthesis of concepts from a variety of sources[1] and has been used to analyze and evaluate a variety of institutions.

The matrix proved to be a very useful analytical as well as programming tool and contributed significantly both to the technicians' and host government institutional leaders' understanding of the institution-building process. It also confirmed my belief that an analytical and evaluative process could be developed upon which realistic institutional goals and strategies could be determined and initiated.

Components of the Matrix. The matrix embodies two major processes—an analytical and an evaluative process. The analytical process deals primarily with the total matrix. The evaluative process is a technique superimposed upon the institution-building and administrative-managerial profile of the matrix through the use of values, which contribute significant insight into institution growth and maturity patterns.

The Analytical Process. The design of the matrix requires analysis of the most significant institutional environmental factors. These factors are identified in checklist fashion. Even though aid donor assistance can only partially meet the overall requirements of an institution, in many instances this aid serves as a significant catalytic agent that is critical to its development. It thus becomes necessary to declare an aid donor a significant institutional environmental factor and worthy of careful analysis. It is for this reason the matrix first calls for an analysis of the USAID technical assistance environment (box A, Figure 3).

USAID Technical Assistance Environment. Perhaps one of the most significant environmental factors in a USAID mission operation is lack of professional continuity. Directors, economists, division chiefs, and program officers come and go with regularity. Each one brings to this assignment his professional talent and experiences as well as his developmental biases. These individuals can have a profound effect, positive or negative, upon host country institutions. For this reason it becomes essential to establish a clear understanding of USAID

INSTITUTION BUILDING MATRIX

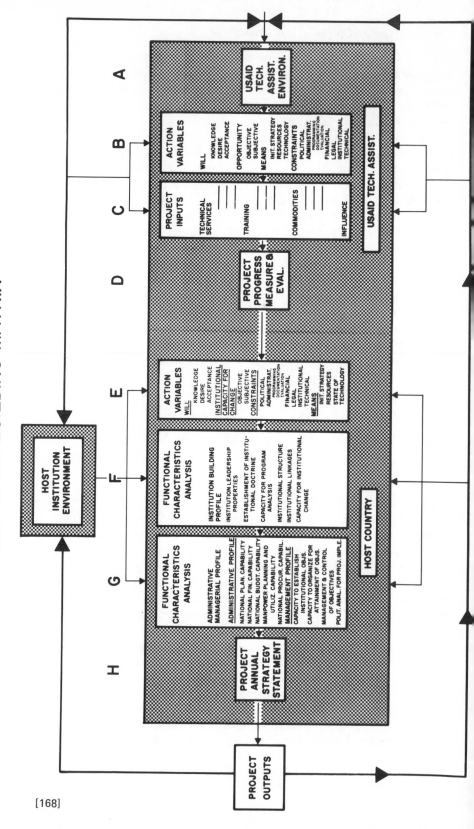

institutional attitudes at a specific point in time, an attitudinal bench mark, if you will. This matrix analysis calls for a description of USAID attitudes in the form of USAID action variables (box B, Figure 3). A discussion of the variables follows.

Will. Significant to effective USAID program development is an objective understanding or judgment of AID/Washington's and USAID mission's overall willingness to embark upon a specific program of institutional development. Such a judgment is usually reflected in AID's overall knowledge of the institution, the role the institution is expected to play in the national development process, and the developmental priority the institution enjoys within the context of the host government's developmental program. The willingness both of the mission and AID/Washington either to embark upon or continue a project should be clearly established and described in basic documentation. Where individual senior AID/Washington and/or mission officers disagree materially, such differences should be identified and recorded. Bench marks should be clearly established so that new officers have an understanding of the significant factors considered as the basis for the formulation of the program, thus providing a sense of continuity.

Means. The means section of the AID variable portion of the matrix should be examined constantly in conjunction with the means section of the host country variable portion.

The methodology or means utilized by AID and the host country through which the institution is to become more viable should be described, keeping in mind that AID resources in most instances are comparatively small and should be supportive of the total institutional resources. The development of AID's initial institutional strategy should be consistent and in harmony with host government total institutional strategy.

It is critical that an all-embracing host government institutional strategy be developed and a clear understanding reached on how the USAID strategy should be linked and supported. Because our input is comparatively small, though critical, its nature should be examined in relationship to USAID total strategy. Both host government institutional strategy and USAID strategy should be formulated, implemented, and/or changed together.

State of Technology. The state of U.S. technology applicable to a specific institution should be carefully compared with the state of the host country technology to determine whether or not the level of U.S. technology to be introduced is compatible with the host government institutional capacity. There have been instances where the U.S. technology introduced has been too sophisticated and complex, causing nonperformance and frustration. There are cases where U.S. institutional experience or technology is too foreign or too U.S.

culture-bound to be effectively introduced. This section is specifically designed to explore these important considerations.

Constraints. In the development and evaluation of AID programs, efforts are usually made to examine host country institutional constraints. I submit that it is equally important to carefully examine USAID program constraints and put them in their proper perspective. The constraints listed on the matrix are self-explanatory.

USAID Project Inputs. USAID project inputs (box C, Figure 3)—whether they be technicians, participant training, or commodities—are usually critical factors in the institution-building process. Because our inputs are usually small in relationship to the total need and catalytic in nature, care must be exercised in the timing and allocation of these inputs so that major impact can be made upon the accomplishment of the institutional goals. A great deal more flexibility is required in utilizing these inputs than exists today, if maximum use is to be made of resources. Effective institutional growth is dynamic; change is constant and unpredictable. Programming of AID inputs is far too static and slow to meet the changing demands of innovative institutions. If emphasis given to institutional development in future years is to be effective, a significant overhaul of the evaluation and decision-making processes for allocation of our resources is required.

Institution Progress Reporting. USAID in-house project reporting is generally related to effective use of AID inputs in accomplishment of specified objectives. This type of reporting is important to USAID mission management as well as to AID/Washington.

The reporting procedure I use in the matrix is significantly different from systems in present use. The procedure is equally effective for use in reporting on technicians, participants, or commodities. For example, the progress reporting chart for technicians lists the major institutional goals, the names of the technicians, their work plan in priority order, and how each individual work plan relates to major objectives by color code. Technician work plans may relate to two or more objectives. A time frame for work progress is also incorporated in the chart. A narrative section is included for recording physical accomplishments. Once the chart is made, it takes minimal time to keep it up to date.

Influence. Rarely is a conscious effort made to develop appropriate influence or leverage strategy to assist more rapid institutional growth. The use of influence can be most effectively linked with USAID inputs, either as a quid pro quo, or more subtly in the context of consensus building. A rational influence strategy should be conceived between the technician and senior officials of the mission. There are times when the mission director, the ambassador, or other influential people can say the right thing at the right time to the right people, which can result in dramatic improvement in the project performance. There are times when AID or senior contract personnel receive the ear of top national leaders which under normal circumstances would not be available to host country institution leaders. More careful consideration should be given to this type of strategy.

Host Government Institutional Environment. Critical to institution building is a perceptive understanding of the environment in which the institution is developing. Understanding of the environmental factors by heads of the local institutions and aid donors is essential if effective use is to be made of resources (box D, Figure 3). The matrix lists a series of action variables (box E, Figure 3) very similar to the variables found on the USAID variable section, with the exception of the institutional capacity for change. This variable is an important factor and should be given careful consideration. The matrix deals with the capacity for change, both in an analytical and in an evaluative manner. This section concerns itself with the analytical process in the hopes of identifying significant change agents, as well as examining the institutional environment for positive signs of change. The other section variables are self-explanatory. I should like to restate the necessity for analyzing simultaneously the means section of the institution environment with the means section of USAID environment.

The Evaluative Process Institution-Building Profile. The core of the matrix is the institution-building profile (box F, Figure 3) based upon the Esman institution-building model. I have used his major categories: (1) institutional leadership properties, (2) establishment of institutional doctrine, (3) capacity for program analysis, (4) institutional structures, (5) institutional linkages, and—a new category—(6) capacity for institutional change. I have taken these six major categories and further broken them down into thirty-seven subcategories (see institutional profile, Figure 4). The rationale for this additional categorization was to increase the number of intuitive and qualitative judgments from seven to thirty-seven factors. These subcategories also made possible the development of a more operational, understandable, evaluative process, and gave much better perception of the institution.

The evaluative process involves the establishment of criteria for the following terms: excellent, good, satisfactory, poor, unsatisfactory (see Figure 4). A base period is selected, in the case of this sample profile, 1961. The institution was evaluated by the chairman of the management department and the campus coordinator, both of whom had been associated with the institution since 1961. Their factor evaluation, the base period, is recorded on the profile in solid black. The next evaluation period was 1965. The evaluation has been recorded in "X" hatching. It can be immediately noted that substantial institutional improvement had taken place. The last evaluative period was 1969

Figure 4

INSTITUTIONAL PROFILE

Evaluation Periods

■ 1961

▧ 1965

░ 1969

INSTITUTIONAL LEADERSHIP PROPERTIES	E	G	S	P	U
POLITICAL VIABILITY			▧	■	
PROFESSIONAL STATUS		░		▧	
TECHNICAL COMPETENCE			▧		■
ORGANIZATIONAL COMPETENCE		░		▧	
CONTINUITY				■	
DELEGATION CAPABILITY	░			▧	
COMMITMENT TO DOCTRINE				▧	
SELF-IMAGE RELATIONSHIP TO INSTITUTION		░	■		
ESTABLISHMENT OF INSTITUTIONAL DOCTRINE					
HAS A CLEAR DOCTRINE BEEN DECLARED?			▧	■	
IS THERE AN INSTITUTIONAL COMMITMENT TO THE DOCTRINE?				■	
IS THE DOCTRINE UNDERSTOOD AND ACCEPTED AND CHAMPIONED BY KEY INSTITUTIONAL LEADERSHIP?			▧	■	
IS THE DOCTRINE CLEARLY RELATED TO THE NEEDS OF THE INSTITUTION?			▧		
DOES THE DOCTRINE ESTABLISH LINKAGES BETWEEN THE OLD AND THE NEW MEMBERS OF THE INSTITUTION--BETWEEN ESTABLISHMENT AND INNOVATORS?		░	▧		
HAS THE DOCTRINE BEEN LEGITIMIZED AND SUPPORTED BY OUTSIDE PUBLICS?					
IS THE DOCTRINAL THEME INTERNALLY CONSISTENT AND ARTICULATED BY INFLUENTIAL PEOPLE?					
DOES THE DOCTRINAL THEME DISTRIBUTE BENEFITS WIDELY?				■	
PRIMARY STIMULUS OR COMBINATION OF STIMULI WHICH CONTRIBUTED TO PROGRAM DEVELOPMENT					
PROGRAM ANALYSIS					
EFFECTIVE ESTABLISHMENT OF OBJECTIVES AND CAPACITY TO IMPLEMENT OBJECTIVES			░	▧	
ESTABLISHMENT OF PRIORITIES WITHIN ESTABLISHED OBJECTIVES			░	▧	
CAPACITY TO MARSHALL AND ALLOCATE RESOURCES TO ACCOMPLISH OBJECTIVES			▧	■	
CAPACITY TO MODIFY PROGRAM IN RESPONSE TO ANALYSIS OF DEPENDABLE FEEDBACK OF EXPERIENCE			▧		
INSTITUTIONAL STRUCTURE					
EXTENT SERVICES ARE USED OR REQUESTED BY PUBLIC ORGANIZATIONS IT IS DESIGNED TO SERVE				▧	
CAPACITY OF THE INSTITUTE TO SURVIVE --MAINTAIN AND EXPAND ITS DOCTRINE AND PROGRAM AND DISTINCT IDENTITY			▧	■	
EXTENT CAPITAL RESOURCES AND FINANCIAL RESOURCES ARE PROVIDED FOR AND EXTENT OTHER ORGANIZATIONS MOBILIZE INFLUENCE BEHIND THE INSTITUTION'S LEADERSHIP AND PROGRAM			■		
THE EXTENT TO WHICH THE PROGRAMS AND PERSONNEL OF THE ORGANIZATION ARE JUDGED TO BE SERVING ACCEPTED OR EMERGENT GOALS			▧	■	
EXTENT WHICH ACTION AND BELIEF PATTERNS ARE INCORPORATED IN THE INSTITUTION		░	▧		
THE DEGREE OF FREEDOM IT HAS TO IMPLEMENT ITS PROGRAM			■	▧	
THE CAPACITY OF THE INSTITUTION TO CONTINUE TO INNOVATE	░				■
INSTITUTIONAL LINKAGES					
EXTENT THE INSTITUTION IS LINKED FAVORABLY WITH ORGANIZATIONS AND SOCIAL GROUPS WHICH CONTROL THE ALLOCATION OF AUTHORITY, PERSONNEL, AND RESOURCES				▧	
EXTENT THE INSTITUTION ENJOYS FAVORABLE LINKAGES WITH ORGANIZATIONS PERFORMING FUNCTIONS AND SERVICES WHICH ARE COMPLEMENTARY IN A IMPLEMENTATION MANNER				▧	■
EXTENT THE INSTITUTION ENJOYS LINKAGES WHICH SUPPLY THE INPUTS AND WHICH USE THE OUTPUTS OF THE INSTITUTION			▧	■	
EXTENT OF LINKAGES WITH OTHER INSTITUTIONS WHICH INCORPORATE NORMS AND VALUES (POSITIVE OR NEGATIVE) WHICH ARE RELEVANT TO THE DOCTRINE OF THE INSTITUTION				▧	■
EXTENT THE INSTITUTE ENJOYS LINKAGES WITH ELEMENTS OF THE SOCIETY WHICH CANNOT BE IDENTIFIED BY MEMBERSHIP IN FORMAL ORGANIZATIONS					
MEASUREMENT OF CHANGE					
ESTABLISHMENT OF NEED AND CLIMATE FOR CHANGE		■			
TRANSFORMATION OF INTENTION INTO ACTUAL CHANGE EFFORTS		■			
STABILIZATION OF INSTITUTION FOR CHANGE			▧		
ACHIEVING EFFECTIVE TERMINAL RELATIONSHIP		░			

and is recorded in dot hatching. Again substantial institutional improvement can be noted.

This evaluative process proposes a systematic guideline for registering clinical judgments of different observers and participants of a developmental effort. When their separate ratings coincide, or fail to be in agreement, it is then possible to investigate the basis of their agreement or their difference.

The evaluation of each one of these factors requires not only the placing of a factor grade on the profile sheet, but a short narrative statement in support of the rationale that determined each rating. Because of space limitation, I will not include in this paper the narrative factor statements. Over time, the institutional profile overlay together with the narrative factor statements gives unusual insight into the nature, problems, and improvement or deterioration of the institutional strengths and weaknesses and permits the establishment or redefining of institutional goals and objectives with more precision and confidence. The evaluation period should be about every two years.

Administrative-Managerial Profile. Lack of administrative-managerial capacity is a major inhibitor to country development and modernization. If institutional improvement and development are to take place, a conscientious effort needs to be made to identify specific administrative and managerial strengths and weaknesses. The administrative-managerial profile (box G on Figure 3) is intended to serve this purpose. The profile is divided into two major elements: (1) administrative and (2) management. I have purposely differentiated administration from management. The administrative portion is intended to define more sharply either strengths or weaknesses in major staff services such as planning, finance, budgeting, personnel, and procurement. Weak staff services usually plague institutions and slow down the pace of institutionalization. Since an institution's administrative procedures are normally prescribed by a national government, progress in improving staff services is usually slow. The particular evaluation method used is identical to the institution-building method. This methodology highlights institutional staff weakness so that, when one institution's profile is compared with others, a number of national staff service weaknesses clearly emerge. This dramatizes and identifies national staff weaknesses both for host government leaders and senior AID officials. Such an evaluation tool simplifies the task of convincing the national government that certain staff services—e.g., personnel management—are seriously inhibiting manpower improvement, as well as institutional modernization and national development.

This evaluation methodology permits the surfacing of staff weaknesses in one or several institutions assisted by a USAID technical division through construction and examination of a division profile. It is also possible to evaluate major institutions in which USAID is involved (this could be as many as 25) and construct a mission profile. Thus if all institution evaluations flag the factor "current cash flow position of Treasury" as *poor,* it becomes clear that unless

Figure 5

Evaluation Periods

- ■ 1961
- ▨ 1965
- ▦ 1969

ADMINISTRATIVE CAPACITY NATIONAL PLANNING CRITERIA	E	G	S	P	U
WHAT IS STATUS OF PROJECT WITHIN PRIORITIES OF THE NATIONAL PLAN?			■		
WHAT IS STATUS OF PROJECT WITHIN NATIONAL MINISTRY?				■	
WHAT IS STATUS OF PROJECT WITHIN THE USAID PRIORITIES?				▨	
NATIONAL FINANCIAL CAPABILITY					
WHAT IS CURRENT FINANCIAL CAPABILITY OF COUNTRY TO SUPPORT PROJECT?			■	▦	
WHAT IS EXTENT OF TREASURY WILLINGNESS TO COMMIT FUNDS?				■	
WHAT IS TREASURY CURRENT CASH FLOW POSITION?					
WHAT IS STATUS OF ADMINISTRATIVE EFFICIENCY OF TREASURY TO MAKE PROMPT PAYMENT?					
NATIONAL BUDGETING CAPABILITY					
IS BUDGETING PROCEDURE ADEQUATE IN ESTABLISHING PROJECT PRIORITIES?				■	
WHAT IS STATUS OF PROJECT AS REFLECTED IN BUDGET DOCUMENT?					
WHAT IS EXTENT BUDGETING IS RELIABLE FOR ALLOTMENT OF FUNDS FOR PROJECT SUPPORT?					
WHAT IS STATUS OF ADMINISTRATIVE EFFICIENCY OF BUDGET AGENCY FOR PROMPT BUDGET ACTION?					
MANPOWER PLANNING AND UTILIZATION CAPABILITY					
TO WHAT EXTENT DO MANPOWER PLANNING UNITS REFLECT PRIORITY OF ASSIGNMENT OF PERSONNEL TO PROJECT?		▦	▨		
ADEQUACY AND COMPETENCY OF ASSIGNED MANPOWER TO IMPLEMENT PROJECT		▦	▨	■	
WHAT IS EXTENT GOVERNMENT IS WILLING TO COMMIT ADEQUATE MANPOWER IN ATTAINMENT OF PROJECT GOAL?				■	
WHAT IS CAPACITY OF PERSONNEL SYSTEM TO RECRUIT AND MAINTAIN ADEQUATE PROJECT PERSONNEL?			■		
NATIONAL PROCUREMENT CAPABILITY					
WHAT IS THE CAPACITY OF THE PROCUREMENT PERSONNEL, PROCEDURES AND FUNDS TO SUPPORT PROJECT?					
WHAT IS EXTENT OF GOVERNMENT WILLINGNESS TO PROCURE SUPPLIES IN SUPPORT OF PROJECT?					
WHAT IS EFFICIENCY OF USAID IN PROVIDING OFFSHORE PROJECT COMMODITIES?					
TO WHAT EXTENT DOES THE PROJECT EFFECTIVELY UTILIZE U.S. PROVIDED COMMODITIES?					
MANAGERIAL CAPACITY **MANAGEMENT BY OBJECTIVES**					
TO WHAT EXTENT ARE OBJECTIVES ESTABLISHED WITHIN PROJECT?			▦	■	
TO WHAT EXTENT IS DATA RELIABLE UPON WHICH OBJECTIVES WERE BASED?			▦		■
TO WHAT EXTENT ARE THE OBJECTIVES SUPPORTED BY MINISTRY LEADERSHIP?				■	
TO WHAT EXTENT DOES A MUTUALITY OF OBJECTIVES EXIST?				■	
NATIONAL CAPACITY FOR ATTAINMENT OF OBJECTIVES					
TO WHAT EXTENT IS MINISTRY ORGANIZED TO IMPLEMENT OBJECTIVES?		▦		■	
TO WHAT EXTENT ARE OBJECTIVES COMMUNICATED AND UNDERSTOOD BY MINISTRY PERSONNEL AND OTHER AGENCIES?			▦	■	
TO WHAT EXTENT ARE MINISTRY STAFF MOTIVATED FOR ATTAINMENT OF OBJECTIVES?		■	▦	▨	
TO WHAT EXTENT ARE THE STAFF EFFECTIVELY DIRECTED OR GUIDED IN ATTAINMENT OF OBJECTIVES?			▦	■	
MEASUREMENT AND CONTROL OF OBJECTIVES					
IS THE PRESENT REPORTING SYSTEM ON STATUS OF PROJECT PROGRESS ADEQUATE?				▨	■
WHAT IS CAPACITY AND INTEREST OF GOVERNMENT TO EFFECTIVELY EVALUATE PROJECT?				▨	■
WHAT IS EXTENT OF FOLLOW-UP MADE AS A RESULT OF EVALUATION?				▨	
WHAT IS CAPACITY OF MINISTRY OR USAID TO RE-PROGRAM OR RE-DIRECT PROJECT OBJECTIVE WHEN REQUIRED?				▨	
POLITICAL ANALYSIS FOR PROJECT IMPLEMENTATION					
TO WHAT EXTENT DOES THE POLITICAL LEADERSHIP SUPPORT THE PROJECT?		■	▨		
EXTENT OF POLITICAL LEADERSHIP GIVEN BY PROJECT DIRECTOR			■		
EXTENT PROJECT DEVELOPS A SENSE OF NATIONAL UNITY AND CITIZEN PARTICIPATION					
EXTENT PROJECT ASSISTS IN PROMOTION OF U.S. FOREIGN POLICY		■	▨		▦
PROJECT INFORMATION DISSEMINATION					
TO WHAT EXTENT ARE THE GOVERNMENT AND PEOPLE AWARE OF THE EXISTENCE AND PROGRESS MADE UNDER PROJECT?					
TO WHAT EXTENT DOES THE PROJECT ENJOY GOOD PRESS AND RADIO COVERAGE?					
TO WHAT EXTENT IS THE USAID IDENTIFIED WITH THE PROJECT?					

overall improvement is made in "cash flow procedures in Treasury" all governmental institutional progress will be impeded.

The administrative element is also designed to give additional support and insight to the linkage section of the institutional profile.

Management Profile. This management profile (box G on Figure 3) is intended to identify major managerial strengths and weaknesses with institutions or projects. The profile is divided into five major categories: (1) establishment of objectives, (2) institutional capacity for attainment of objectives, (3) measurement and control of objectives, (4) political implications of objectives, and (5) information dissemination—which is again supportive of the linkage section of the institutional profile. The total management element is also designed to be supportive and permit greater perception of the program analysis section of the institution profile.

For purposes of clarity and better understanding, two completed administrative-managerial profiles have been included. One is the assisting institutions management profile (Figure 5), and the other is the host institutions management profile (Figure 6). It should be noted that a narrative statement is also included, giving the rationale for the factor grades.

I have found that the above evaluation procedure gives the host government institutional leaders, the AID technical staff, and AID senior staff personnel a better insight into institutional strengths and weaknesses and enables them to chart a more precise course of corrective action.

Institutional Strategy Statement. The objective of the entire analytical-evaluative process is to provide a rational framework upon which an institutional development strategy (box H on Figure 3) can be designed. The analytical-evaluative technique is intended to clearly identify major institutional strengths and weaknesses and permit improvement strategies and courses of action to be devised which will be instrumental in moving weak institutional factors from right to left on the profiles. The evaluation and strategy statement should be completed about every two years. This allows enough time to pass and events to transpire to make the evaluation meaningful. The process is too abrasive and time-consuming to be done more often.

The process gives the institutional leader good insight into the nature of his institution, permits the presentation of more critical and precise institutional goals or objectives, enables the institution to divert manpower and resources to more clearly defined objectives and problem areas, and charts a more orderly, well-balanced course for institutional improvement and viability.

Evaluation of Institutional Inputs and Outputs. A conscious effort should be made to measure the effect of inputs and outputs upon the nature of the institution and its capacity to change and improve its viability. Have the technicians' services contributed to or assisted in correcting weaknesses

Figure 6

Evaluation
Periods

1968

1969

ADMINISTRATIVE CAPACITY / NATIONAL PLANNING CRITERIA	E	G	S	P	U
WHAT IS STATUS OF PROJECT WITHIN PRIORITIES OF THE NATIONAL PLAN?		1968			
WHAT IS STATUS OF PROJECT WITHIN NATIONAL MINISTRY?			1968		
WHAT IS STATUS OF PROJECT WITHIN THE USAID PRIORITIES?	1968				
NATIONAL FINANCIAL CAPABILITY					
WHAT IS CURRENT FINANCIAL CAPABILITY OF COUNTRY TO SUPPORT PROJECT?		1968			
WHAT IS EXTENT OF TREASURY WILLINGNESS TO COMMIT FUNDS?			1968		
WHAT IS TREASURY CURRENT CASH FLOW POSITION?				1968	
WHAT IS STATUS OF ADMINISTRATIVE EFFICIENCY OF TREASURY TO MAKE PROMPT PAYMENT?			1968		
NATIONAL BUDGETING CAPABILITY					
IS BUDGETING PROCEDURE ADEQUATE IN ESTABLISHING PROJECT PRIORITIES?				1968	
WHAT IS STATUS OF PROJECT AS REFLECTED IN BUDGET DOCUMENT?				1969	1968
WHAT IS EXTENT BUDGETING IS RELIABLE FOR ALLOTMENT OF FUNDS FOR PROJECT SUPPORT?				1968	
WHAT IS STATUS OF ADMINISTRATIVE EFFICIENCY OF BUDGET AGENCY FOR PROMPT BUDGET ACTION?				1968	
MANPOWER PLANNING AND UTILIZATION CAPABILITY					
TO WHAT EXTENT DO MANPOWER PLANNING UNITS REFLECT PRIORITY OF ASSIGNMENT OF PERSONNEL TO PROJECT?				1968	
ADEQUACY AND COMPETENCY OF ASSIGNED MANPOWER TO IMPLEMENT PROJECT				1969	1968
WHAT IS EXTENT GOVERNMENT IS WILLING TO COMMIT ADEQUATE MANPOWER IN ATTAINMENT OF PROJECT GOAL?			1969		
WHAT IS CAPACITY OF PERSONNEL SYSTEM TO RECRUIT AND MAINTAIN ADEQUATE PROJECT PERSONNEL?			1968		
NATIONAL PROCUREMENT CAPABILITY					
WHAT IS THE CAPACITY OF THE PROCUREMENT PERSONNEL, PROCEDURES AND FUNDS TO SUPPORT PROJECT?			1968		
WHAT IS EXTENT OF GOVERNMENT WILLINGNESS TO PROCURE SUPPLIES IN SUPPORT OF PROJECT?			1968		
WHAT IS EFFICIENCY OF USAID IN PROVIDING OFFSHORE PROJECT COMMODITIES?			1968		
TO WHAT EXTENT DOES THE PROJECT EFFECTIVELY UTILIZE U.S. PROVIDED COMMODITIES?			1969		
MANAGERIAL CAPACITY / MANAGEMENT BY OBJECTIVES					
TO WHAT EXTENT ARE OBJECTIVES ESTABLISHED WITHIN PROJECT?	1968				
TO WHAT EXTENT IS DATA RELIABLE UPON WHICH OBJECTIVES WERE BASED?			1968		
TO WHAT EXTENT ARE THE OBJECTIVES SUPPORTED BY MINISTRY LEADERSHIP?			1969		
TO WHAT EXTENT DOES A MUTUALITY OF OBJECTIVES EXIST?			1969		
NATIONAL CAPACITY FOR ATTAINMENT OF OBJECTIVES					
TO WHAT EXTENT IS MINISTRY ORGANIZED TO IMPLEMENT OBJECTIVES?				1969	1968
TO WHAT EXTENT ARE OBJECTIVES COMMUNICATED AND UNDERSTOOD BY MINISTRY PERSONNEL AND OTHER AGENCIES?			1968		
TO WHAT EXTENT ARE MINISTRY STAFF MOTIVATED FOR ATTAINMENT OF OBJECTIVES?		1969			
TO WHAT EXTENT ARE THE STAFF EFFECTIVELY DIRECTED OR GUIDED IN ATTAINMENT OF OBJECTIVES?		1969			
MEASUREMENT AND CONTROL OF OBJECTIVES					
IS THE PRESENT REPORTING SYSTEM ON STATUS OF PROJECT PROGRESS ADEQUATE?		1968			
WHAT IS CAPACITY AND INTEREST OF GOVERNMENT TO EFFECTIVELY EVALUATE PROJECT?				1969 / 1968	
WHAT IS EXTENT OF FOLLOW-UP MADE AS A RESULT OF EVALUATION?				1968	
WHAT IS CAPACITY OF MINISTRY OR USAID TO RE-PROGRAM OR RE-DIRECT PROJECT OBJECTIVE WHEN REQUIRED?				1968	
POLITICAL ANALYSIS FOR PROJECT IMPLEMENTATION					
TO WHAT EXTENT DOES THE POLITICAL LEADERSHIP SUPPORT THE PROJECT?				1968	
EXTENT OF POLITICAL LEADERSHIP GIVEN BY PROJECT DIRECTOR		1968			
EXTENT PROJECT DEVELOPS A SENSE OF NATIONAL UNITY AND CITIZEN PARTICIPATION				1968	
EXTENT PROJECT ASSISTS IN PROMOTION OF U.S. FOREIGN POLICY	1968				
PROJECT INFORMATION DISSEMINATION					
TO WHAT EXTENT ARE THE GOVERNMENT AND PEOPLE AWARE OF THE EXISTENCE AND PROGRESS MADE UNDER PROJECT?				1968	
TO WHAT EXTENT DOES THE PROJECT ENJOY GOOD PRESS AND RADIO COVERAGE?				1968	
TO WHAT EXTENT IS THE USAID IDENTIFIED WITH THE PROJECT?			1968		

identified in the profiles? Have returned participants had a constructive influence upon the institution? Are the institutional outputs, whatever they are, adequately serving the institution's clientele? In what way do the institutional outputs or inputs make it possible for the institution to place less and less dependence upon donor assistance? In what ways do the outputs feed back into the institution to strengthen the institution's capability to provide better services to its clientele?

Conclusion. The matrix is a simple schematic chart identifying major elements of institution building arranged in an understandable manner.

The matrix with the supporting profiles would be of value to AID technicians and institutional leaders even if the analysis and evaluations were not made. The matrix in and of itself provides a good checklist by asking the right questions, and in this manner it could help the institutional leaders become more aware of the significant elements of institution building.

In most developing countries, unfortunately, institutions are strongly identified with a single leader and viability of the institution is linked to its leader. This factor makes evaluation of institutional leadership properties as a bilateral exercise difficult because of the sensitivities involved. Maturity of the institution is reflected in its willingness to participate jointly in this type of analytical evaluative exercise. When practicable, the analysis should be a joint venture; when not practicable, unilateral analysis is a worthy in-house USAID exercise.

Analysis and evaluation of five institutions have shown leadership properties to be the most sensitive area. At the same time, the importance of such analysis and evaluation, if leadership properties are to be better understood, is of paramount importance. The most difficult factor for both the host country institutional leaders and U.S. technicians to understand, but probably the most significant, is the concept of establishing institutional doctrine. Evaluating the capacity for institutional change is also proving troublesome to comprehend.

Making the Institution-Building Matrix Operational

The institution-building matrix, as described above, is still in the developmental-experimental stage. Testing its operational value by applying it to a variety of projects is still required. The following methodology is suggested both as a procedure for testing the model and training senior AID officers in institution-building analysis and evaluation.

A traditional formal academic program is not envisaged. I see the need for the training to be closely associated with universities and their professional staff, however, in the nature of professional guidance, selected readings, auditing appropriate seminars, and conducting some applied research in institution development. It is important that senior functional officers gain greater appreciation and knowledge of technical fields other than their own. An

[178]

APPLICATIONS

integrated training cadre of senior AID professionals would provide this opportunity. A balanced team of senior AID officers, five or six, consisting of the following types of officers—a deputy director and chiefs of the following divisions: program, agriculture, education, public administration, and capital development. These individuals should be selected to train as an integrated team so that they would have an opportunity to interact one with the other during the training period. A resource person competent in this subject matter should be selected to prepare curricula and guide the training program.

Outstanding professors or other competent individuals would be selected to direct segments of the training exercise. They would prepare selected reading materials concerned with their specific segment and identify knowledgeable individuals to act as resource persons. Those participating would study together, discussing their findings with each other. Each officer would look at institution building in light of his own functional specialty and relate his studies and experience to that of others in the group. After reading and group discussion, they would meet with their resource person who would then suggest additional reading or assistance from other resource people. At the completion of the training period the officer would go into the field to determine its operational value.

Ten major projects in each of the following areas—capital development, agriculture, education, public administration—which have institution-building characteristics, should be selected on a worldwide basis. The functional specialists would be responsible for analyzing and evaluating their assigned institutions in general keeping with the institution-building matrix. They would meet with the host government institution directors, USAID chiefs of party, USAID division chiefs. They would be responsible, in collaboration with the others, to analyze and evaluate the institution, and to write all narrative statements, including the program strategy statement for review by the mission and host government institutional leaders. To place as little burden on mission personnel as possible, most of the evaluative work and writing should be prepared by the AID/Washington specialists. I would estimate that about ten days would be required to make the analysis, complete narrative statements and prepare the strategy.

On large institution-building projects, the economist or the deputy director should join the functional specialists in the preparation of the analysis.

When the functional specialists have completed their first five institutional analyses, they should meet at a convenient location, review their experiences, and make the first initial refinement of the process. They would then make the last five analyses, come back to Washington for a comprehensive review of their experiences, refine the process, prepare case studies and operational manuals.

Once the above is completed, the agency could tool up for a massive training program for AID personnel in institution-building analysis and evaluation.

The advantages of this type of training approach are as follows:

1. It would permit the senior officer to concentrate his studies in those areas most significant and relevant to the agency's needs.

2. The training need not correspond to the academic year.

3. It provides the trainee greater latitude for specialized study and research in keeping with USAID and objectives and also complements the officer's own interests and capabilities.

4. It provides for greater and more intimate professional association.

5. It permits each officer, through the integrated study team approach, to gain knowledge, insight and appreciation of institutional development problems associated with major functional areas.

6. This type of training approach could be tried on a limited basis, then evaluated, and a more refined program designed and applied in a more general program for other senior AID officers as well as other high-level professional employees of the host government.

7. Senior AID officers are now primarily responsible for the development of specific technical area strategies, program design, implementation, and management of mission projects, guidance, review, and evaluation of contract technical teams who are responsible for specific project implementation with the host government. To effectively assume this new role and carry out the implied responsibilities, the senior officer needs an array of additional skills, techniques, and broader insights into the institution-building process. Senior AID officers serving overseas need more in their luggage than just their professional training and experience, especially in view of the emphasis being placed upon institution building as an important part of national development.

NOTE

1. Wade Jones, AID/Washington, personal correspondence.

TECHNICAL ASSISTANCE AND INSTITUTION BUILDING: AN EMPIRICAL TEST

WILLIAM S. POOLER

Syracuse University

RICHARD L. DUNCAN

San Diego State College

WILLIAM S. POOLER is Assistant Professor of Sociology at the University of Syracuse, after receiving his Ph.D. in 1970 from the University of Michigan. He has a general interest in development, particularly as it relates to population and formal organization mechanisms. His most recent publication is "Population and Social Development" in M. Stanley, editor, *Frontiers in Development,* New York: Basic Books, 1971.

RICHARD L. DUNCAN has studied and worked in Latin America over the past twenty years. From 1952 to 1963 he was with AID and predecessor agencies in a variety of positions in Pakistan, Cuba, and Mexico. In 1964 he became Associate Director of the Technical Assistance Research Project at the Maxwell School at Syracuse University. This project involved an overall review of technical assistance activities. While there, he worked closely with members of the Inter-University Program in Institution Building. He has since worked with the Ford Foundation in Venezuela on the development of a graduate school of administration and is presently a social science advisor on educational planning to the Ministry of Education in Brazil, under an AID contract to San Diego State College Foundation. During the course of his academic and administrative career he has participated in the design, implementation, and evaluation of many institution-building projects.

TECHNICAL ASSISTANCE AND INSTITUTION BUILDING: AN EMPIRICAL TEST

W I L L I A M S. P O O L E R

Syracuse University

R I C H A R D L. D U N C A N

San Diego State College

INTRODUCTION

The Inter-University Research Program in Institution Building has proposed a framework to describe and explain a process of institutional development in both developed and developing societies. As a part of this effort, a theoretical orientation has been developed which specifies the dimensions, and within dimensions, the variables involved in institution building.[1] The goal of this research is to empirically test the relationships implied by the formulated scheme while emphasizing the role of technical assistance. Also, suggestions are made for revising and extending the orientation.

It should be recognized at the outset that institutions, as used in the context of this research, are defined in a particularistic manner. They are specific formal organizations which over time have developed a capacity to act as agents for the larger society by providing valued functions and services. More than this, they serve as models for defining legitimate normative and value patterns, conserving and protecting them for the larger society. In dealing with the problem of how to introduce innovative techniques in developing societies, we assume that an effective way to do this is by creating and supporting formal organizations which

AUTHORS' NOTE: This chapter is a revision of Richard L. Duncan and William S. Pooler, "Technical Assistance and Institution Building," a research report supported by the Inter-University Program in Institution Building, Pittsburgh, 1968 (mimeo).

utilize these innovations and corresponding technology in such a manner that, over time, given changes in the existing institutional complex of the society, these organizations take on the mantle of institutions. These new institutions then provide a means for gaining acceptance of new technology, managing temporary problems with greater effectiveness, and providing additional innovations as they are required. They become part of the institutional matrix of society and assist in achieving its long-range goals.

The institution-building framework posits three dimensions significant to understanding the process of institution building. First, there is an internal organization dimension which includes variables dealing with leadership, doctrine, program resources, and internal structure. Second, there is a linkage dimension which includes variables dealing with enabling support in the recipient environment and the existence or emergence of functionally related activities in the society. Further, this dimension deals with a normative consideration which specifies the presence or emergence of compatible normative orientations by already existing institutions, and a pattern of diffusion of norms, values, and techniques from the created organization qua institution to other segments of the society. Third, there is a transaction dimension which involves the ways in which the nascent institution gains support for itself, sets up resource exchanges, structures the environment, and transfers norms and values. For the purposes of this research, the framework is put in a time perspective which implies that there is a life-cycle to institution building and that efforts to institutionalize created formal organizations should vary as the life-cycle stages of the process change.

To isolate and research the role of technical assistance in institution building, two dimensions of the original framework have been kept—internal organization and environmental linkages; and the dimension of time, to examine maturation, has been added.[2] Internal organization variables and environmental linkages, while they provide the means to focus on both internal and external dimensions of institutions, by themselves constitute a static frame of reference. With the introduction of time, a dynamic dimension is added. This is accomplished by positing three stages which are then used to trace the development of the created organization from organization to institution.

To isolate the effects of technical assistance, the contributions of technical assistance have been differentiated from the contributions of other factors, essentially within the recipient society. While it is recognized that factors other than technical assistance and recipient society efforts do have consequences for the institution-building process, the particular focus of the study and the limitations imposed by the data precluded any systematic consideration of them. The major thrust of the research, then, is an examination of the contributions of organized technical assistance efforts to the institution-building process, and the insights into the process provided by this orientation.

Some Preliminary Considerations

The Concept of Technical Assistance. The problem of defining an institution has offered and will continue to offer difficulties in both the conceptual and practical realm. Because of the objectives of this research, the definition set forth above, while somewhat unique, is particularly adapted to the purposes of this research.

Technical assistance, on the other hand, is defined in so many ways as to require some attempt to clarify the activity and its relation to institution building.[3] In the most pragmatic sense, the definition is derived from the projects used in the research where government and private agencies are engaged in activities they call technical assistance. It cannot be assumed, though, that for both donors and recipients technical assistance activities are defined in similar ways across projects. A review of technical assistance shows that there is wide variation in the nature, rule, and approach of projects that are so classified. For example, colonial sedrants remaining in their jobs with their salary partly or fully paid by the former metropolitan power are classified as technical assistance. Some missionary activities are similarly designated. The United Nations operational and executive programs and a number of U.S. government projects which involve only training are also called technical assistance.

In general, the standard program of major technical assistance agencies involves the provision of personnel, training, and equipment. The focus is usually on the achieving of some particular development objective, but these, too, vary widely. Neither does technical assistance concentrate exclusively on institution building, though it is a strong emphasis in many programs. The question of how to define such a variety of activities is, therefore, problematic. Fortunately, there are a few common elements which can be sorted out as encompassing technical assistance in general terms and these, taken together, constitute the definition used in the research.

Technical assistance is first of all *purposive;* it can be easily separated from traditional diffusion and acculturation which has been occurring among cultures for thousands of years.

Technical assistance is *cooperative.* It requires agreement on purpose and means between a donor agency and a recipient government. Either party participating in technical assistance is free to withdraw or to allow activities to languish until they are terminated.

Technical assistance involves an *international transfer of knowledge and skill through individuals or agencies of a donor,* and with a defined relationship to individuals involves groups or organizations of a recipient in the *accomplishment of mutually agreed objectives.*

The Nature of the Data. Extensive and careful analysis was required to uncover evidence related to the different dimensions and variables posited by the institution-building model. Fortunately, there has been a growing body of reports and other studies which emphasize the institution-building context of technical assistance.[4] But problems of operationalization and analysis were complicated by the inconsistency of the data within reports and lack of comparability across reports. The lack of comparability is the major factor accounting for the small number of cases used in the research and points to the need to gather data using a common framework, such as the "Guiding Concepts," as a frame of reference.[5]

Disappointment in finding relatively few complete cases, from which we could draw information about most of the detailed aspects of institutional growth and participation of technical assistance, was reduced when it was found that the larger volume of general materials provided a basic structure to support the research. Much of this data provided a broader basis for the design of a coding system and assisted in the determination of the significance of different isolated facts in the specific projects which were finally coded. Therefore, the final n of forty-six cases which, in some cases, does not include coding all phases, is by no means an indication that these cases form the entire base of the analysis. The refining of the concepts, the design of the coding system, and the information required to effectively extract the necessary and relevant material from the cases which are included in the analysis resulted from long, detailed, and sometimes frustrating examination of a large volume of technical assistance activities. It is precisely this problem of breaking down the concepts and developing the coding system which will now be treated briefly.

Breaking Down the Concepts into the Preliminary Elements of the Coding System

One of the important first steps in the development of the coding system was to break down the concepts into a series of categories which would allow for the proper classification of data from the reports available.[6] The classification of instruments such as joint operations, individual technicians, university contracts, or of types of activity such as agricultural credit banks, planning and research, and higher education, involved few difficulties. The question of operational or advisory, however, was more difficult to separate. Joint operations is normally a system by which technical assistance personnel form a part of the operating arm of the agency, but this has varied in degree and over time. In other cases, such as in planning boards, technical assistance advisors provided a limited amount of operational support under certain circumstances, but were generally involved in training and advising. In still other cases there were single advisors for organizations whose efforts were strictly limited to advisory services at different levels with no discernible operational participation. To eliminate some complexity it was decided to call any project in which technical assistance personnel performed any operation an "operational project"; all other projects were labelled "advisory."

There were relatively few problems in classifying institutions as new or reconstituted, since the latter category included restructuring, modifying old institutions, introducing new functions, and so forth. Similarly, the kinds of institution were easily identified; and the two broad categories of rural and urban services provided mechanisms into which all activities, not easily assigned to more specific categories, would fit.

The problem of determining the emphasis of technical assistance was one of considerable difficulty. Leadership had to be divided into provisional subcategories such as the existence of transition plans, the amount of training, and the degree of internal support for the leadership. To identify doctrine, evidence of a developing philosophy of operation and/or some organizational norms, either borrowed or developed internally, were established as criteria. Emphasis on program was assigned according to the importance placed by the donor on particular outputs of the institution and indicators of such activity. When attention in reports was given to outputs such as increasing the volume of loans, setting up demonstration plots, and the like, the project was coded as having a program emphasis.

Insofar as technical assistance contributed to the development of a staff and to organizational development and change, internal structure was coded positively. The amount and nature of the resources both human and physical which were used in the project by both the donor and recipient provided a significant clue to the resource emphasis of the project. It will be noted that while it was possible to reduce the internal variables of the institution into their component parts, much of the coding depended on searching throughout the reports for enough facts and supporting clues which would support judgments about the emphasis of technical assistance in a given case. A technique of independent coding by the individual researchers with different backgrounds made possible a minimization of a particular person's bias.

Breaking down the linkage concepts into meaningful statements which could be found in the material available was another of the difficult aspects of establishing the coding system and required a number of initial attempts which proved less than satisfactory. Here again the large mass of material which was available was of invaluable assistance, even though many of the case materials and the interview statements could not ultimately be coded. The unused material provided a greater understanding of linkage relationships and internal variables and thus assisted in refining the concepts to fit the data which were available for coding. Because of the continuous comparison between concepts and data, it was possible to identify such items as authority and resources within enabling linkages and state them in such a way that specific data references provided a basis for coding these and other linkage variables.

An additional factor, also of importance in the linkage variables, is the question of whether technical assistance or the host country was the principal in the transactions involving different linkages. In functional relationships, for example, there could be complementary technical assistance projects that would support the development of functional linkages, or there could be complementary institutions in the recipient environment which would provide the basis for maturing functional relationships. In the same manner, the influence and prestige of technical assistance may well provide the basis for grants of authority in enabling linkages or the use of mass media to develop diffused linkages. Further, as the institution matures, it may provide the basis for influencing normative behavior of other institutions, or technical assistance may provide the basis for other means of expanding the institution's influence. In the latter case it will be important to try to determine what happens to this normative relationship during the course of the three phases.

Some of the linkages were extremely difficult to break down. Normative linkages, for example, sometimes show up only in very specific circumstances, i.e., when there are branches of the institution created and operated under their control, or when there is specific evidence in the case histories that other agencies had adopted a similar approach in the administration of their organization or in carrying out particular functions. Newly created institutions have a variety of influences on the other institutions in the environment in relatively subtle and informal ways. One of the most common ways is for persons trained in the new institution to move into important positions in other institutions in the society. None of the reports on presently coded cases mention such occurrences, but from previous experience and examination of programs in different countries we know this to be so. Therefore, when the normative linkages are noted in the data, they result from significant overt recorded effects.

The questions of diffused linkages also represented a serious coding problem. There are a number of cases in which relationships with the clientele, the use of mass media, and the particular actions of technical assistance or recipients in carrying out of institution-building projects have been so significant as to be noted in different reports. However, there is considerable indication from interviews and other data gained on previous projects that diffused linkages with the public and clientele are oftem important factors in the growth of an institution, but tend to be of an informal nature. As a consequence, they are not mentioned in many of the materials which were available to us.

When the initial attempt was made to conceptualize similarity—that is, the degree to which the technical assistance project is different from organizational forms found in the recipient society—it was thought one category would be sufficient. In pretesting the coding scheme, we became aware of the multidimensional nature of this concept and decided to break it down into some component parts. Four components of similarity were constructed which specify the nature of a project in terms of its similarity of function, similarity of content, similarity of philosophy of operation, and similarity to societal value system when compared to what already exists in the recipient society.

Similarity of function refers to how an activity is performed, i.e., in what particular ways are resources organized to accomplish whatever is being undertaken? Similarity of content refers to the specific nature of the activity.

Given the fact that a function is organized in a certain manner, similarity of philosophy of operation or method then looks at the rules or norms used to run the organization. Finally, similarity to societal value system refers to those values that lie behind the operating rules. Obviously the four distinctions are not absolutely clear, mutually exclusive, or even exhaustive, but they do get at important distinctions of similarity and provide a useful starting point.

Development of the Time Phasing and Criteria for Success

During the initial examination of variables, no provision was made for different time phases in a project. However, early in the development of the coding system, it became clear that there were changes in the different variables over time. At first an attempt was made to use two time phases, but further testing uncovered the need for three time phases. They are elaborated as follows: The first time phase involved the beginnings of technical assistance, the period of organization, and initial functioning of the organization. The second period remained flexible throughout the study and is defined as a transitional period at which time there were changes in the significance and configuration of the inputs to the various internal and external variables. The third phase is a mature or terminal period when it would normally be expected to find indications of institutionalization and either the reduction or withdrawal of technical assistance. It was necessary to set certain approximate minimums and maximums, at least on Phase I and Phase III, in order to get some comparability of information. After finding that ten years eliminated cases which met approximate criteria for the third phase, it was decided that projects with less than eight years' development would not be coded in all three phases. Projects terminated prior to four years would be coded in the first phase and in the second phase as much as the data would allow. Any project less than four years old would then have to have special circumstances or additional material which would make it useful in the development of the study. Projects which ran between four and eight years were coded in the first two time phases.

There were a few cases in which the duration had been between two and four years and particular reasons why they could be accepted as cases for coding. In one case, for instance, continuous technical assistance was provided for only two years, but an evaluation study detailing the development of the project was carried on some eight years after the project had begun. In this particular case it was not possible to code any variables in the third phase (except success), but the volume of data made it possible to code two time phases of the project. There were other problems involved with the time phasing including a determination as to the point at which Phase II could be coded. Usually the attempt to find changes in the internal linkage variables was successful, but it was not always possible to clearly delineate between the phases.

In reviewing the completed coding, it was noted that there were some cases in which certain variables remained constant throughout the three phases. There were, however, enough variables which did change in each case to provide some basis for believing that we had, in fact, been able to conceptualize the institution-building process in three time phases.

A critical point in the development of the coding system was setting up criteria for evaluating successful institution building. This problem has been the source of difficulty for planners, administrators, evaluators, and research personnel alike. No definitive answer has been developed in the literature and there is bound to be considerable variation in the criteria for success in accordance with geographic, developmental, and substantive factors. Nevertheless, an attempt to achieve some agreement was attempted. The elements laid out in the "Guiding Concepts" served as a beginning. (1) Successful institutions survive and continue to carry on the functions which they were designed to accomplish. (2) Successful institutions also have a relatively greater degree of autonomy in the determination of the use and the obtaining of their funds than unsuccessful ones. These, then, became the first two of five utilized criteria. In addition, a variety of other factors were discussed and compared with the data which had been reviewed. The preliminary additional criteria which stood the test of the case materials were: (3) structural impact defined as evidence of societal structural change to accommodate the emergence of the institution as a result of institutional output, services, or other effects which it has on the environment; (4) the degree to which institutional norms are recognized as being legitimate. (that is, are the services desired, and/or is the approach which the institution is using to accomplish its activities beginning to be considered the appropriate way to accomplish such activities); (5) the degree to which institutional norms have been incorporated (that is, to what degree other institutions in the society have been influenced by the normative patterns which have been developed by the institution). (See page 224 for coding criteria.)

As the case material was reviewed it became evident that an overall estimate of successful institutional development would have to be constructed, since no one of the five elements by itself would be an adequate indicator. Two different cumulative measures were developed. The first measure is for time Phase II and does not include the fifth element of success, normative incorporation. This, because little data were available to code this element in Phase II, when normative incorporation appears to be unlikely to occur. The second measure is for time Phase III which does include all five elements and allows for greater discrimination within elements.

The summary score for Phase II can be thought of as providing an indicator for future success. The elements are coded 0 or 1 depending upon whether or not there are any indications in the data. For time Phase III, the summary score represents the degree to which the organization has successfully made the transition to an institution. Here the elements are coded 0, 1, or 2—with 0 representing no evidence, and 2 representing significant evidence.

Selecting the Institution-Building Cases

There were generally three criteria for selecting the cases. First, did the case fall within the specifically defined category we had established for institution building? Second, was there a significant and identifiable technical assistance component concerned with the development of the institution? Third, were there enough data on the institution and the technical assistance project to provide the basis for coding the individual case?

The criterion for institution building has remained rather flexible in the studies up to this point. In part, this was due to the fact that institution building has been an implicit, if not explicit, objective of a great many different kinds of technical assistance projects over the years. The creation of autonomous organizations such as rural credit banks, planning boards, and universities can be instances of institution building. So can developing departments within ministries, setting up a specific office within an agency, creating an extension or home economics program with a ministry of agriculture, or starting a small-range management program actually restricted to a small geographic segment of a recipient society. Institution-building projects can require massive inputs of capital and personnel over a period of time, such as a civil air transport organization. Conversely, only small amounts of capital and personnel might be required in another institution-building project—for example, a small hotel school.

Given the wide variety of possible projects and kinds of efforts expended, what, then, can be used to classify projects as belonging to a relatively exclusive category of institution-building projects? The specific designation "institution building" is reserved for those projects which tehnical assistance and the recipient society cooperatively designate as institution-building efforts in the long-range objectives or goals of the projects. This is either explicitly stated or strongly implied in the specification of the aims of the projects. This is our first criterion. Does the case history report of a technical assistance project specifically state that the particular project being worked on is intended to develop into an institutional form in the recipient society?

The second and third criteria were tested for only after the first criterion was met. This was accomplished by attempting to code each case according to the developed coding system. When each case had been broken down into a series of coded categories, a determination was made as to the completeness of the information in terms of the technical assistance effort (the second criterion) and in terms of the recipient society's effort, the time phase changes, the success criteria, and so forth (the third criterion). When all three criteria were met, the case was included in the analysis.

Coding Procedure and Tabular Presentation

After the institution-building cases were selected according to the discussed criteria, each selected case was coded independently by each investigator using the developed coding scheme. When this was completed, the researchers met and discussed the categories coded for each case. In most instances there was agreement that the appropriate codes were utilized. Where differences were uncovered, the case material was reread by each person and, after reviewing them, agreement reached on the most appropriate code.

When all the cases had been coded according to the coding system (Appendix 1) they were then punched on IBM cards. This is a fairly mechanical process which essentially involved small numerical transformations to fit the punch card scheme. In some instances new variables were created, but again this involved only a mechancial operation—that of combining existing codes.

The IBM cards were then punched and the tabular data obtained by using a counter-sorter. The procedure decided on was to use the combined success scores in time Phases II and III as dependent variables and the others as predictor or independent variables. Except for the first table, which deals with the correlation of the combined success scores in Phase II with that of Phase III, the tables demonstrate the relationship between each selected independent variable and the combined success score in Phase II and Phase III.

Preliminary Methodological Note

It might be implied in what has been said thus far that we have used a tautological approach and hence have insured findings consonant with the underlying theoretical orientation. It is true that the forty-six project histories that make up the coded cases for the present study were among those used to help create the coding scheme which represents an operationalization of the framework of institution building. At the time of initial examination, though, these data were part of a larger volume of material and were referred to only in order to determine what was available and to construct variables which could serve as a bridge between the theoretical framework and existing empirical data.

During this phase of the research no attention was paid to relationships of variables or in fact even to the kinds of cases that could be thought of as institution-building projects. The assumption was that somewhere in the mass of reports we had available there would be a number of cases which could be adjudged to be instances of attempts at institutionalization. Priorities dictated that we first find out if there were any fit between the existing data sources in all their variability and the theoretical orientation. If this proved to be so, then we could go back over the material and select case histories which could be included in the analysis.

One could argue that there is some contamination in proceeding this way. But the writers feel it is minimized because the main thrust of the study is not the specification of variables, but the examination of the dynamic interrelationships among the variables and the insights they give us in understanding the process of institutionalizing innovations in developing societies.

RESULTS AND DISCUSSION

Before presenting the data, it is important to remind the reader of the tentative nature of the relationships to be discussed. The overwhelming consistency 'of all the results bodes well for the fruitfulness of the approach. Particular relationships, though, should be treated as something less than conclusive evidence. This is so because of the subjective judgments involved in writing up the case history material used as data for this report and in fitting this case history material to the developed coding scheme. Also, the "Guiding Concepts" document, the theoretical orientation around which the research has been built, is pitched at an abstract level, making the operationalization procedure difficult and thus possibly affecting the validity of our results.

Nonetheless, given these limitations and others implied in our discussions of procedure, the results appear to offer significant promise for the approach. For the present we assume that there is a canceling of the biases across case history reports both in terms of their being written up and coded.

The combined success scores in Phase II (the second time phase, which is a transitional stage in the development of an institution) and Phase III (the point in time when the organization is institutionalized) serve as our dependent variables. The success score in Phase II can be thought of as an indication of the institutional potential of an organization at some midpoint in its development, while the success score in Phase III can be thought of as an evaluation of the degree to which the organization has been institutionalized, given enough time for the process to have taken place. The success scores are referred to as combined success scores because the summary figure is arrived at by summing the 0 or 1 scores for four success criteria in Phase II, and 0, 1, or 2 scores for five success criteria in Phase III. To simplify presentation, the combined scores are dichotomized for each of the two phases into high and low success categories. In Phase II there are 46 cases, 24 or 52 percent of which are high success cases. In Phase III there are 30 cases that were coded for all three phases, 14 or 47 percent of which are low success cases and 16 or 53 percent which are high success cases.

The degree of consistency of scores from Phase II to Phase III for those projects coded in these two time phases can be seen in Table 1. Because of the nature of the data, 16 of the 46 cases in Phase II could not be coded in Phase III. Of the 30 cases coded for all three times phases, 24 or 80 percent of them are either low or high success cases in both of the last two phases. There is some variation across the high and low success categories, with the former showing a greater degree of consistency. Of the high success cases in Phase II, 11 or 92 percent of them are still high success in Phase III. For low success cases, 13 or 72 percent of the 13 in Phase II remain low in Phase III. The indications are that cases which appear to be successful in the intermediate stages tend to maintain their development and, according to the selected success criteria, become

TABLE 1

Summary of the Relationship of Success Scores for Phase II
(potential) and Phase III (conclusions)
(based on the 30 cases coded for all three phases)

	High Success	Low Success	Total
1. Phase II (potential)	12	18	30
2. Phase III (conclusions)			
A. Correctly predicted	11	13	24
B. Incorrectly predicted	1	5	6
3. Index of Reliability	92%	72%	

TABLE 2A

The Kind of Technical Assistance in Phase I and Success
Potential in Phase II

	Success Potential in Phase II					
	Low Success (potential)		High Success (potential)		Total	
Kind of Technical Assistance in Phase I	n	%	n	%	n	%
Joint operations	—	—	2	100	2	100
Contract	12	57	9	43	21	100
Direct hire	11	50	11	50	22	100
Equipment and/or training	1	100	—	—	1	100
Total	24	52	22	48	46	100

TABLE 2B

The Kind of Technical Assistance in Phase I and
Success in Phase III

	Success in Phase III					
	Low Success		High Success		Total	
Kind of Technical Assistance in Phase I	n	%	n	%	n	%
Joint operations	—	—	2	100	2	100
Contract	8	53	7	47	15	100
Direct hire	5	42	7	58	12	100
Equipment and/or training	1	100	—	—	1	100
Total	14	47	16	53	30	100

institutionalized. Cases which are rated as low success, however, do not necessarily end up as non-institutionalized.

Almost all of the cases from which data were tabulated and analyzed are either contract or direct hire technical assistance projects; a very few were joint operations.

In analyzing the relationship between success or success potential and kind of technical assistance, the two joint operations cases will not be treated except to say that they both exhibited high success potential. The direct hire projects were somewhat related to high success potential, but there is not a large difference between them and contract cases.

Table 2B shows that what little difference obtained between contract and direct hire cases is magnified when related to actual success in Phase III. Thus one can tentatively conclude that direct hire projects have a somewhat greater likelihood of being successful institution-building projects.

Why should this be so? Unfortunately, at this time there are no definitive answers, but certain possibilities come to mind. Technical assistance involves getting agreement between parties by relying heavily on cooperation. Contract projects require agreement between more parties than direct hire. Thus, direct hire projects are potentially less likely to involve conflict and misunderstanding and hence may tend to be more successful. It also might be that we are dealing with a majority of cases which do not involve overly complex technology and thus direct hire projects are more suitable for this kind of endeavor. If this is so, it would explain why some of the contract projects demonstrated high success. There is also the possibility that the persons writing the evaluation reports used as data allowed their own biases to enter into the reports. These people were, in the main, direct hire personnel of one or another agency and possibly were predisposed to accent the successful features of the direct hire projects they were investigating.

Whether a new organization was created or an existing organizational (institutional) form was changed seems to have a bearing on the success of the institution-building effort. For Phase II (Table 3A) and even more so for Phase III (Table 3B), starting fresh with a new organization tends more often to result in success. This would seem to make sense in that old ways of doing things and old allegiances do not have to be broken down or destroyed before the new effort can be instituted. All of the projects are innovative in nature. Where there is a lack of competition in terms of no already existing traditional means for achieving desired ends, some of the resistance is avoided that would be generated if more traditional means had been in use.

Table 4 compares the approach of technical assistance in the initial stage of the project to success potential for institutionalization. An original hypothesis was that, in most institution-building projects, donor personnel would have to take some operational responsibility in the initial stages for there to be success. The data tend to bear out this contention. This finding casts some doubt on the

TABLE 3A
Institutional Situation and Success Potential in Phase II

| | Success Potential in Phase II | | | | | |
| | Low Success (potential) | | High Success (potential) | | Total | |
Institutional Situation	n	%	n	%	n	%
New situation	14	50	14	50	28	100
Changed old situation	10	56	8	44	18	100
Total	24	52	22	48	46	100

TABLE 3B
Institutional Situation and Success in Phase III

| | Success Potential in Phase III | | | | | |
| | Low Success | | High Success | | Total | |
Institutional Situation	n	%	n	%	n	%
New situation	6	40	9	60	15	100
Change old situation	8	53	7	47	15	100
Total	14	47	16	53	30	100

TABLE 4
Initial Approach of Technical Assistance and Success Potential in Phase II

| | Success Potential in Phase II | | | | | |
| | Low Success (potential) | | High Success (potential) | | Total | |
Initial Approach of Technical Assistance	n	%	n	%	n	%
Operational	8	33	16	67	24	100
Advisory	16	73	6	27	22	100
Total	24	52	22	48	46	100

position of those who argue that operational participation by donor personnel is not an acceptable function of technical assistance.

That an operational approach to institution-building projects should be temporary—that is, should be followed only in the initial stages of the projects—becomes evident in examining Tables 5A and 5B. The majority of projects which evidenced no change in approach, that were either operational or advisory throughout the history of the project, tended to be less successful. Referring back to Table 4, any success that was encountered was probably a function of maintaining an unchanging operational stance. But of those cases that did change their approach, 80 percent of the cases that started with operational technical assistance personnel and at a later stage switched to advisory technical personnel were successful projects.

While there were a relatively small number of projects that evidenced a switch from an operational to an advisory approach by technical assistance, the high percentage of successful projects in this category is encouraging support for the hypothesis that, as an organization becomes institutionalized, the role of donor personnel should change from direct participation in the operational activities of the organization to one of greater emphasis on advisory services. Attention should be paid to getting indigenous personnel to operate the organization, but only after this is some stable organization to operate.

Thus far, results have been presented which bear on the general nature of the projects analyzed and the general character of the technical assistance effort. The next section of the results deals with intra-organizational concerns and attempts to portray the contributions of technical assistance and donor activities in this area insofar as they bear on the process of institution building.

The "Guiding Concepts" document specified five variables within an organizational structure which were important dimensions to consider when building an institution. Table 6 demonstrates the relationship between the number of these variables or dimensions emphasized by technical assistance and success. In essence, it refers to technical assistance taking a narrow or wide intra-organizational approach and the consequences for institution building.

Clearly, the more dimensions emphasized, the greater the probability of success. This might be a different way of measuring involvement or commitment by technical assistance. If it is, it tends to reinforce the findings noted in previous tables dealing with initial operational participation of technical assistance and the switch from an operational to an advisory approach at a later period in the maturation process. That the switch from operational to advisory does not mean less involvement can be supported in part from the findings in Table 6. The character of the approach of technical assistance changes in highly successful projects, but not the level of involvement.

One of the factors identified and related to the coding system was the existence of arrangements, plans, or specific preparations for transition to recipient leadership of, and thus responsibility for, a project. This was hypothesized as a critical factor in institutional development. These arrange-

TABLE 5A

**Change in Approach of Technical Assistance (phases I and II)
and Success Potential in Phase II**

| | Success Potential in Phase III | | | | | |
| | Low Success (potential) | | High Success (potential) | | Total | |
Change in Approach of Technical Assistance	n	%	n	%	n	%
No change	20	65	11	35	31	100
Change—operational to advisory	2	15	11	85	13	100
Change—advisory to operational	2	100	—	—	2	100
Total	24	52	22	48	46	100

TABLE 5B

**Change in Approach of Technical Assistance (phases I to III)
and Success in Phase III**

| | Success in Phase III | | | | | |
| | Low Success | | High Success | | Total | |
Change in Approach of Technical Assistance	n	%	n	%	n	%
No change	11	61	7	39	18	100
Change—operational to advisory	2	20	8	80	10	100
Change—advisory to operational	1	50	1	50	2	100
Total	14	47	16	53	30	100

TABLE 6

**Number of Intra-Organizational Variables Emphasized
by Technical Assistance in Phase I and Success in Phase III**

| | Success in Phase III | | | | | |
| | Low Success | | High Success | | Total | |
Number of Intra-Organizational Variables Emphasized by Technical Assistance in Phase II	n	%	n	%	n	%
1 through 3	10	67	5	33	15	100
4+	4	27	11	73	15	100
Total	14	47	16	53	30	100

ments, where they were found in the case histories, varied from the highly specific (i.e., a manning table specifying dates and times that shifts of leadership and directives would take place from donor to recipient personnel) to relatively unstructured arrangements whereby the recipient leadership group within the organization gradually assumed control.

Surprisingly there was only sparse mention in the case histories of transition plans for leadership, and hence it was meaningless to code this category by time phases. Thus the variable was dichotomized into those cases where there was mention of this anywhere in the report and these cases where there was not. Table 7A and 7B show the degree to which transition plans are related to success. It is interesting to note that 87 percent of the cases with transition plans in some phase were coded as having high success potential in Phase II. However, in Phase III, only 67 percent of the cases having transition plans were coded as high success. In both time phases, the lack of transition plans leads to little success. It is, of course, consistent with the idea of institution building to posit that planning for leadership transition is at least indirectly related to the execution of indigenous leadership takeover, and that this should be highly related to success in institution building. What is somewhat intriguing is the smaller magnitude of the relationship that exists in Phase III when compared to Phase II. One explanation for this might be that emphasis on intra-organizational factors is important early in the process of institution building, while linkage variables assume increasing importance at a later time. If this is so, then the success score for Phase III is contaminated by the linkage configuration (environmental factors), and hence the relationship between intra-organizational factors and Phase III success scores may be somewhat weaker or stronger than would be the case if a multivariate approach was adapted and the linkage configuration held constant. This would not be the case for Phase II where intra-organizational factors assume overriding importance.

Yet another explanation might be that transition plans, started late in the institution-building process, reflect organizational problems. It could be that the indigenous personnel were of such low calibre that their eventual takeover was questionable, or that the technical assistance personnel assumed too strong an operational stance and found it difficult to extricate themselves. Thus, leadership transition plans had to be delayed or undertaken with such caution that the institutionalization of the organization was jeopardized.

Training indigenous leadership was often mentioned in the case histories, as Table 8 demonstrates. This activity, in the different time phases, was postively related to the success scores. The table demonstrates that early emphasis on training leadership is related to high success. The relationship changes though when one relates constant or later attention to leadership and success. The fact that early attention to training is positively related to institution building and, further, that this finding is consonant with our interpretation of the institution-building process, lends credence to the analysis.

TABLE 7A

**Leadership Transition Plans Emphasized by Technical
Assistance and Success Potential in Phase II**

Leadership Transition Plans Emphasized by Technical Assistance	Success Potential in Phase II					
	Low Success (potential)		High Success (potential)		Total	
	n	%	n	%	n	%
Yes	2	13	13	87	15	100
No	22	71	9	29	31	100
Total	24	52	22	48	46	100

TABLE 7B

**Leadership Transition Plans Emphasized by Technical
Assistance and Success in Phase III**

Leadership Transition Plans Emphasized by Technical Assistance	Success in Phase III					
	Low Success		High Success		Total	
	n	%	n	%	n	%
Yes	3	33	6	67	9	100
No	11	48	10	52	21	100
Total	14	47	16	53	30	100

TABLE 8

**Training Leadership Emphasized by Technical Assistance
and Success in Phase III**

Training Leadership Emphasized by Technical Assistance	Success in Phase III					
	Low Success		High Success		Total	
	n	%	n	%	n	%
Only phase I and II	3	33	6	67	9	100
All phases	8	47	9	53	17	100
Late or no emphasis	3	75	1	25	4	100
Total	14	47	16	53	30	100

As was the case with leadership transition plans, "internal support for leadership" was infrequently noted and hence we had to dichotomize this variable. For this variable to be given a positive value for a particular case, there had to be some demonstration that the technical assistance activity was directed at legitimizing the internal authority structure. Where this actively was not noted or where technical assistance efforts were directed at giving support for leadership outside of the organization, in the recipient environment, the variable was assigned a negative value. The latter effort was coded positively for a linkage variable, enabling support.

Table 9 points out the strong relationship that exists between internal support for leadership within the organization and the success of institution building. The high discrimination power of the variable demonstrates the significance of this activity for technical assistance and adds strength to the argument that, in order for the organization to develop an institutional mantle, a strong internally integrated organization must be built. The cases where doctrine was emphasized in Phases I and II were successful half the time. But where it was emphasized in all three time phases, over two-thirds of the cases were successful. Why this disparity? One explanation might be that attention to doctrinal concerns indicates a continuing commitment to the institution-building effort. Also, the acceptance by the larger recipient society of the organizational doctrine is essential for the success of the project. Thus what we have categorized as "attention to internal doctrine" might actually be an attempt by the organization to encourage acceptance by the environment. This would be consistent with the general suggestion that Phase III projects must pay maximum concern to building environmental linkages. There is some indication that constant program outputs do result in more success but this cannot be considered a valid generalization. Undoubtedly, some projects do benefit from program outputs, but which ones and why still remain problematic.

That technical assistance must pay early attention to building a viable internal organizational structure if there is to be the development of an institution is evident from Table 12.

This finding is consistent with those presented earlier and provides additional basis for the inference that there is a need to build a strong organization to insure the emergence of a new institution. Further, the strength of the relationship, when looking at early effort in this direction, points to the significance of different kinds of technical assistance efforts depending on the maturation stage of the institution.

Further evidence for this assertion is forthcoming from Table 13.

It is almost self-evident that a major function of technical assistance is to provide resources, material, and men as inputs for the project. But it is not as evident that continued resource emphasis on the part of technical assistance has negative consequences for successful institution building. From Table 13 it would seem that keeping the project dependent on technical assistance resource inputs beyond Phase II will result in something less than an institutional form. It

TABLE 9

Internal Support for Leadership Emphasized by Technical Assistance and Success in Phase III

Internal Support for Leadership Emphasized by Technical Assistance	Success in Phase III					
	Low Success		High Success		Total	
	n	%	n	%	n	%
Yes	6	33	12	67	18	100
No	8	67	4	33	12	100
Total	14	47	16	53	30	100

TABLE 10

Doctrine Emphasized by Technical Assistance and Success in Phase III

Doctrine Emphasized by Technical Assistance	Success in Phase III					
	Low Success		High Success		Total	
	n	%	n	%	n	%
Only phases I and II	5	56	4	44	9	100
All phases	5	33	10	67	15	100
Other (including No Emphasis)	4	67	2	33	6	100
Total	14	47	16	53	30	100

TABLE 11

Program Outputs Emphasized by Technical Assistance and Success in Phase III

Program Outputs Emphasized by Technical Assistance	Success in Phase III					
	Low Success		High Success		Total	
	n	%	n	%	n	%
Only phase I and II	6	50	6	50	12	100
All phases	4	40	6	60	10	100
Other (including No Emphasis)	4	50	4	50	8	100
Total	14	47	16	53	30	100

TABLE 12

Internal Structure Emphasized by Technical Assistance
and Success in Phase III

Internal Structure Emphasized by Technical Assistance	Success in Phase III					
	Low Success		High Success		Total	
	n	%	n	%	n	%
Only phases I and II	2	17	10	83	12	100
All phases	4	57	3	43	7	100
Other (including No Emphasis)	8	73	3	27	11	100
Total	14	47	16	53	30	100

seems reasonable to assume that the organization constantly needs resources. Successful projects thus are able to get resources by nature of their own initiative; i.e., linkage relationships that have been established with the environmental complex in the recipient society.

From the relationships analyzed thus far, it would seem that technical assistance is instrumental in helping a project from its inception as an organization until it develops into an institution. Further, the data suggest that when dealing with matters internal to the organization, treating it as a closed system if you will, technical assistance is most effective when efforts are made early in the life-cycle and attention is paid to withdrawing support in the later stages. It has also been demonstrated that a wide focus dealing with all facets of organization is more effective than a narrow focus. And finally, in terms of the relative importance of the five internal organization variables, leadership, internal structure, and resources were most clearly related to successful institution building, but mainly when emphasized in the early stages of the project. Doctrine and program output were significantly less related to success. For this reason, one might tentatively conclude they should be given somewhat

TABLE 13

Resources Emphasized by Technical Assistance and
Success in Phase III

Resources Emphasized by Technical Assistance	Success in Phase III					
	Low Success		High Success		Total	
	n	%	n	%	n	%
Only in phases I and II	3	25	9	75	12	100
All phases	5	56	4	44	9	100
Other (including No Emphasis)	6	67	3	33	9	100
Total	14	47	16	53	30	100

TABLE 14A
Technical Assistance Efforts to Encourage Recipient Authority
Support and Success Potential in Phase II

Technical Assistance Efforts to Encourage Authority Support	Success Potential in Phase II					
	Low Success (potential)		High Success (potential)		Total	
	n	%	n	%	n	%
Low	9	53	8	47	17	100
High	15	26	14	74	29	100
Total	24	47	22	53	46	100

less priority. This last remark, is of course, somewhat tempered by the wide-versus-narrow focus issue raised above. It also might be a function of those who wrote up the reports being unaware of doctrine considerations.

The final section of the result presentation deals with the development of environmental linkage configurations, technical assistance and recipient society efforts in this direction, and their relation to success potential and success. In this segment we will be able to say something more positively about the recipient society contribution. When dealing with intra-organizational concerns, the recipient society influence was one that was implied rather than specifically stated.

The effort that technical assistance makes in an attempt to gain grants of authority from the recipient society's power structure (enabling body) is positively related to the success of the project. This kind of activity can be quite variable, ranging from such activities as using the technical assistance agreement as a means to assure continued support, to the short-circuiting of normal communication patterns in order to make the needs of the organization known to persons capable of insuring continued grants of authority. The data demonstrate that this kind of activity is minimally related to success potential (Phase II) and highly related to ultimate success (Phase III). The initial

TABLE 14B
Technical Assistance Efforts to Encourage Recipient Authority
Support and Success in Phase III

Technical Assistance Efforts to Encourage Authority Support	Success in Phase III					
	Low Success		High Success		Total	
	n	%	n	%	n	%
Low	9	82	2	18	11	100
High	5	26	14	74	19	100
Total	14	47	16	53	30	100

hypothesis would be that efforts to gain enabling support should result in successful institution-building projects. Even though the data seem to verify part of our general conception of institution building, this interpretation can be somewhat misleading. The kind of effort put forth by technical assistance is probably a function of the degree of commitment the recipient power structure feels toward the project. The degree to which this group is committed to the project is directly related to the effectiveness of technical assistance in encouraging this kind of activity. Thus in dealing with the power structure of the recipient society, technical assistance would seem to be relatively powerless as regards a crucial linkage being formed between the newly created organization and the existing institutional network, unless this commitment is also present. This powerlessness is further verified by Table 15. Here, low or small effort to encourage resource support results in high success potential. A contradictory finding? No. It is rather an indication of recipient executive commitment; and where commitent is high, little effort has to be expended by technical assistance.

The assumption underlying the interpretation of Tables 14A, 14B, and 15 is that technical assistance personnel are aware of the crucial nature of strong enabling linkages and become involved in activity to insure their emergence to the degree that there are indications of a favorable outcome. Given the primitive nature of the research, it seems to be a tenable assumption.

Strong support for the importance of recipient society direct involvement in building enabling linkages comes from Tables 16 and 17.

In those instances where authority grants were made, 76 percent of the cases proved successful; and where resource grants were made, a high proportion—73 percent—of the cases also proved successful. While these relationships are very strong and tend to substantiate at least part of the interpretation being made, nevertheless some problems remain.

An even stronger case could be made if it could be shown that the enabling linkages were formed early in the life-cycle of the project; and at some time prior to the emergence of the organization as an institution, the enabling linkages were withdrawn and the project remained successful. For there truly to be institutional development, other linkages (i.e., functional) that have been developed between the institution and the environment should serve as enabling purpose. Thus while the data seem to indicate the general interpretation of institution building, our conclusions remain quite tentative.

One might expect that what was true of enabling linkages would be true of functional linkages (complementary activities) in terms of technical assistance encouragement and recipient society commitment. As Tables 18 and 19 show, this is not at all the case.

For functional linkages to develop, there must be some correspondence between the activities of the two-or-more organizations or institutions involved. At the outset it was noted that the newly created organizations incorporate innovative techniques and hence the need for technical assistance. This being so, the recipient society is not in a position to set up the proper functional linkages

TABLE 15
Technical Assistance Efforts to Encourage Recipient Resource
Allocation and Success Potential in Phase II

Technical Assistance Efforts to Encourage Recipient Resource Allocation and Success Potential in Phase II	Success Potential in Phase II					
	Low Success (potential)		High Success (potential)		Total	
	n	%	n	%	n	%
Low	7	41	10	59	17	100
High	17	59	12	41	29	100
Total	24	52	22	48	46	100

TABLE 16
Recipient Authority Grants and Success in Phase III

Recipient Authority Grants	Success in Phase III					
	Low Success		High Success		Total	
	n	%	n	%	n	%
Low	10	77	3	23	13	100
High	4	24	13	76	17	100
Total	14	47	16	53	30	100

TABLE 17
Recipient Resource Allocation and Success in Phase III

Recipient Resource Allocation	Success in Phase III					
	Low Success		High Success		Total	
	n	%	n	%	n	%
Low	11	58	8	42	19	100
High	3	27	8	73	11	100
Total	14	47	16	53	30	100

without guidance from technical assistance personnel, no matter how high the level of commitment. Thus technical assistance effort in this direction is highly related to successful institutional development. Similarly, recipient activity to develop functional linkages is also positively related. Here we assume recipient activity is guided by the advice of technical assistance and, further, as in the interpretations above, commitment to the project is high and enduring.

Where there are already existing organizations or institutions in the recipient environment which can be characterized as competing activities for the new organization—e.g., perform the same function using more primitive means—control of these activities leads to more successful institution building. As Tables 20 and 21 demonstrate, both technical assistance effort to get the recipient to initiate controls and actual controlling activity by the recipient are highly related to success. Pointing out that competing institutions exist and preparing means to control them are necessary activities in terms of bringing them to the attention of the recipient. When this is accomplished, the recipient, if committed to the project, will take necessary action to insure the continuance of the new project. Also, it might be that other technical assistance operations are extant in the society and the introduction of a new project results in reassessing the goals of some other projects to prevent duplication and overlapping of activities. Further, the technical assistance operation might have been started to eliminate some older form of activity which, while it performs a useful function for the recipient society, does so in an uneconomical manner. If this is so, one would expect action on the part of the recipient to phase out this older form. There are many reasons why competing projects would be controlled. The fact that the control activity is generated by both the technical assistance effort and recipient effort is shown by the data and is consistent with the general interpretation. Little or no emphasis on controlling competing activity is related to low success, both for technical assistance and the recipient. Thus one would assume that newly created organizations must replace some already existing forms, and that the exercise of control in this area is important for the process of institution building.

Technical assistance efforts to encourage normative linkages, secure mass media support, and generally achieve a favorable image for the project are somewhat related to success. This same activity undertaken by the recipient, though, is more highly related to success. Thus one might conclude that, when dealing with the later phases of the life-cycle of a project and the more abstract kinds of linkages that develop, the activity of the recipient society is more crucial than technical assistance efforts. One exception to this might be in the area of building up a clientele for the newly created organization. Here, as Tables 22 and 23 show, both technical assistance and recipient efforts are vital. Again, one can maintain that recipient activity is probably more crucial for the building of strong environmental linkages. This must be qualified, though, by the idea that where the creation of ties between the new organization and the recipient environment requires the knowledge and understanding of the innovative

TABLE 18
Technical Assistance Efforts to Establish Complementary
Activities and Success in Phase III

Technical Assistance Efforts to Establish Complementary Activities	Success in Phase III					
	Low Success		High Success		Total	
	n	%	n	%	n	%
Low	10	77	3	23	13	100
High	4	24	13	76	17	100
Total	14	47	16	53	30	100

TABLE 19
Recipient Efforts to Establish Complementary Activities
and Success in Phase III

Recipient Efforts to Establish Complementary Activities	Success in Phase III					
	Low Success		High Success		Total	
	n	%	n	%	n	%
Low	11	73	4	27	15	100
High	3	20	12	80	15	100
Total	14	47	16	53	30	100

TABLE 20
Technical Assistance Efforts to Control Competing Activities
and Success in Phase III

Technical Assistance Efforts to Control Competing Activity	Success in Phase II					
	Low Success		High Success		Total	
	n	%	n	%	n	%
Low	11	58	8	42	19	100
High	3	27	8	73	11	100
Total	14	47	16	53	30	100

technology incorporated into the new organization, technical assistance efforts become crucial.

It would seem that it is in Phases II and III of a project when most linkage-building activities takes place and when, if little attention is paid to these environmental relationships, little success will obtain. One could hazard an educated guess and hypothesize that Phase II is probably more important than Phase III. This is so because if no environmental linkages are built in Phase II, the project will become overly dependent on technical assistance support. Withdrawal of that support will less likely be compensated for by increased dependence on environmental linkages; because even if the linkages are there, they will still be weak, since they have been only recently formed. If the linkages are organized in Phase II, there might well be pressures to decrease technical assistance support in Phase III because of the available support alternatives in the recipient environment. If this is so, the process of institution building is facilitated.

In addition to comparing efforts to promote environmental linkages in particular phases by technical assistance and/or the recipient society, and relating a general measure of linkage building activity to success, we also looked at the consistency of effort across time phases in building and strengthening different linkages which a new organization must form prior to effective institutionalization. For purposes of this study, "consistent effort" is defined as positive activity across all three phases; no activity in Phase I and positive activity in the later two phases; or positive activities in the early phases with neutral activity in Phase III. These patterns are characterized as consistent in terms of the institution-building process. Thus, following the earlier discussion of linkage formation, early attention to creating and maintaining environmental relationships with the new organization is necessary with respect to the emergence of an institution. No activity in the last time phase is assumed to be an indicator of the formation and operational status of the linkages. Constant effort across all three time phases is also considered consistent. This is so because of the recognition that the formation of environmental linkages is variable across societal contexts and projects. Where difficulties are encountered in building linkages, constant effort is required. Also, our end point was chosen somewhat arbitrarily, and hence for some projects the final success measures might reflect some phase of the project between the first of what could be many transition stages and the final stage. Further, constant effort is an indirect indicator of general commitment to the project, both for technical assistance and recipient, and as was noted above, this is a vital consideration in successful institution building. Non-consistent effort, of course, is any pattern different from the ones discussed. The main patterns included in this category would be no effort at all and negative or dysfunctional effort.

Tables 24 and 25 show a high positive relationship between the final coding of success and consistent efforts by both technical assistance and recipient.

TABLE 21
Recipient Efforts to Control Competing Activity and
Success in Phase III

Recipient Efforts to Control Competing Activity	Success in Phase III					
	Low Success		High Success		Total	
	n	%	n	%	n	%
Low	11	65	6	35	17	100
High	3	23	10	77	13	100
Total	14	47	16	53	30	100

TABLE 22
Technical Assistance Efforts to Encourage a Clientele
and Success in Phase III

Technical Assistance Efforts to Encourage a Clientele	Success in Phase III					
	Low Success		High Success		Total	
	n	%	n	%	n	%
Low	9	82	2	18	11	100
High	5	26	14	74	19	100
Total	14	47	16	53	30	100

TABLE 23
Recipient Efforts to Encourage a Clientele and Success in Phase
III (based on the 30 cases coded for all three phases)

Recipient Efforts to Encourage a Clientele	Success in Phase III					
	Low Success		High Success		Total	
	n	%	n	%	n	%
Low	11	92	1	8	12	100
High	3	17	15	83	18	100
Total	14	47	16	53	30	100

TABLE 24

**Technical Assistance to Encourage Recipient Authority Support
Across Phase I to III and Success in Phase III**

Technical Assistance Effort to Encourage Recipient Authority Support Across Phase I to III	Success in Phase III					
	Low Success		High Success		Total	
	n	%	n	%	n	%
Consistent effort	5	26	14	74	19	100
Nonconsistent effort	9	82	2	18	11	100
Total	14	47	16	53	30	100

Because of agreement, prestige, or their capacity to contribute both capital and technical resources to development in the society, donor agencies have recourse to relatively high levels within the recipient power structure. Thus technical assistance is in a position to exercise considerable influence in encouraging grants of authority. This finding tends to confirm the wisdom of indigenous leadership within the organization taking action to obtain the cooperation of technical assistance agencies in getting grants of authority in situations where they are unable to do so on their own.

The strong relationship in Table 25 demonstrates that grants of authority by recipient enabling bodies are crucial for institution building. From both a theoretical and an empirical standpoint one can almost categorically state that the degree to which the recipient authority structure is willing to invest autonomy in the new organization is a direct reflection of the degree to which there will be successful institutionalization. This is one of the few places where recipient actions directed toward internal matters in the organization have positive results for the organization.

The relationships between success potential and attention to resource inputs for both donor and recipient are shown in Tables 26 and 27.

TABLE 25

**Recipient Authority Support Across Phases I to III and
Success in Phase III**

Recipient Authority Support Across Phases I to III	Success in Phase III					
	Low Success		High Success		Total	
	n	%	n	%	n	%
Consistent support	4	24	13	76	17	100
Nonconsistent support	10	77	3	23	13	100
Total	14	47	16	53	30	100

TABLE 26

Technical Assistance Effort to Encourage Recipient Resource Allocation Across Phases I to III and Success in Phase III

Technical Assistance Effort to Encourage Recipient Resource Allocation Across Phases I to III	Success in Phase III					
	Low Success		High Success		Total	
	n	%	n	%	n	%
Consistent effort	11	48	12	52	23	100
Nonconsistent effort	3	43	4	57	7	100
Total	14	47	16	53	30	100

TABLE 27

Recipient Resource Allocation Support and Success in Phase III

Recipient Resource Allocation Support	Success in Phase III					
	Low Success		High Success		Total	
	n	%	n	%	n	%
Consistent support	3	27	8	73	11	100
Nonconsistent support	11	58	8	42	19	100
Total	14	47	16	53	30	100

TABLE 28

Technical Assistance Effort to Encourage Recipient Complementary Functional Linkages Across Phases I to III and Success in Phase III

Technical Assistance Effort to Encourage Recipient Complementary Functional Linkages Across Phases I to III	Success in Phase III					
	Low Success		High Success		Total	
	n	%	n	%	n	%
Consistent effort	4	25	12	75	16	100
Nonconsistent effort	10	71	4	29	14	100
Total	14	47	16	53	30	100

These relationships are somewhat weaker, especially so for technical assistance, than the previous patterns just discussed. While resource inputs are important for the organization, particularly in the early phases of the project, the consistency of effort in this area is not as vital as was the case with grants of authority. It is true though that consistent recipient resource inputs bodes well for the organization, and this is further documentation for the importance of general recipient effort in setting up enduring patterns of relationships between the organization and its environment. Support is also offered for the commonsense conclusion that as a project tends to become institutionalized, less effort is required by technical assistance to promote grants of resources.

In previous remarks, the importance of building functional or complementary linkages in the environment for institutional development was discussed. Tables 28 and 29 provide further support for this idea. As with all the tables dealing with consistency of effort to either encourage or actually build environmental linkages, some of the similarity between the tables is a function of using the same remarks in the case histories to code different variables. But if the similarity was only a function of coding two variables with the same score, the relationships in Tables 28 and 29 would be weaker than those in 18 and 19. That this would be so comes from the fact that in the former tables, evidence of encouragement or actual support could be coded as non-consistent effort if it does not follow the constructed definitions of consistency. Some of the strength of the relationship noted in the latter table would disappear unless there were a one-to-one correlation between no encouragement or no actual support and lack of consistency, a highly unlikely occurrence. Thus there is at least partial support for the idea that efforts to encourage or provide support for environmental linkages not only should be provided, but they should be provided in a manner consistent with the theoretical orientation revolving around institution building, i.e., those patterns which the research defines as consistent.

Tables 28 and, in particular, 29 point to the importance of consistent attention to the building of complementary linkages. While it appears that the existence of activity directed at the encouragement of complementary linkages

TABLE 29
Recipient Support for Complementary Functional Linkages
Across Phases I to III and Success in Phase III

Recipient Support for Complementary Functional Linkages Across Phases I to III	Success in Phase III					
	Low Success		High Success		Total	
	n	%	n	%	n	%
Consistent support	3	19	13	81	16	100
Nonconsistent support	11	79	3	21	14	100
Total	14	47	16	53	30	100

TABLE 30
Technical Assistance Effort to Encourage Recipient Mass Media
Support Across Phases I to III and Success in Phase III

Technical Assistance Effort to Encourage Recipient Mass Media Support Across Phases I to III	Success in Phase III					
	Low Success		High Success		Total	
	n	%	n	%	n	%
Consistent effort	2	29	5	71	7	100
Nonconsistent effort	12	52	11	48	23	100
Total	14	47	16	53	30	100

by technical assistance is vital, there is even stronger support for the idea that actual effort by those in the recipient environment has a greater effect on the institutionalization of a technical assistance project. This is yet another piece of evidence that points to the crucial role the recipient plays in terms of developing necessary environmental relationships with reference to the organization.

Tables 30 and 31 refer to the relative contribution of technical assistance encouragement and recipient activity in terms of building, in a consistent manner, normative and diffuse environmental linkages, and the consequences of this activity for successful institution building.

As regards normative and diffuse linkages, the recipient society seems to make more consistent efforts than technical assistance. Also, consistent mass media support by the recipient resulted in a somewhat higher percentage of successful projects than did technical assistance encouragement, although both were high. Again, one can tentatively conclude that, when considering those linkage relationships that come to prominence at the end of the life cycle of the institution-building process, the recipient society effort is more effective and vital when compared to technical assistance. Probably technical assistance effort is needed in certain situations, but the specifications of these situational contexts is not possible, given the quality of the data and analytical tools now available.

TABLE 31
Recipient Mass Media Support Across Phases I to III and
Success in Phase III

Recipient Mass Media Support Across Phases I to III	Success in Phase III					
	Low Success		High Success		Total	
	n	%	n	%	n	%
Consistent support	1	11	8	89	9	100
Nonconsistent support	13	62	8	38	21	100
Total	14	47	16	53	30	100

There are some other tentative conclusions that emerge from an analysis of these latter tables. For instance, where consistent effort is expended by either technical assistance or the recipient society in building a favorable image for the organization, the project *always* proved successful. One could hazard a guess that this type of activity is not undertaken unless many favorable indications of success for a project are already evident and it is recognized that the creation of a favorable image of the project in the recipient society will further insure success. This linkage relationship occurs at the end of the life-cycle process. Hence, it is possible that image building is a function of having personnel and resources free because of the successful conclusion of other activities related to the total enterprise.

Technical assistance and recipient are both heavily involved in building a clientele for the new organization, heavily involved in a consistent manner. The recipient societies' efforts are somewhat more effective, but both donor and recipient seem to recognize the crucial importance of this activity. As with other data dealing with the consistency factor, recipient consistency is equal to or greater than technical assistance consistency. This is probably so because of the advisory and supportive role technical assistance plays in building environmental linkages. Technical assistance provides relatively short spurts of assistance and, though this aid may last for long periods of time, it is relatively intermittent. As a result, for institutionalization to be successful, those within the organization as well as those in the recipient environment who are committed to the project must develop a conscious approach to forming enduring clientele relationships for there to be success.

Two final considerations concerning consistency and environmental linkages: first, the degree of consistency of effort by either technical assistance or recipient is directly related to the degree of success the project enjoyed as regards institution building; second, the fact that the case histories included reference to efforts to build environmental linkages mainly in Phases II and III, with an emphasis on Phase III, points to the necessity of considering different facets of the institution-building process at different stages of its life-cycle. Because of the generally stronger relationships betwen recipient effort and success when compared to donor, one can hypothesize that technical assistance, to optimally aid a developing society, should become heavily involved in the beginning stages of the process. As the organization matures and begins to become institutionalized, technical assistance should gradually become less involved and assume an advisory rather than an operational role.

The final table has to do with the degree of similarity of content the project has to other activities carried on in the recipient society and how this relates to success.

This table was included because it was the only table dealing with the four different categories of similarity (content, function, philosophy of operation, and societal value system) that shows any significance for successful institution

TABLE 32
Similarity of Content and Success Potential in Phase II

	Success Potential in Phase II					
	Low Success (potential)		High Success (potential)		Total	
Similarity of Content	n	%	n	%	n	%
Similar	3	23	10	77	13	100
Dissimilar	21	64	12	36	33	100
Total	24	52	22	48	46	100

building. As one would expect, the greater the similarity the greater chance of success, although the relationship is not particularly strong.

It is apparent from the limited relationship reported and the lack of significance of the other categories of similarity that we will have to revise the coding scheme for these variables. We feel the general idea of a fit between what is being introduced into the society and what already exists is an important consideration. Obviously though, our operationalization of this idea is far from perfect, and there has to be some rethinking of how one can measure this dimension.

CONCLUSIONS

This report represents a first attempt to empirically study the process of institutionalization. Particular attention was paid to the role of technical assistance, which was treated as an external input into a newly created organization which embraces innovative technology. One of the stated goals of both technical assistance and the decision makers in the recipient environment concerned the institutionalization of the patterns of activity with their attendant technological complexity which were incorporated in the organization. Those who were directly concerned with any specific instance of institution building engaged in a series of concerted efforts to achieve this end, sometimes cooperating with others, sometimes alone. Discovering the patterns of effort which contributed most to institution building has been the goal of the research.

A central theme which ties in many of the findings has to do with the relationship of technical assistance and recipient efforts as regards intra-organizational and intra-societal concerns. The projects which were most successfully institutionalized were those in which technical assistance personnel dealt with matters internal to the social organization, and the recipient society effort was directed toward building linkages or imbedding the new organization into the existing institutional structure in the society. In general, the greater the involvement of technical assistance personnel in creating the organization and giving it enduring structure, the greater the evidence of success. This, of course, is tempered by the fact that technical assistance activity should be undertaken with the understanding that eventually it will be phased out. Thus attention must be paid to setting up mechanisms which insure the continued existence of the organization when it is manned solely by indigenous recipient personnel.

The authority technical assistance personnel possess in the recipient society is delegated to them by common agreement with the recipient power structure. It is usually specific to a particular project. Thus when dealing with the already existing institutional configuration in the recipient society, technical assistance people are relatively powerless. If a project is going to assume an institutional form, some change or accommodation to the newly emerging institution must occur. It follows then that effort to bring about societal structural change necessary for institutional development must be made by that element in the recipient society empowered to bring about such changes—the legitimate constituted authority structure. Thus, as our data have shown, the greater the involvement of recipient power structure in building environmental linkages between the new organization and the existing recipient institutional complex, the greater the success in institution building.

Although this division of labor between donor and recipient is functional for successful institution building, there are important exceptions where technical assistance effort is required in terms of forging environment linkages, and recipient activity is needed to build a strong organization. For a strong organization to be formed, the recipient society must provide enabling grants of authority and adequate resources, both in terms of men and materials. It is crucial for the recipient power structure to grant sufficient authority to the delegated indigenous leadership of the new organization and further to protect the organization from outside interference, particularly in the early stages of the project. Technical assistance effort to encourage this kind of activity is also vital. Some of this is accomplished by prior project agreement and some by short-circuiting the chain of command and appealing to the top of the recipient power structure, through either formal or informal channels. Here technical assistance gets involved in linkage-building activity, even though the enabling linkages are temporary. If successful institution building takes place, functional linkages with other recipient institutions provide a positive alternative to enabling linkages by creating a pattern of legitimate interdependencies and giving the organization a needed measure of autonomy.

As was noted previously, the creation of functional linkages requires some knowledge of the innovative technology being introduced and how it can be utilized. Technical assistance personnel are experts specifically hired because of their knowledge in these techniques. Hence they are most able to guide the formation of the kinds of functional linkages that should be established. In such a manner, technical assistance can play an important role in building functional linkages. Further, when building a strong organization, part of the technical assistance effort is directed at giving the recipient leadership element some appreciation of the need for environmental linkages, particularly functional, and hence in this sense it is involved in building a bridge between the new organization and the existing societal structure.

Beyond the idea of a division of labor between donor and recipient and the noted exceptions, a second important theme for institution building involves the idea of time phases associated with a general process. Not only should certain activities be performed, but also there is an appropriate time sequence attached to when they should be undertaken if there is to be successful institutional development. In the beginning of a project technical assistance is heavily involved in building a strong organization, training recipient personnel, and exercising influence with the recipient society power structure to secure enabling grants of authority and resources. It is at this stage of the process that technical assistance might have to assume an operational rather than an advisory stance. The recipient effort at this time is mainly directed at providing grants of authority and resources in the form of qualified personnel and adequate material.

With the onset of the second stage, technical assistance begins to provide for transition plans for leadership; build up an awareness, both within the organization and within the recipient environment, of necessary functional linkages; assume a greater advisory role with little if any emphasis on operation; and in general set up procedures to effect a turnover to indigenous recipient personnel. The recipient society effort is directed at setting up functional linkages, starting to build a clientele (with technical assistance guidance), insuring continued support for the organization, and starting to publicize the organization in the environment such that normative and more diffuse linkages might be activated.

The third stage is one where technical assistance activity is considerably reduced, usually to some minimal advisory services or continuing consultation. By this time, if there has been success in building an institution, the organization should now have some autonomy by virtue of its place in the recipient society's institutional configuration. Recipient efforts are mainly directed at further publicizing the new institution and gaining greater acceptance for it. The latter is accomplished by encouraging normative and diffuse linkages. At the end of the third and final stage, both donor and recipient assistance should be no longer needed and the institution should be a quasi-independent functioning entity in the society.

It must be apparent that the discussion of a somewhat exclusive series of activities for both recipient and donor and the timing of these activities is a highly simplified explanation of a very complex process. Further, we have commented on this process at a fairly abstract level, for the most part ignoring the "nuts and bolts" procedures that constitute each of the different kinds of activities we have mentioned. Still, given its primitive nature, we believe a beginning has been made to pin down what is involved in the process of institution building and how one goes about accomplishing it. The data presented do tend to back up most of the explanation. Assuming the validity of the data, the following additional general points have developed from the analysis:

1. All of the tables are internally consistent, with each other and with the theoretical framework. Thus the variables that were created do discriminate and hopefully, with revision and expansion, are capable of helping illuminate the process of institution building.

2. Institution building is a generic process that can be thought of as analytically divorced from specific projects in specific societal settings. This was a crucial assumption we started with that allowed us to analyze the material the way we did. That it has some validity has been borne out by the results of the analysis. Further, if future analysis continues to uphold the validity of this assumption, our findings and explanations of this general process should prove useful in a variety of settings exclusive of technical assistance efforts.

3. Institution building is a time consuming process. We have adopted eight years as an operational cutoff point, saying that a project will not be institutionalized prior to this time. Of course, this was an arbitrary decision, in part dictated by the nature of the data. Actually, the length of time needed to complete a successful institution-building project will vary beyond a certain minimal time. Some of the factors that will influence time are: complexity of technology being introduced, the level of development of the society, the stability of the recipient political order, the quality and stability of recipient leadership and other personnel who are involved in setting up the organization, the quality and stability of technical assistance personnel involved, the degree of fit between what the project is introducing and what exists in the recipient society, and the need for the innovation.

Although we did not directly measure the variable, the level of commitment of both donor and recipient seemed to have an important bearing on the institutionalization process. Enduring interest, willingness to provide resources and other necessities, and patience all are vital ingredients.

Much of the work on this research represents a promise of useful findings rather than definitive explanation. It is apparent that effort will have to be expended to revise the coding scheme and to expand it to include relevant variables that came to light as a function of this first effort.

APPENDIX 1. A Tentative Coding System for Institution-Building Technical Assistance Projects with Specification of Items as Needed

1. KIND OF TECHNICAL ASSISTANCE
   A. Joint Operations
      (1) Joint Account
      (2) Host and donor personnel directly involved in operations
   B. Institutional Contract
      (1) University
      (2) PASA
      (3) Other
   C. Individual Contract—consultant
   D. Direct Hire Individual
   F. Equipment
   G. Training

2. INSTITUTIONAL SITUATION
   A. New
   B. Reconstituted

3. KIND OF INSTITUTION
   A. Planning and/or Research (any kind of planning or research)
   B. Higher Education
   C. Secondary and Vocational
   D. Development (or Credit) Bank
   E. Rural Services
   F. Urban Services
   G. Resource Development

4. APPROACH OF TECHNICAL ASSISTANCE
   A. Operational
   B. Advisory

(Note: If technical assistance provides any operational personnel to the project, it is classified as operational.)

5. EMPHASIS OF TECHNICAL ASSISTANCE (Internal to Institution)
   A. Leadership
      (1) Definite transition plans
      (2) Training
      (3) Internal support for leader
   B. Doctrine (philosophy of operation, planning)
   C. Program (outputs)
   D. Internal Structure (including mechanisms to handle institution-environmental relations)
   E. Resources (throughput potential)

6. ENVIRONMENTAL CONDITIONS (Scale −1 to +1)
   A. Enabling Linkages (coded in Phases I, II, and III)
      (1) Technical Assistance
         (a) Authority:

+1 means that the donor has taken some action to encourage the recipient country's authority structure to support and protect the institution.

−1 means that the donor has done nothing in supporting the institution, although there is a minimum which the donor must do in order to maintain the project.

         (b) Resources:

+1 means that the donor has provided as much resources, both human and financial, as could be absorbed by the project.

0 means that the donor has provided that minimum of resources so that the progress of the project is not impeded by the lack of donor contributions.

−1 means that there have been serious delays or an important lack of resources at a time when they were needed.

      (2) Other than Technical Assistance
         (a) Authority:

+1 means that the recipient enabling bodies have supported or were encouraged to support the institution by influences other than those of technical assistance and allowed ample powers to determine and undertake such activities as were necessary at the time.

−1 means that an institution's role has been seriously limited and its opportunity to determine its program has been infringed upon in some way.

         (b) Resources:

+1 means that there have been very few problems in obtaining funds, personnel, and such other resources as were needed.

−1 means that there were serious delays or problems in obtaining funds or personnel which seriously impeded the progress of the institution.

   B. Functional linkages (coded in Phases I, II, and III)
      (1) Technical Assistance
         (a) Complementary:

+1 means that there were other technical assistance activities which encouraged the provision of inputs, supporting services or used the outputs of the institution.

−1 means that technical assistance could have encouraged functional support but did not, or prevented such functional relationship through inaction or resistance but not through developing competition.

(b) Competitive:

+1 means that if there were competing projects, these conditions were mitigated by policy determinations defining the scope of each agency or some other form of avoidance or mutual agreement without direct cooperation. If there were no competing projects, technical assistance provided conditions which precluded their emergence.

−1 means that there were technical assistance activities with similar program outputs to the same clientele which were actively competing with the institution for influence and program development.

(2) Other Factors:

(a) Complementary:

+1 and −1 are the same as in Item 1 except they refer to organizations within the recipient environment.

(b) The same as (1) b).

(Note: The assumption is made that where institutions or groups have set up functional or enabling linkages with the institution being studied, normative linkages also exist. Where functional or enabling linkages do not occur or are thwarted, it is assumed that normative reasons can at least partially account for the noted conditions. The degree to which these assumptions are met might prove to be explanatory factors in institution building.)

(The "transactions" noted in the Esman and Blaise paper serve as indicators of "institution-environment" activity.)

C. Normative Linkages—Independent of Functional and enabling Linkages (coded in Phases II and III)

(1) Technical Assistance:

+1 means that technical assistance was involved in influencing normative behavior of other existing institutions in the recipient standards if they already exist.

0 means that no consideration was given to normative linkages.

−1 means that technical assistance took action in the environment which served to create or maintain normative linkages antithetical to the project's emergence as an institution.

(2) Factors other than TA: Same as under Part 1 but the results are from the action of organizations in the recipient government.

D. Diffused Linkages (coded in Phases II and III)

(1) Technical Assistance:

(a) Mass Media:

+1 means that the efforts of the technical assistance mission to provide publicity significantly influenced the image of the institution with the various publics whose understanding and support it required.

−1 means that the activities of technical assistance had no particular value in increasing the knowledge and understanding of the institution through mass media.

(b) Clientele:

+1 indicates that technical assistance had made a particular contribution to the building of a clientele which would benefit from and thereby support the institution.

0 means that the technical assistance agency made efforts at building a clientele, but there were no indicators of appreciable success.

−1 means that no efforts were made to develop a clientele.

(c) Other:

+1 means that some special action on the part of technical assistance, i.e., the supporting of field research, demonstration, or such other activity, has in some way increased the influence or improved the image of the institution within the environment.

−1 means that no such action was taken.

(2) Other: All three (a), (b), and (c), have the same criteria as in Number 1 except that the actions taken are those by some element or organization within the recipient environment.

(Note: This project is primarily concerned with the influence of Technical Assistance on institution building in developing countries. For that reason the variables dealing with "institution-environmental relations" have been dichotomized to partial out those relations that are a function of Technical Assistance and those that are not.)

7. SIMILARITY (coded in Phases I, II, and III)
   A. Similarity of Function (how activity performed)
      (1) Similar
      (2) Dissimilar
   B. Similarity of Content
      (1) Similar
      (2) Dissimilar
   C. Similarity of philosophy of operation or method
      (1) Similar
      (2) Dissimilar
   D. Similarity to the societal value system
      (1) Similar
      (2) Dissimilar

8. DURATION—the time elapsed since project initiation to the date of analysis

  A. Less than 5 years
  B. 5 to 8 years
  C. More than 8 years

(Note: If project has continued less than 8 years, only Phase I and Phase II are coded. If less than 5 years, Phase II will be coded insofar as possible.)

9. SUCCESS (Scale 0 to 1 cumulative Phase I); (Scale 0 to 2 cumulative Phase II)

  A. Autonomy:
  0 means that the institution is still subject to superior authority for internal policy decisions and has no insured allocation of funds.

  2 means that the institution enjoys considerable independence, including major internal policy decisions, and is able to acquire needed resources.

  B. Survival:
  0 means that the institution no longer exists or is being phased out.

  2 means that the institution exists and exercises a recognized functional responsibility.

  C. Structural Impact
  2 means that because of the institutional outputs there is evidence of societal structural change to accommodate the emergence of the new institution.

  1 means that the institutional outputs primarily affect clientele structural relations.

  0 means no structural change.

  D. Degree to institutional norms are recognized as being legitimate
  2 means society-wide recognition.

  1 means clientele recognition.

  0 means no appreciable recognition.

  E. Degree to which institutional norms have been incorporated
  2 means that other institutions in the society in some way adopted or imitated the normative patterns which have been developed by the institution.

  1 means that agencies directly related either to the agency or to the same clientele incorporated some of the normative patterns of the institution.

  0 means that there was no incorporation of the institution's normative patterns by other agencies.

(Note: "Success potential" is the cumulative success score in Phase II divided by 5. "Success" is cumulative score in Phase III divided by 10.)

NOTES

1. Milton J. Esman and Hans C. Blaise, "Institution-Building Research-The Guiding Concepts," Pittsburgh: Inter-University Program in Institution Building, 1866 (mimeo).

2. The transactions dimension is imbedded in the analysis and interpretation. Essentially the aim of the research is to formulate the patterns and kinds of transactions necessary to build institutions.

3. The possibilities of selection are extensive. The following are a few of the definitions representing administrative and operational definitions:

a. Roscoe Martin, "Technical Assistance: The Problem of Implementation." Public Administration Review, Vol. XII, No. 4: 258.

b. Jahangir Amuzegar, *Technical Assistance in Theory and Practice: The Case of Iran*, New York: Frederick A. Praeger, 1966, p. 30.

c. Fernand Vrancken, *Technical Assistance in Public Administration: Lessons of Experience and Possible Improvements*, final version of the general report XII International Congress of Administrative Sciences, Brussels: International Institute of Administrative Sciences, 1963, p. 17.

d. *AID Manual*, Order 1301.1, paragraph IIA.

4. The Ford Foundation, for example, has a variety of internal reports and other documents which examine the institution-building process with unusual perception. See also Hiram S. Phillips, "Handbook for Development: Changing Environments and Institutions, prepublication draft, June 1967, which provides some important analysis and insights on the operational process of institution building.

5. A three-year research study conducted by the Maxwell School of Syracuse University and sponsored by AID gathered a large amount of information on the administrative practices of most technical assistance agencies. The material we had available included most of the published literature on technical assistance both in books and journal articles. It also contained a large volume of reports from the Technical Assistance Research Project at Syracuse, from the United Nations, the major foundations, AID and many other technical assistance programs. In addition to this, we had internal material from different agencies. For example, we had the material of the AID Technical Assistance Study Group files which included 1,100 interviews organized according to selected problems. The Technical Assistance Research Project itself had also conducted 1,500 interviews of headquarters and field personnel in different agencies by some twelve faculty members and eight graduate assistants. It produced many reports and working papers dealing with most aspects of technical assistance problems, several bearing directly on the institution-building problem. Even though it was later found that much of the materials could not be converted into coded cases, they were studied for such data and insights as they could provide.

6. For a complete description of the variables coded and the definitions of variables, see Appendix 1 "A Tentative Coding System for Institution-Building Technical Assistance Projects with Specification of Items as Needed."

FIELD APPLICATION OF INSTITUTION BUILDING

R A L P H H. S M U C K L E R

International Studies and Programs
Michigan State University

RALPH H. SMUCKLER, who joined Michigan State University as an instructor in Political Science in 1951, is presently Dean of International Studies and Programs and Professor of Political Science at Michigan State University. He has participated actively in the Pittsburgh-based Inter-University Research Program in Institution Building, serving as Chairman during its early years and after his return from Pakistan in 1969, where he served from 1967 as Ford Foundation Representative supervising the Foundation programs in agriculture, education, family planning, and administration in both East and West Pakistan. He served in Vietnam on two tours, totaling over three years between 1955 and 1959, as a member of Michigan State University's technical assistance contract group in positions of Research Coordinator, Assistant Chief Advisor, and Chief Advisor. At Michigan State and in his assignments abroad, he participated in numerous institution-building efforts.

FIELD APPLICATION OF INSTITUTION BUILDING

RALPH H. SMUCKLER

International Studies and Programs
Michigan State University

The institution-building concepts, as defined by Milton Esman and the Inter-University Research Program in Institution Building, were intended from the outset to meet a double test: usefulness in research to social scientists concerned with development, and practical applicability to improve the task of those actively engaged in building institutions. Usefulness in research can be seen in the case studies which have actually used the concepts or some portion of them and by the role of the Esman institution-building model in the research conducted by Committee on Institutional Cooperation researchers—the so-called CIC/AID study. The applicability and helpfulness of the institution-building model in real-life technical assistance effort is just now beginning to be put to test by Thomas W. Thorsen and others who are using the model in evaluation and related activity in the field.[1]

This paper will consider a number of applications—ways in which the concepts are now helpful and, if put to use properly, should lead to more focused, effective institutional development assistance.

Much of the impetus for the IB program came from a sense of frustration on the part of university people who had been engaged professionally in technical assistance work abroad over long periods of time. Although they sensed that the process in which they were engaged was researchable and generic in nature, they did not find the concepts and analysis at hand which would make their individual experiences cumulative, reasonably transferable from one setting to another, and available to newcomers to the effort. Those who were helping to

[229]

build a new institute of administration in Thailand were dealing with variables much like their predecessors in a similar effort in the Philippines and akin to the institution-building effort at the National Institute of Administration in Saigon. Similarly, those helping to create a new teacher-training school in Thailand or a new university in Nigeria were confronting issues of leadership, doctrine, resource availability, and so on, which were also observable in the work of advisors helping to fashion a development planning unit in Pakistan or in Colombia. Although the environments varied greatly, the need for various types of linkage with the environment surrounding each project were about the same. At least the linkage categories seemed definable in similar ways.

The sense of frustration and the obvious need to describe more clearly the process itself led directly to the efforts to define institution-building concepts and process variables; thus, given their origin in practical situations, the institution-building concepts should have obvious applicability. They should find increasing use in the field at the same time that their meaning is being probed, refined, and expanded through research.

The IB product has been variously described as composing a model, a heuristic device, a set of definitions, and a number of interrelated categories. There has been some disagreement as to exactly what to label the thing. Since we are concerned here with field application, the definition of what it is seems less crucial. We can accept operationally the Esman framework, abbreviated as follows: [2]

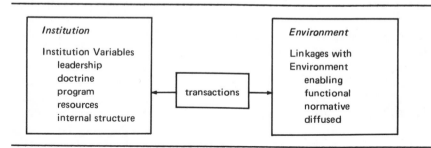

The definitions and clusters of variables as set forth by Esman suffice for our purposes and whether labelled institution-building model or concepts or descriptive categories should make little difference for purposes of application.

Clearly there are some things which the institution-building concepts cannot do since they are not intended to ease the work of all persons in technical assistance, or even all those very broadly concerned with some questions closely related to institution building. There are also limitations imposed by the fact that the concepts are still somewhat general, a bit vague, and need considerable refinement based on research.

The institution-building concepts should be seen by practitioners as relating only to the institution-building process: the putting together of new or revitalization of old organizations which (a) embody change, (b) foster new, hopefully progressive action, and (c) are supported locally.[3] The technical assistance personnel need not be foreigners; they may be nationals of the country in which the institution is located. The important point is that the concepts have applicability under varying, limited circumstances, and are of almost no help to those engaged in technical assistance or development activity other than institution building. Thus, they tell the economic analyst or planner very little. They have nothing much to say to the immediate needs of the tax policy specialist or the wheat research man, except when he, in order to spread an innovative technique, helps to organize a local cooperative to buy better seeds, works to reorganize an existing organization or to build a new one, and to maintain machinery needed to institutionalize agricultural modernization practices.

Institution-building concepts are of little help in making choices of priority among alternative administrative sectors, such as education, health, family planning, agriculture. The concepts may help to clarify in which fields the institution-building effort would be less difficult, but would not be of much help in specifying which field is to be placed first in importance.

Similarly, the concepts would not be very helpful to those considering national development strategies or priorities in a broad context. Even if one sector—e.g. agriculture—is given high rank in national plans, the institution-building concepts would not be useful in determining which agricultural institutions ought to be brought into being or revised or what the balance should be between institutional investment and other development efforts within the sector. The choice between strengthening or revitalizing agricultural research or funding imports of farm machinery or other production inputs or modifying a particular public policy must be based on other grounds, using guidelines other than those provided by the institution-building model. In such choices, it is reasonable to assume that the institution-building share of the technical assistance or development effort will not diminish, especially since a well-built and progressive institution has the quality of surviving political upheaval, retaining ability to contribute after other changes are lost. Thus, it should continue to receive major attention from development strategists.

Furthermore, at present the institution-building concepts can be of only modest help in making policy choices in specific project strategy choices once an institution-building effort is under way. Hopefully, a few years from now, more refined concepts will serve this need. At present, research about development policies is still too sparse, and generalizations are at best suggestive. In most cases, use of the concepts as presently defined would not yet yield a high probability of success in predicting which choices would have what consequences, when establishing a specific array of enabling linkages or a particular pattern of institutional leadership.

These are important practical limitations. Even their brief statement suggests that limited portion of the development task for which the model is intended, the preliminary nature of our conceptualization, and the first-stage nature of our institution-building research. Having noted the negative first, what can be stated affirmatively?

The main positive contribution of the institution-building framework at this stage of definition is that it offers the practitioner a set of concepts and relationships which yields a sharper insight into the process of strengthening institutions. It provides a more systematic nomenclature for discussion among those engaged in institution building. Since institution building is a major component of concerted modernization efforts generally, this contribution is important. The larger number of personnel—local and foreign—who are engaged in institution building under the label of agricultural development, a planning effort, an educational or family-planning project, can benefit from this conceptual approach to viewing their task. They may call their project by a different name and define major goals without reference to institution building per se, but they ignore this improved vantage point at a price. Although some raise intuitively the type of questions suggested by the institution-building model, some queries may be missed even by experienced personnel without the sharper focus provided by this more systematic approach.

There are numerous examples, in the developing world as well as in the United States, of useful economic research and planning being accomplished over a number of years of an assistance project without the concurrent institutional build-up which would sustain the planning process over a much longer period. A specific agricultural research project is easier to undertake than the building of the institutional mechanism for continuing and multiplying modernization practices. The short-run accomplishment may be fine; the long-run payoff turns out to be minor. These types of semi-failures argue for concerted attention to the institution-building component in technical assistance; they also point up the need for just as systematic and pointed an approach to institution building as the technical side of any such program. And that is where the institution-building model comes in—to be used by the economist or agriculturist as well as the public administration specialist abroad.

Fortunately, at this early stage of research and conceptualization—and due to the practical orientation of IB—the model does not demand a high level of social science sophistication to be useful. As research and refinement continue, we can expect the model to require more specialized knowledge to enable the practitioner to make full use of increasingly rich data and specific application.

At the present time, use of the model enhances the chances of successful institution building. It also provides greater insight into measures of success or failure. It can serve as an instrument for project evaluation.

In addition, the concepts provide a useful means of comparison among various institution-building efforts in any country and between several. It facilitates transfer of knowledge born of experience from one situation to another. It does this by providing a framework for research and by supplying data (or experience) categories, so that the sensitive and analytical practitioner can more easily move from one situation to another without always starting afresh. He will more easily identify similar characteristics or linkages. He will have a better idea about the range of questions which are pertinent.

These positive and practical contributions will be made more specific later in this paper. They are not earthshaking, and some experienced and thoughtful development specialists may, at this stage, learn little new from the concepts. But for most development specialists, the institution-building concepts can already provide meaningful assistance in the difficult tasks they face.

The institution-building concepts, in their attempt to be relevant to both researchers and practitioners, run the risk of being acceptable to neither. Specifically, the practitioner (who is usually an agriculturist or educator rather than a social scientist) worries about the formality, the "jargon." He is put off by the need to deal with doctrine, or enabling or normative linkages. These terms are actually at a minimum in the model and represent a quest for added precision which is a precondition to comparison, to data accumulation, and to deeper understanding of the process. Furthermore, the minimal and careful use of jargon moves us one step away from everyday words which too often mean different things to different people. Finally, if the practitioner actually finds other terminology so much more comfortable that he must stick with it, he should first establish in his own mind some reasonable equating of his own phraseology to that of the IB framework so that nothing is lost in the translation.

The concepts may also seem too general to be put to use at present. As we penetrate more deeply, more precise application and usefulness will be possible. For example, some of the research is moving the leadership concept in institution building into a more elaborate set of patterns of leadership, and this in turn will eventually suggest to the practitioner choices among different successful patterns of leadership in varying circumstances. [4]

On balance, the model receives more severe criticism from social science researchers who see it as not precise enough—as presently formulated—to yield useful research hypothesis. To some it is a peculiar mix of rather traditional public administration constructs with sociology and organizational theory.

Clearly, the set of institution-building concepts is sufficiently general at this stage to permit expansion and redefinition by both researchers and practitioners. The concepts represent a beginning. There is still plenty of room for variation, subcategorization, and expansions. For example, the concept of "doctrine" and the assertion of its importance in the model as one of the institutional variables calls for thoughtful, more specific definition in line with experience.

Furthermore, since institution building is only one part, though an important part, of the general development or technical assistance effort, use of these concepts systematizes somewhat only this one part of the total. It imposes few rigidities when viewed in this larger context. There are major areas still open for modification, innovation, and, hopefully, improvement.

Before turning to more specific questions of practical application, two comments might be added on the value of the very general nature of the model. First, because it is general, it has usefulness to development efforts either with or without a technical assistance or foreign component. Second, from an American viewpoint, it is not limited to a foreign setting. It may well have usefulness within present domestic attempts to build or modify domestic institutions so as to link them more effectively with their environment.

The members of the consortium were convinced that the model has considerable applicability to the American domestic scene. While their own research was largely overseas, there was one domestic field study.[5]

SOME PRACTICAL APPLICATIONS

The institution-building concepts provide no help in estimating which institution should be strengthened or started. Once this policy decision has been made, they become distinctly useful in project planning. They provide an essential checklist of items to be carefully considered in evolving the strategy for a successful effort.

Each of the major clusters of institutional variables as set forth in the IB model—leadership, doctrine, program, resources, and structure—suggests a set of questions which can become highly specific in a project context. Some of the questions are obvious; others less so. Some are answerable; others can be answered with only a low probability of accuracy.

Consider the set of variables within the doctrine category. In building a new university in an African country, it suggests that planners should take into account these types of question:

1. What philosophy of education should prevail at the new institution? That is, toward what broad societal purposes should it be directed? What blend of varying higher educational traditions or innovations should it accept as its own or seek to identify in the foreseeable future?

The answer to these types of questions help to decide admission policy, the schools or departments to be given initial priority, relationships within the environment, initial staff appointments, and so forth. We have seen examples of universities established in a popular mold, with an avowed "common man" orientation or "land-grant" purpose, which because of initial leadership appointments immediately veered in an "oxbridge" direction. In the United States, we have recently experienced a conflict between open admission policies and restricted admission criteria based on documented evidence of preexisting technical qualifications. In the developing world, this issue is only now coming up. Far more crucial has been the policy question on whether or not professional education should begin immediately after the completion of high school, as is the European custom, or whether the American liberal arts model should be inserted between high school graduation and entrance into medical or social work education.

2. How can the institutional doctrine be made clear?

3. Can the doctrine become an asset in the building and operation of the institution? If used properly, it may be able to hasten growth of productive esprit which in turn will enable the fledgling institution to sustain itself within its environment. If overstressed, the doctrine may generate premature traditionalist opposition or open hostility which could endanger the growth of the university. "Productive esprit" might be seen as an *incipient professional social movement,* which turns the program into a technical cult, asserting and defending its innovation against competing dogmas in the environment.[6]

If institutional doctrine is closely tied to a tested technology with clearly desired production implications—for example, a training institution in some specialized technical field—it may find that frequent, clear identification with the technology, which is really part of the doctrine, is a great asset in accomplishing "institutionality," which is the goal of the whole effort.[7]

4. What relationships or linkages are suggested by the institutional doctrine? Various types of linkages included in the checklist ought to be considered— enabling, functional, normative, diffuse. For example, if the university is to have scientific agricultural goals as important components of its purpose, certain natural bonds in the society are suggested, as would be the case if it is to be a technically oriented institution.

Consider some of the questions which should be raised concerning functional linkages. As a new university is being planned its planners should examine the environment well enough to estimate:

(a) Which schools will be the main suppliers of students to the new university?
(b) Which organizations—schools, offices, agencies, businesses, and the like—will be the main consumers of the university's product, both graduates and research?
(c) Which organizations can be expected to provide what types of financial and other inputs into the new university?

Institution builders should consider at the outset—and periodically as the new institution grows—which pattern of ties with such outside organizations will enable the new institution to fulfill its purpose.

The institution-building model provides a checklist for project planners and development strategists, whether the effort is to receive technical assistance from abroad or not. But if it is to be aided from abroad, the institution-building model takes on an added usefulness. It then becomes the basis for intensive discussion between local leaders and the initial technical assistance project leaders who are jointly planning the pattern of assistance. Without such a specific institutional emphasis and checklist, important questions might be overlooked in the haste to bring functional improvement in agricultural research, in economic planning, in use of family planning, or public health personnel. The technical assistance project planning or survey team personnel are always sure to include the functional outside expert who raises questions related to his specialty; but in the past such teams have not always had persons attuned to the institution-building questions, and, as a result, many have not been raised in time.

During the planning period, there should be intensive discussion of the institution-building task. The IB model facilitates such discussion. Each term should be defined by the technical assistance visitors and by the host leaders. Linkages should be discussed. Preliminary views on strategy and priorities should be brought out and discussed. Such discussions early in the project's development will increase probability of success later, and will help, among other things, to define the nature of the technical assistance input.

These discussions—centering around the types of questions mentioned above—will bring out the need for certain types of new data and further inquiry. Longer-term research may be called for. For example, a new university with a heavy technical emphasis should have some manpower data available before it opts too heavily for the specifics of one technology or another. If such data are not available, the necessary research will be suggested. Leaders of a new university must have a realistic view of their consumers—both the feeder schools from which they expect students and the institutions likely to accept their graduates. Without such evidence, a new university may develop at great expense without optimum utility to those who maintain it.

To summarize, during the planning phase, the institution-building concepts in their present form have direct applicability in providing a checklist of significant questions to be considered, a clearer basis for discussion between local leaders and outside technical assistance leaders, and in suggesting data gaps and possible supporting research needs.

In their present form, the institution-building concepts are also useful in guiding staff selection when no technical assistance component is envisaged for the project. It has already been pointed out that careful definition of institutional doctrine may affect choice of the institution's vice chancellor or president. Similarly, analysis of the linkage pattern to be sought may veto certain leadership appointments or suggest strong endorsements of others. For instance, a review may favor as choice for president an individual who is committed to appointing experienced academic leaders to positions of technical leadership, rather than a politician identified with the belief that the spoils system dictate the allocation of subleadership posts. Conversely, if a new institution is in a keen struggle for political support, its president may have to be someone with the right political connections, even if this will thereby lead to a downgrading of persons with a technical education background. In such an event, a strong deputy with program planning skills might be recommended, with an appropriate and agreed-upon division of labor between him and his politically chosen superior.

Even more clearly, appointments to the technical assistance team should be influenced by the institution-building model. If a certain pattern of leadership is planned for the new institution, the technical assistance team leader must be selected to fit into the pattern. If the primacy of some of the institution-building questions becomes apparent in the early discussions, the technical assistance team composition should reflect these observations. In a sizable technical assistance team engaged in institution building abroad, the team leader should be as familiar with the institution-building concepts as he is with his own specialty. His agronomist and the engineer should also be conversant with the conceptual framework.

This suggests, also, the usefulness of the institution-building concepts in preparing staff for overseas service—the orientation function. All personnel moving into a technical assistance position abroad should have some knowledge of the institution-building process. Whether this exposure—or immersion—occurs just prior to departure for abroad or as part of on-the-job training at post is of no consequence. The important goal is to orient the professional toward leaving behind institutional strength when he departs from his post abroad, not just a specific task accomplishment in his special field. Other things being about equal, the practitioner who is familiar with the components of the institution-building model and can think easily in these categories, relating his actions to institution-building goals and tasks, expands his accomplishments abroad. This could be accomplished by providing practitioners, before they leave for the field, with a chance to analyze an institution with which they are already familiar. The analytic model thus learned then can be applied more easily to new institutions to help each practitioner learn from his own knowledge and to utilize it for the analysis of situations that will be new.

Since the institution-building model is general in terminology and applicability, it is more easily used in orientation than existing materials. That is, the experience of agriculturalists in Iran can be seen as relevant to the engineers in Taiwan or public administration advisors in Thailand, since all can talk about and analyze their institution-building experiences in terms of concepts and categories of variables, such as types of linkages within differing settings. Case studies become more useful.

While the project is under way, the institution-building concepts can facilitate communication between technical assistance personnel and their counterparts. Here again the concepts provide a checklist for discussion and periodic internal examination. Such discussions may help to clarify critical weaknesses and new choices within project strategy.[8] For example, as a new institute of business administration takes shape abroad, the institution-building framework may point to a need to establish a deliberate set of relations with certain business leaders in the community, or may point out the contradictory nature in a given society of serving both the academic need of university affiliation and, at the same time, the practical need of preparing graduates for specific types of jobs. These discussions may suggest identifying new members of an institute advisory panel (to enhance functional linkages); or new service functions to be undertaken (as a part of program variables); or regularized communications with certain authorities (to assure enabling linkages); or publishing a clear restatement of purpose and progress toward institutional goals (clarifying institutional doctrine).

In using the institution-building concepts for internal evaluation or review by outsiders, there is some danger that we can get caught in a tautological box, i.e., having defined institution building in a specific way, to measure success in line with the definition whether it squares with broader experience or not. If we do not prematurely rigidify definition and categories, we should be able to avoid this trap. Furthermore, so much of the institution-building model is tied, through the concept of linkages, to the specific institutional environment that the model's application in evaluation exercises should be shielded from logical difficulties and those of unrealism. Indeed, the ever-changing environment suggests the need for continuous and systematic monitoring with appropriate changes in criteria for success.

The model is useful in gauging progress toward institutional maturity. J. A. Rigney finds that the IB model serves as a very useful device for evaluation and "maturity testing." He suggests a series of questions derived from the model. He also points out a number of operational difficulties in using the model for this purpose: lack of familiarity with the terminology on the part of project personnel, resistance to evaluation if there is any chance that adverse comment will result, questions of timing, and others. Most of these difficulties appear to be manageable if the IB model were to become a part of planning and implementation phases of institution-building efforts more generally. [9]

One other application of the institution-building model ties to participant training—i.e. preparation of future staff members of the new or revitalized institution. It is not unusual for a number of future staff from one institution to be in the United States at one time for advanced degree work. The institution-building model as specifically applied to the future staff members' home institution could be the basis for useful mid-sojourn training. A report from home and ensuing discussion could center around the data categories suggested in the model. While this could not replace the usual anecdotal sessions, it would provide a framework for serious and more systematic analysis of the institution to which they will be returning, and a way of viewing the strategy for strengthening it. The initially abstract terms of the model would soon be translated into significant reality for each of the participants.

APPLICATION SHORTCOMINGS

The IB model can be seen as having usefulness in aspects of project planning, staff selection and orientation, counterpart discussions, internal review and external evaluation, and in participant training. As the preceding discussion indicates, it fails at this time to give us specific guidance; but continuing research should expand its contribution in practical application in the future. We should arrive at the point where, given certain circumstances, we can predict the probability of success offered by different course of institution-building decision or strategy.

At present, we can make gross estimates and base decisions on them. For example, we sense that the chance of institution-building success is enhanced when a clear new technology which is highly desired in the society forms a main ingredient in the doctrine of the institution. We know generally that "strong" local leadership (in whatever form) provides more assurance of success over the long run than if the chief technical assistance person steps into the leading role. The institution-building concepts, if used for research and applied by practitioners in their present form, should hasten our ability to become far more specific in the future.

Therein lies one of the problems of application. The concepts run the risk of being rejected as too general, too "common-sensible," and, therefore, not worth the effort. Rejection on this basis would be foolishly shortsighted. Experience yields plenty of examples to show the need to systematize in this field and to begin to take advantage of the practical gains to be made by use of the model even in its present condition and generality.

Several other shortcomings mentioned earlier should be examined and balanced in summary. One, the language itself runs the risk of scaring away those practitioners not accustomed to employing even this moderate level of social science abstraction. Since the model is relatively uncomplicated and jargon-free, it is worth the effort to master it and try it in practice. The discussion of potential benefits above and knowledge of past failures should sufficiently justify the effort.

Finally, the model falls short of promising to provide a complete strategy. Concepts can be used to describe testable propositions. Our present model does not include such propositions. There are still many questions which, even with comprehensive research and accurate data, it will not answer, e.g., which of alternate institutions should be strengthened in a particular setting and circumstances, and for what reasons.

Because the IB model is not designed to offer the full and final answer does not mean it cannot be highly useful within its domain. But even there, to the impatient, the institution-building model may be discouraging. Institution-building research will take time and some patience and those working in institution-building situations will receive only general, rather limited assistance from the model during the immediate years ahead. Had we started with this more systematic approach—and the research to support it—about twenty years ago when the main international assistance to institution building began, we might now be far along in attaining levels of certainty in prediction in these efforts. To those who are now impatient, we can offer the firm rejoinder—reinforced with the weight of experience—that the institution-building process is crucial, is far more complicated than one thinks, and requires a blend of patience and insight. The institution-building model offers a good approach to the latter.

NOTES

1. See Thomas W. Thorsen, "The Institution-Building Model in Program Operation and Review," Chapter 8 above.

2. See Milton J. Esman, "The Elements of Institution Building," Chapter 1 above, for definitions.

3. "Institution building may be defined as the planning, structuring, and guidance of new or reconstituted organizations which (a) embody changes in values, functions, physical and/or social technologies, (b) establish, foster, and protect new normative relationships and action patterns, and (c) obtain support and complementarity in the environment." Esman, Chapter 1 above.

4. Milton Esman points out that the original set of concepts, left deliberately simple at the outset, is now being considerably elaborated and enriched by the field investigations. "The Institution-Building Concepts—An Interim Appraisal," Pittsburgh: Inter-University Research Program in Institution Building, 1967 (mimeo)

5. Anwar Quereski, "The California State Training Division: A Study of Institution Building," Los Angeles. Ph.D. dissertation, University of California, 1967.

6. The theory and development of such professional movements were analyzed in a study completed some years ago by Joseph W. Eaton, *Stone Walls Not A Prison Make,* Springfield, Ill.: C. C Thomas, 1962.

7. "Institutionality" means that the organization has attained self-sustaining qualities without losing its ability to produce within the society. See Esman, Chapter 1, above, for definition. John Hanson, in his study *Education, Nsukka* in which he applies the IB concepts, considers an organization institutionalized to the extent it is prized in its environment.

8. Thorsen has found the matrix based on the IB model to be useful in this phase. "The matrix in and of itself provides a good checklist by asking the right questions and in this manner helps the institutional leaders become more aware of the significant elements of institution building." See Thorsen, Chapter 8, above.

9. J. A. Rigney, "The Institution-Building Model in Project Review and Maturity Testing," paper delivered at AID-CIC Conference on Institution Building and Technical Assistance, Washington, December 4-5, 1969.

SELECTED
BIBLIOGRAPHY

SELECTED BIBLIOGRAPHY

Compiled by J A M E S   J.   A L I B R I O

University of Pittsburgh

BIBLIOGRAPHICAL STUDIES

Aid for International Development Program (AID). Inquiries regarding documentation of research, seminars, and other activities funded by the Agency for International Development in the field of institution building may be addressed to the Technical Assistance Methodology Division, Bureau for Technical Assistance, Washington, D.C. 20523. In making such inquiries it would be helpful to indicate special areas of interest (e.g., technical assistance methodology, agriculture, development administration).

Brode, John, *The Process of Modernization: An Annotated Bibliography of Socio-cultural Aspects of Development.* Cambridge: Harvard University Press, 1969.

Frey, Frederick W., editor, *Survey Research on Comparative Social Change: A Bibliography,* Cambridge: M.I.T. Press, 1969.

Katz, Saul M. and Frank McGowan, editors, *A Selected List of Readings on Development.* Prepared for the U.S. Delegation to the United Nations Conference on the Applications of Science and Technology for the Benefit of Less Developed Areas, Washington, D.C.: Agency for International Development, 1963.

[243]

Kaufman, Harold F., Lucy Cole, and Kenneth P. Wilkinson, *Community Structure and Participation: A Program and Bibliography,* State College, Miss.: Mississippi State University, 1967.

BOOKS AND ARTICLES

Adams, Walter and John A. Garraty, *Is the World Our Campus?* East Lansing: Michigan State University Press, 1960.

Adelman, Irma and Cynthia Morris, *Society, Politics and Economic Development,* Baltimore: Johns Hopkins Press, 1967.

Anthony, Robert N., *Planning and Control Systems—A Framework for Analysis,* Boston: Harvard University, Graduate School of Business Administration, 1965.

Arensberg, Conrad M. and Arthur H. Niehoff, *Introducing Social Change: A Manual for Americans Overseas,* Chicago: Aldine, 1964.

Argyris, Chris, *Integrating the Individual and the Organization,* New York: Wiley, 1964.

Argyris, Chris, *Interpersonal Competence and Organizational Effectiveness,* Homewood, Ill.: Irwin-Dorsey; London: Tavistock, 1962.

Ashby, Eric, *African Universities and Western Tradition,* Cambridge: Harvard University Press, 1964.

Ashen, Melvin, "The Management of Ideas," Harvard Business Review, Vol. XLVII, July-August 1969: 99-107.

Asher, Robert E., editor, *Development of the Emerging Countries—An Agenda for Research,* Washington, D.C.: Brookings Institution, 1962.

Bakke, E. Wight and Chris Argyris, *Organizational Structure and Dynamics: A Framework for a Theory,* New Haven: Yale University Press, 1954.

Banfield, Edward C., *The Moral Basis of a Backward Society,* Chicago: University of Chicago Press and Free Press, 1958.

Barringer, Herbert R., George I. Banksten, and Raymond W. Mack, editors *Social Change in Developing Areas: A Reinterpretation of Evolutionary Theory,* Cambridge: Schenkman, 1965.

Battersby, Albert, *Network Analysis for Planning and Scheduling,* New York: Wiley, 1970.

Becker, Howard S., et al., editors, *Institutions and the Person: Papers Presented to Everett C. Hughes,* Chicago: Aldine, 1968.

Bendix, Reinhard, *Nation-Building and Citizenship: Studies of our Changing Social Order,* Garden City, N.Y.: Doubleday, 1969.

Benham, Frederic, *Economic Aid to Underdeveloped Countries,* London: Oxford University Press, 1962.

Bennis, W. G., Kenneth Benne, and Robert Chin, *The Planning of Change,* New York: Holt, Rinehart & Winston, 1961.

Benveniste, Guy, *Bureaucracy and National Planning: A Sociological Case Study in Mexico,* New York: Praeger, 1970.

Birkhead, Guthrie, *Institutionalization at a Modest Level: Public Administration Institute for Turkey and the Middle East,* Pittsburgh: University of Pittsburgh, Graduate School of Public and International Affairs, March 1967.

Black, Cyril Edwin, *The Dynamics of Modernization: A Study in Comparative History,* New York: Harper & Row, 1966.

Blair, Thomas L., *The Land to Those Who Work It: Algeria's Experiment in Workers' Management,* Garden City, N.Y.: Doubleday, 1969.

Blaise, Hans C. and Rodriguez, Luis A., *Introducing Innovation at Ecuadorian Universities,* Pittsburgh: University of Pittsburgh, Graduate School of Public and International Affairs, 1968.

Brown, R.G.S., *The Administrative Process in Britain,* London: Camelot Press, 1970

Bruton, Henry J., *Principles of Development Economics,* Englewood Cliffs: Prentice-Hall, 1965.

Burns, Tom and George M. Stalker, *The Management of Innovation,* London: Tavistock; Chicago: Quadrangle, 1961.

Byrnes, Francis C., *Americans in Technical Assistance: A Study of Attitudes and Responses to Their Role Abroad,* New York: Praeger, 1965.

Caiden, Gerald E., *Administrative Reform,* Chicago: Aldine, 1969.

Carlson, Sune, *Development Economics and Administration,* Stockholm: University of Uppsala, Institute of Business Studies, 1964.

Carroll, T. F., *Rural Institution and Planning Change,* Geneva: United Nations Research Institute for Social Development, n.d.

Cleveland, Harlan, et al., *The Overseas Americans,* New York: McGraw-Hill, 1960.

Conference on Institution Building and Technical Assistance, *Proceedings of A Conference Held in Washington, D.C., December 4 and 5, 1969,* sponsored by the Agency for International Development, Department of State, and the Committee on Institutional Cooperation, Evanston, Ill., edited by D. Woods Thomas and Judith C. Fender, Washington, D.C.: Agency for International Development, n.d.

Cowan, L. Gray, James O'Connell, and David G. Scanlon, editors, *Education and Nation Building in Africa,* New York: Praeger, 1965.

Davis, Russell G., *Planning Human Resource Development: Educational Models and Schemata,* Chicago: Rand McNally 1966.

Dobyns, Henry, et al., *Methods of Analyzing Cultural Change,* Ithaca: Cornell University, ERP Document Number VII-12, 1957.

Dobyns, Henry, et al., *Strategic Intervention in the Cultural Change Process,* Ithaca: Cornell University, ERP Document Number VII-11, 1967.

Domergue, Maurice, *Technical Assistance—Definition and Aims, Ways and Means, Conditions and Limits.* Paris: Organisation for Economic Co-operation and Development, 1961.

Duhl, Leonard, *The Urban Condition,* New York: Basic Books, 1963.

Duncan, Richard L. and William S. Pooler, *Technical Assistance and Institution Building,* Pittsburgh: University of Pittsburgh, Graduate School of Public and International Affairs, 1967.

Eaton, Joseph W., "Community Development Ideologies," International Review of Community Development, No. 11, 1963: 37-50

Eaton, Joseph W., *Influencing the Youth Culture: A Study of Youth Organizations in Israel,* Beverly Hills: Sage, 1970.

Ellsworth, David F., *Extent of Administrative Unity Within the Technical Assistance Complex,* Lafayette, Ind.: Purdue University, 1968.

Emery, F. E. and E. L. Trist, "Socio-technical Systems," in C. W. Churchman and M. Verhulst, editors, *Management Sciences Models and Techniques,* Vol. 2, New York: Pergamon Press, 1961.

Esman, Milton J., "Institution Building in National Development," in Gove Hambidge, editor, *Dynamics of Development,* New York: Praeger, 1964.

Esman, Milton J., "The Institution Building Concepts—An Interim Appraisal," Pittsburgh: University of Pittsburgh Inter-University Research Program in Institution Building, 1967 (mimeo)

Esman, Milton J. and Hans C. Blaise, "Institution Building Research: The Guiding Concepts," Pittsburgh: University of Pittsburgh, Inter-University Program in Institution Building, 1966 (mimeo).

Esman, Milton J. and Fred Bruhns, "Institution Building in National Development: An Approach to Inducting Social Change In Transitional Societies," in Hollis W. Peters, editor, *Comparative Theories of Social Change,* Ann Arbor, Mich.: Foundation for Research in Human Behavior, 1966.

Esmay, Merle L., "Institutionalization of the Facultad de Agronomia at Calcarce, Argentina," in Michigan State University, East Lansing, International Program, Papers in International and World Affairs, 1969 Series, July 3, 29-50.

Fayerweather, John, *International Business Management: A Conceptual Framework,* New York: McGraw-Hill, 1969.

Foster, George M., *Traditional Cultures, and the Impact of Technological Change,* New York: Harper, 1962.

Frankel, Charles, *The Neglected Aspect of Foreign Affairs,* Washington, D.C.: Brookings Institution, 1965.

Gant, George F., "The Institution Building Project," *International Review of Administrative Science,* Vol. XXXII, No. 3, 1966: 219-225.

Gautam, O. P., J. S. Patel, and T. S. Sutton, *A Method of Assessing Progress of Agricultural Universities in India,* New Delhi: Indian Council of Agricultural Research, 1970.

Glick, Philip M., *The Administration of Technical Assistance—Growth in the Americas,* Chicago: University of Chicago Press, 1957.

Goodsell, Charles T., *Administration of a Revolution: Executive Reform in Puerto Rico under Governor Tugwell—1941-1946,* Cambridge: Harvard University Press, 1965.

Gross, Bertram M., editor, *Action Under Planning,* New York: McGraw-Hill, 1967.

Gross, Bertram M., *The Managing of Organizations,* 2 vols., New York: Free Press, 1964.

Gross, Bertram M., "What Are Your Organization's Objectives? A General-Systems Approach to Planning," Human Relations, Vol. XVIII, August 1965: 195-216.

Guest, Robert H., *Organizational Change: The Effect of Successful Leadership,* Homewood, Ill.: Irwin-Dorsey, 1962.

Hagen, Everett E., *On the Theory of Social Change—How Economic Growth Begins,* Homewood, Ill.: Dorsey Press, 1962.

Hagen, Everett E., *Planning Economic Development,* Homewood, Ill.: Irwin, 1963.

Haire, Mason, editor, *Modern Organization Theory,* New York: Wiley, 1959.

Hamilton, B. L. St. John, *Problems of Administration in an Emergent Nation, A Case Study of Jamaica,* New York: Praeger, 1964.

Hamilton, William B., editor, *The Transfer of Institutions,* Durham: Duke University Press, 1964.

Haq, Mahbubul, *Strategy of Economic Planning: A Case Study of Pakistan,* Karachi: Oxford University Press, 1963.

Hanna, Paul R., editor, *Education: An Instrument of National Goals,* New York: McGraw-Hill, 1962.

Hanson, John W., *Education Nsukka: A Study in Institution Building Among the Modern Ibo,* East Lansing, Mich.: Michigan State University, 1968.

Harbison, Frederick and Charles A. Myers, *Education, Manpower and Economic Growth,* New York: McGraw-Hill, 1964.

Hillery, George A., Jr., *Communal Organizations: A Study of Local Societies,* Chicago: University of Chicago Press, 1968.

Hills, Richard Jean, *Toward a Science of Organization,* Eugene: University of Oregon, Center for the Advanced Study of Educational Administration, 1968.

Hirschman, Albert O., *Journeys Toward Progress: Studies of Economic Policy-Making in Latin America,* New York: Twentieth Century Fund, 1963.

Hirschman, Albert O., *The Strategy of Economic Development,* New Haven: Yale University Press, 1961.

Honey, John C., *Planning and the Private Sector: The Experience in Developing Countries,* New York: Dunellen, 1970.

Hodges, Wayne, *Company and Community: Case Studies in Industry-City Relations,* New York: Harper, 1958.

Horowitz, Irving Louis, *Three Worlds of Development,* New York: Oxford University Press, 1966.

Institution Building and Education: Papers and Comments, Bloomington, Ind.: Indiana University, Comparative Administration Group, Department of Government, 1968.

Institution Building and Technical Assistance. See Conference on Institution Building and Technical Assistance.

Israel's Program of International Cooperation, Jerusalem: Ministry for Foreign Affairs, Division for International Cooperation, 1970.

Janowitz, Morris, *Institution Building in Urban Education,* New York: Russell Sage Foundation, 1969.

Johnson, R. A., F. E. Kast, and J. E Rosenzweig, *The Theory and Management of Systems,* New York: McGraw-Hill, 1963.

Jones, Garth, *Planned Organizational Change: A Set of Working Documents,* Los Angeles: University of Southern California, 1964.

Kahn, Alfred J., *Studies in Social Policy and Planning,* New York: Russell Sage Foundation, 1969.

Katz, Israel and Harold Silver, *The University and Social Welfare,* Jerusalem: The Magnes Press and Hebrew University, 1969.

Katz, Saul M., "Guide to Modernizing Administration for National Development," Pittsburgh: University of Pittsburgh, Graduate School of Public and International Affairs, 1965.

Katz, Saul M., "A Systems Approach to Development Administration: A Framework for Analyzing Capability of Action for National Development," in Papers in Comparative Public Administration No. 6, Washington, D.C.: Comparative Administration Group, American Society for Public Administration, 1965.

Kaufman, Harold F. and Kenneth Wilkinson, *Community Structure and Leadership: An Interactional Perspective in the Study of Community,* State College, Miss.: Mississippi State University, 1967.

Kelman, Herbert B. and Raphael S. Ezekiel, *Cross National Encounters,* San Francisco: Jossey-Bass, 1970.

Klayman, Maxwell I., *The Moshav in Israel,* New York: Praeger, 1970.

Kroeger, Louis J., editor, *Reflections on Successful Technical Assistance Abroad,* Washington, D.C.: Agency for International Development, 1957.

Kulp, Earl M., *Rural Development Planning: A Systems Analysis and Working Method,* New York: Praeger, 1970.

Laufer, Leopold, *Israel and the Developing Countries: New Approaches to Cooperation,* New York: Twentieth Century Fund, 1967.

Lawrence, Paul R. and Jay W. Lorsch, *Developing Organizations, Diagnosis and Action,* Reading: Addison-Wesley, 1969.

Lerner, Daniel and Lucille Pevsner, *The Passing of Traditional Society: Modernizing the Middle East,* New York: Free Press, 1958.

Lewis, W. Arthur, *Development Planning: The Essentials of Economic Policy,* New York: Harper & Row, 1966.

Likert, Rensis, *New Patterns of Management,* New York: McGraw-Hill, 1961.

Lin, Nan, Donald Leu, Everett M. Rogers and Donald F. Schwartz, *The Diffusion of an Innovation in Three Michigan High Schools: Institution Building Through Change,* East Lansing: Michigan State University, Institute for International Studies in Education and Department of Communication, 1966.

Lippitt, Ronald, Jeanne Watson, and Bruce Westley, *Dynamics of Planned Change,* New York: Harcourt, Brace, 1958.

Maddison, Angus, *Foreign Skills and Technical Assistance in Economic Development,* Paris: Development Centre of the Organisation for Economic Cooperation and Development, 1965.

March, James G. and Herbert A. Simon, *Organizations,* New York: Wiley, 1958.

Martindale, Dan Albert, *Institutions, Organizations and Mass Society,* Boston: Houghton Mifflin, 1966.

Martz, John D., *The Dynamics of Change in Latin American Politics,* Englewood Cliffs: Prentice-Hall, 1965.

McClelland, David C., *The Achieving Society,* Princeton, N.J.: D. Van Nostrand, 1961.

McGregor, Douglas, *The Human Side of Enterprise,* New York: McGraw-Hill, 1960.

Miller, Norman N., "The Political Survival of Traditional Leadership," Journal of African Studies, Vol. VI, No. 2, 1968: 183-201.

Miller, Norman N., *Research in Rural Africa,* Published by Canadian Journal of African Studies at Loyola College and African Studies Center, Michigan State University, 1969.

Millikan, Max F., editor, *National Economic Planning,* New York: National Bureau of Economic Research and Columbia University Press, 1967.

Montgomery, John D. and William J. Siffin, editors, *Approaches to Development: Politics, Administration and Change,* New York: McGraw-Hill, 1966.

Moseman, Albert L., editor, *Agricultural Sciences for the Developing Nations,* Washington, D.C.: American Association for the Advancement of Science, 1964.

Myrdal, Gunnar, *Rich Lands and Poor,* New York: Harper, 1957.

Naik, K. C., *A History of Agricultural Universities,* New Delhi: Committee on Institutional Cooperation and Agency for International Development, 1968.

Nayar, P.K.B., *Leadership Bureaucracy and Planning in India: A Sociological Study,* New Delhi: Associated Publishing House, 1969.

O'Connell, Jeremiah, *Managing Organizational Innovation,* Homewood, Ill.: Irwin, 1968.

Perlmutter, H. V., "A Conceptual Guide for the Organization Building Process," Lausanne, Switzerland: Institut des Etudes de Methodes de Direction de l'Entreprise, Mimeo No. HPBE 109, 1965.

Perlmutter, H. V., *Toward a Theory and Practice of Social Architecture,* London: Tavistock Pamphlet No. 12, 1965.

Phillips, Hiram S., *Guide for Development: Institution-Building and Reform,* New York: Praeger, 1969.

Pieris, Ralph, *Studies in the Sociology of Development,* Rotterdam: Rotterdam University Press, 1969.

Pinto, Aluizio, "The Brazilian Institute of Public Administration: A Case Study of Institution Building in Brazil," Los Angeles: University of Southern California, 1968 (dissertation).

Pinto, Rogerio, Feital, S., *The Political Ecology of the Brazilian National Bank for Development (BNDE): A Study of Politics, Development and Public Administration,* Washington, D.C.: Organization of American States, Research Cooperation Project, 1969.

Ponsioen, J. S., *National Development,* The Hague: Mouton, 1968.

Porter, Willis P., "College of Education, Bangkok, Thailand: A Case Study in Institution Building," Pittsburgh: University of Pittsburgh, Graduate School of Public and International Affairs, 1967 (mimeo).

Propp, Kathleen M., *The Establishment of Agricultural Universities in India: A Case Study of the Role of USAID-U.S. University Technical Assistance,* Urbana, Ill.: University of Illinois, College of Agriculture, 1968.

Propp, Kathleen M., Harold D. Guither, Earl Regnier and William Thompson, *AID-University Rural Development Contracts, 1951-1966,* Urbana, Ill.: University of Illinois, 1968.

Pye, Lucian W., *Aspects of Political Development,* Boston: Little, Brown, 1966.

Pye, Lucian W., editor, *Communications and Political Development,* Princeton: Princeton University Press, 1963.

Pye, Lucian W., *Politics, Personality and Nation Building,* New Haven: Yale University Press, 1962.

Raj Panday, Devendra, *Nepal's Central Planning Organization: An Analysis of Its Effectiveness in a Inter-Organizational Environment.* Pittsburgh: University of Pittsburgh, 1969.

Reining, Conrad C., *The Zande Scheme: An Anthropological Case Study of Economic Development in Africa,* Evanston, Ill.: Northwestern University Press, 1966.

Resnick, Idrian N., editor, *Tanzania: Revolution by Education,* Arusha: Longmans of Tanzania, 1968.

Reuveny, Jacob, *A Framework for Comparative Cultural Analysis of Administrative System,* Pittsburgh: University of Pittsburgh, 1966 (dissertation).

Riggs, Fred W., *Administration in Developing Countries—The Theory of Prismatic Society,* Boston: Houghton Mifflin, 1964.

Riggs, Fred W., *Frontiers of Development Administration,* Durham: Duke University Press, 1971.

Rigney, J. A., *The IB Model in Project Review and Maturity Testing.* See Conference on Institution Building and Technical Assistance.

Rigney, J. A., J. K. McDermott, and R. W. Roskelley, "Strategies in Technical Assistance," North Carolina Agricultural Experiment Station, Technical Bulletin No. 189, December, 1968.

Rivkin, Arnold, editor, *Nations by Design: Institution Building in Africa,* Garden City, N.Y.: Doubleday, 1968.

Roberts, Glyn, *Volunteers in Africa and Asia,* London: Stanhope Press, 1965.

Roberts, Karlene H., "On Looking at the Elephant: An Evaluation of Cross-cultural Research Related to Organizations," Psychological Bulletin, Vol. LXXIV, No. 5, 1970: 327-350.

Rogers, Everett M., *Diffusion of Innovations,* New York: Free Press, 1962.

Rogers, Everett M., Richard E. Joyce, Donald J. Leu and Frederic J. Mortimore, *The Diffusion of Educational Innovations in the Government Secondary Schools of Thailand,* East Lansing: Michigan State University, 1969.

Rose, Arnold M., editor, *The Institutions of Advanced Societies,* Minneapolis: University of Minnesota Press, 1958.

Roskelley, R. W., *Pre-Contract Planning,* Logan, Utah: Utah State University, n.d.

Roskelley, R. W. and J. A. Rigney, "Measuring Institutional Maturity in the Development of Indigenous Agricultural Universities," Logan, Utah: Utah State University, Department of Sociology, n.d. (mimeo).

Rostow, Eugene V., *Planning for Freedom,* New Haven: Yale University Press, 1960.

Rural Development Research Project, *A Summary Report of the CIC-AID Building Institutions to Serve Agriculture,* Lafayette, Indiana: Purdue University, n.d.

Schultz, Theodore W., *Economic Crises in World Agriculture,* Ann Arbor, Mich.: University of Michigan Press, 1965.

Selznick, Philip, *Leadership in Administration,* Evanston, Ill.: Row, Peterson, 1957.

Selznick, Philip, *TVA and Grass Roots,* Berkeley: University of California Press, 1953.

Sherman, Harvey, *It All Depends: A Pragmatic Approach to Organization,* University, Ala.: University of Alabama Press, 1966.

Sherwood, Frank P., *Institutionalizing the Grass Roots in Brazil: A Study in Comparative Local Government,* San Francisco: Chandler, 1967.

Sherwood, Frank P., *Social Exchange in the Institution-Building Process: Rewards and Penalties in the Brazilian School of Public Administration,* Pittsburgh: University of Pittsburgh, Graduate School of Public and International Affairs, 1967.

Siegel, Gilbert B., *Development of the Institution Building Model,* Pittsburgh: University of Pittsburgh, Graduate School of Public and International Affairs, 1966.

Siffin, William J., *The Institution-Building Perspective: Properties, Problems and Promise,* Bloomington, Ind.: University of Indiana, 1969.

Siffin, William J., *The Thai Bureaucracy—Institutional Change and Development.* Honolulu: East-West Center Press, 1966.

Siffin, William J., *The Thai Institute of Public Administration: A Case Study in Institution Building,* Pittsburgh: University of Pittsburgh, Graduate School of Public and International Affairs, ERP Document No. VII-2, March 1967.

Siffin, William, *Summary Report.* See Conference on Institution Building and Technical Assistance.

Sigmund, Paul E., Jr., editor, *The Ideologies of the Developing Nations,* New York: Praeger, 1963.

Silvert, K. H., editor, *Expectant Peoples: Nationalism and Development,* New York: Random House, 1963.

Sirkin, Gerald, *The Visible Hand: The Fundamentals of Economic Planning,* New York: McGraw-Hill, 1968.

Smart, Lyman F., editor, *Proceedings of the Regional Conference on Institution Building,* Logan, Utah: Utah State University, 1970.

Snyder, Louis L., *The Dynamics of Nationalism,* Princeton: D. Van Nostrand, 1964.

Sofer, Cyril, *The Organization from Within,* London: Tavistock, 1961.

Spicer, Edward H., editor, *Human Problems in Technological Change: A Casebook,* New York: Russell Sage Foundation, 1952.

Staley, Eugene, *The Future of Underdeveloped Countries,* New York: Praeger, 1961.

Strassmann, W. Paul, *Technological Change and Economic Development: The Manufacturing Experience of Mexico and Puerto Rico,* Ithaca: Cornell University Press, 1968.

Sufrin, Sidney C., *Technical Assistance Theory and Guidelines,* Syracuse: Syracuse University Press, 1966.

Sufrin, Sidney C., *Transactions of Trade Unions and Government in Developing Societies,* Pittsburgh: University of Pittsburgh, Graduate School of Public and International Affairs.

Swerdlow, Irving, editor, *Development Administration: Concepts and Problems,* Syracuse: Syracuse University Press, 1963.

Taylor, Donald A., *Institution Building in Business Administration: The Brazilian Experience,* East Lansing: Michigan State University, 1968.

Thayer, Philip W. and William T. Phillips, editors, *Nationalism and Progress in Free Asia,* Baltimore: Johns Hopkins Press, 1956.

Thomas, D. Woods and Judith G. Fender, editors, *Proceedings: Conference on Institution Building & Technical Assistance.* See Conference on Institution Building and Technical Assistance.

Thomas, D. Woods, William L. Miller, Harry R. Potter, and Adrian Aveni, editors, *Institution Building: A Model for Applied Social Change,* Cambridge: Schenkman, 1971.

Thompson, Carey C., editor, *Institutional Adjustment: A Challenge to a Changing Economy,* Austin: University of Texas Press, 1967.

Thompson, William N., Harold D. Guither, Earl H. Regnier, and Kathleen M. Propp, *AID-University Rural Development Contracts and U.S. Universities,* Urbana: University of Illinois, 1968.

Thurber, Clarence E. and Edward W. Wiedner, *Technical Assistance in Training Administrators,* Bloomington: Indiana University, Department of Government, 1962.

Tinbergen, Jan, *The Design of Development,* Baltimore: Johns Hopkins Press, 1958.

Tinbergen, Jan, *Development Planning,* New York: McGraw-Hill, 1967.

United Nations, *The Administration of Economic Development Planning: Principles and Fallacies,* New York: United Nations, 1966.

United Nations, Department of Economic and Social Affairs, *Appraising Administrative Capability for Development,* New York: United Nations, 1969.

United Nations, Public Administration Branch, *Appraising Administrative Capability for Development;* A Methodological Monograph Prepared by the International Group of Studies in National Planning (INTERPLAN), New York: United Nations, 1969.

United Nations, Agency for International Development, *Science, Technology and Development;* United States Papers Prepared for the United Nations Conference on the Application of Science and Technology for the Benefit of Less Developed Areas, Washington, D.C.: Agency for International Development, 1962-1963.

United States, Agency for International Development, Public Administration Service, *Modernization of Government Budget Administration,* Washington, D.C.: Agency for International Development, 1962.

Vermeulin, A. and C. Saunders, *A Study in Development.* Rotterdam: Rotterdam University Press, 1970.

Walinsky, Louis J., *The Planning and Execution of Economic Development,* New York: McGraw-Hill, 1963.

Walker, Charles R., *Modern Technology and Civilization: Introduction to Human Problems in the Machine Age,* New York: McGraw-Hill, 1962.

Warnken, Philip F., *Strategies for Technical Assistance,* Columbia: University of Missouri, 1968.

Waterston, Albert assisted by C. J. Martin, August T. Schumacher and Fritz A. Steuber, *Development Planning: Lessons of Experience,* Baltimore: Johns Hopkins Press, 1965.

Wayt, William A., *AID, Agriculture, and Africa: A Perspective on University Contract Projects,* Columbus: Ohio State University, n.d.

Weitz, Raanan, *From Peasant to Farmer: A Revolutionary Strategy for Development,* New York: Twentieth Century Fund, 1971.

Wiedner, Edward W., *Development Administration in Asia,* Durham: Duke University Press, 1970.

Willner, Dorothy, *Nation-Building and Community in Israel,* Princeton: Princeton University Press, 1969.

PERIODICALS*

American Journal of Agricultural Economics, Varden Fuller, editor, American Agricultural Economics Association, Cornell University, Ithaca, New York, 1919.

Published five times a year, this journal covers a wide scope of national and international agro-economic questions on both the micro and macro levels.*

American Journal of Economics and Sociology, Will Lessner, editor, American Journal of Economics and Sociology, Inc., New York, 1941.

Aims at a "constructive synthesis in the social sciences" through the reporting of the results of original research designed for the understanding of contemporary economic and social processes. Journal is effective for the scholar, college student, or interested layman who is seeking analysis of economic problems and situations, or by one who is seeking studies of the interrelationships between economics and sociology, history, and political science. Two important areas covered are the sociological aspects of economic institutions and the economic aspects of social and political institutions. Besides United States studies, others are concerned with foreign situations. While the articles are thoroughly documented, the style is nontechnical. Authors are professors and government officials.

Asian Survey, Robert A. Scalapino, editor, Institute of International Studies, University of California, 1961.

Studies the economic, political and social problems of Asia in contemporary settings. Five or six scholarly articles appear in each monthly issue, frequently accompanied by charts and tables. The impressive list of contributors—Norman Palmer, Sung Chik Hong, A. G. Norani, Donald J. Monro—makes *Asian Survey* an outstanding journal on contemporary Asian problems.

British Journal of Sociology, Terence Morris, editor, Routledge and Kegan Paul, London, 1950.

*With the exception of those annotations marked with an asterisk, all annotations were taken in whole or in part, from Bill Katz and Barry Gargal, *Magazines for Libraries,* New York: R. R. Bowker, 1969, by permission of the publishers. Age of periodical is shown by year of inauguration in main entry.

Sponsored by the London School of Economics and Political Science, this journal presents scholarly articles ranging over the fields of theoretical and applied sociology. The editors state that there is no attempt to favor any "school center, country, or variety of sociology," and an effort is made to represent fairly social anthropology, social administration, and several relevant areas of history, philosophy, and social psychology.

Co-Existence: A Journal for the Comparative Study of Economics, Sociology and Politics in a Changing World, Rudolf Schlesinger, editor, Pergamon Press, New York.

As the full title suggests, this journal covers a wide range of articles from the various disciplines relating to development and change. Each edition is balanced with economic, political, and sociological analysis.*

Community Development Journal, Marjorie DuSantoy, editor, Oxford University Press, 1970.

Short descriptive articles on community problems and development effort ranging from local social welfare programs to national institutions.*

Comparative Education Review, Harold J. Noah, editor, Comparative Education Society, New York, 1956.

Basic journal in comparative and international education. Each number averages ten to fifteen articles of both a descriptive and analytical nature. The level of scholarship is high; the style relatively difficult. As the magazine stresses international coverage, it has some interest for political scientists and sociologists; but the primary audience is the professional educator.

Comparative Political Studies. Sage Publications, Beverly Hills, California, 1968.

A model statistical approach to political science, with emphasis on material of interest primarily to the teacher and graduate student. Its scope is international; papers are normally by subject experts and require background for understanding.

Current Sociology. Basil Blackwell, Oxford, England, 1959.

This publication of the International Sociological Association is primarily a lengthy annotated bibliography of material in a given subject area. Each issue concentrates on a particular point of interest and is preceded by a "Trend Report" on the topic and/or several papers of related interest. The main text is both in English and French; the annotations, a combination. Coverage is international, and a run of the periodical can give the individual one of the best single sources of information on all major subjects related to sociology, e.g., demography, underdeveloped nations, human organizations, social issues, and so on.

Economic Development and Cultural Change, Bert F. Hoselitz, editor, Research Center in Economic Development and Cultural Change, University of Chicago Press, 1952.

A well-written journal primarily concerned with developments in the emerging nations of the world. Economic, political, and cultural activities are examined, and an effort is made to link all factors relevant to development. The material is technical, but because it covers such a wide range of social and political issues, it will be of interest to a great number of scholars and graduate students.

Environment and Behavior, Gary H. Winkel, editor, Sage Publications, Beverly Hills, California, 1969.

Environment and Behavior has been brought into being to report rigorous experimental and theoretical work focusing on the human behavior at the individual, group, and institutional scale.*

Human Organization, Marion Pearsdall, editor, Society for Applied Anthropology, University of Kentucky, Lexington, Kentucky, 1941.

Devoted to the scientific investigation of the principles of human behavior and the application of these principles to practical problems. Man is viewed holistically as a biological and psychological organism and as a social being existing in a changing physical and cultural environment. Anthropology provides the major framework, but inter-disciplinary approaches to problems confronting change agents in many cultures are featured.

Human Relations: A Journal of Studies Toward the Integration of the Social Sciences, Eric L. Trist, editor, Plenum Publishing Corp., New York, 1947.

International in scope, with three editorial committees (Europe, U.K. and USA). Increasingly concerned with social problems and the "identification of conditions which will render decision making more opposite and social action more effective." There is an average of seven articles per issue, which are either reports on research proposals carried out by the author or extensive monographs based on thorough and extensive reading and rethinking of theory and procedural design. The articles are primarily devoted to the psychological and sociological aspects of group process, systems, interpersonal relations, and interaction.

Industrial and Labor Relations, Robert H. Ferguson, editor. New York State School of Industrial and Labor Relations, Cornell University, Ithaca, New York, 1947.

This interdisciplinary journal in the field of industrial and labor relations publishes articles covering such topics as personnel administration, industrial sociology and psychology, labor economics, labor history, and labor law. Approximately six articles appear in each issue, the majority being written by faculty members of various universities. Every number has a section where current topics of interest are considered by leading experts, with a symposium of several essays written by the "pros."

International Development Review, Andrew E. Rice, editor, Society for International Development, Washington, D.C., 1959.

A well-written, readable journal devoted to the economic development of the emerging nations. Articles are practical documented, and usually in English. Those in French or Spanish have English abstracts. News of the United Nations, film reviews, and short perceptive book reviews round out the average issue. Valuable magazine for difficult-to-find information on smaller nations.

International Journal of Comparative Sociology, K. Ishwaran, editor, E. J. Brill, Publishers, Leiden, the Netherlands.

Coverage of world-wide research and developments in sociology. The primary aim is "the furtherance of pure research in the field." The scholarly studies describe and interpret social situations with comparisons to other countries. The evaluative and descriptive reviews submitted by scholars from all over the world provide a sampling of new materials in the field from nonwestern areas. Occasionally an entire issue is devoted to a single topic, which draws information from different cultures. For example, there have been presentations on the relationship between politics and social change, and kinship and geographic mobility. Primarily for the scholar and college student interested in an international and comparative view of sociology.

International Review of Administrative Sciences. International Institute of Administrative Sciences, Brussels, Belgium, 1928.

The International Institute of Administrative Sciences aims at "disseminating the general principles of public administration, comparing the experience of different countries in this field . . . for the improvement of administrative science."*

International Review of Education. Martinus Nijhoff Publishing, 's Gravenhage, Netherlands, 1955.

Dedicated to achieving international intercommunication on all aspects of education. Highly technical articles in English, French, and German are typical. The average issue has 3 to 8-page-long articles, varying numbers of shorter articles, and book reviews. There is often a particular concern with experimental programs, such as the use of computers in teaching. An occasional issue is devoted to a special topic, usually under a guest editor and including a bibliography on the topic.

Journal of Asian and African Studies, K. Ishwaren, editor, E. J. Brill Publishers, Leiden, Netherlands, 1966.

Although issued quarterly, recent practice has been to publish double numbers of some 160 pages twice a year. Issues center on specific subjects of interest to any scholar involved with man and society in developing nations of Asia and Africa, e.g., sociology of Japanese religion, and traditional and modern institutions in Asia and Africa. Emphasis is on sociology, but contributors come from other disciplines such as political science, history, anthropology, and related social sciences. The material represents original research, is well documented, and is an excellent source of references for the specialist.

Journal of Comparative Administration, Peter Savage, editor, Sage Publications, Beverly Hills, California, published in cooperation with the

Comparative Administration Group of the American Society for Public Administration, 1969.

This journal seeks theoretical and empirical articles which focus on the interdisciplinary and/or international concerns of public organizations, viewed in a comparative context. It also includes a "Research Notes" section which reports on-going research projects, research designs, and preliminary findings; review articles are also sought.

Journal of Conflict Resolution; for Research Related to War and Peace, Elizabeth Converse, editor, Center for Research on Conflict Resolution, University of Michigan, 1957.

Conflict here stands for war, and the sponsoring group publishes articles which consider problems relating to war and to peace. Authors cover a wider spectrum of interests from political science and economics to literature and art. The five to six scholarly articles touch on historical implications of war in all parts of the world. Concerned, as well, with the effects of communication, the magazine should have wide appeal to any serious student of psychology, history, or sociology.

Journal of Human Relations, Ralph T. Templin, editor, Center State University, Wilberforce, Ohio, 1952.

Approaches human relations from all disciplines in the belief "that the human conditions require the light of every science in order to increase social awareness and to establish more meaningful practical relationships." There are usually eight non-technical articles, of 10 to 12 pages, written by professors and laymen in the fields of literature, philosophy, education, sociology and other social sciences. Authors have dealt with the necessity of identifying and constructing meaningful national goals and the psychological factors inducing warfare. Occasionally, several articles will present a symposium on various aspects of a topic like poverty. Regular features include: "The Record"—a factual and unbiased study of a controversial matter, such as the Arab-Israeli conflict; "Research Studies and Abstracts"—a brief presentation of a current study; "Human Frontiers"—a short article of theory and thought on frontier questions; "Focus on Human Conditions"—a critical evaluation of trends, programs and habits, and so forth; and "Context of Growth"—articles on educational aspects of human relations.

Journal of Interamerican Studies and World Affairs, Ione S. Wright, editor, Sage Publications, Beverly Hills, California, 1959.

Sponsored by the Center of Advanced International Studies at the University of Miami, this publication consists of some five to eight articles on various aspects of Latin American politics, social conflicts, and economics. Authors are prominent American scholars, as well as scholars from various Latin American Universities.

Journal of Modern African Studies, David and Helen Kimble, editors. Cambridge University Press, New York, 1963.

This journal offers a quarterly survey of politics, economics, and related topics in contemporary Africa and seeks to promote a deepened understanding of what is happening in Africa today, by selecting authorities from various fields. Political science professors, U.S. officials, and economics and history teachers, give this journal a broad scope. . . . To keep the scholars and librarians up to date, a section entitled "Africana" publishes resumés of the work of institutes and centers for African Studies.

Journal of Social Issues, B. H. Raven, editor, Ann Arbor, Michigan, 1945.

Sponsored by the Society for the Psychological Study of Social Issues, this journal seeks to bring theory and practice into focus on human problems of the group, community and nation. The goal is to communicate scientific findings in a non-technical manner without the sacrifice of professional standards. Each issue has a guest editor and seven articles on different aspects of a single topic like bilingualism or cultural change in small communities. Authors are professors or specialists in the field.

Rural Sociology, W. Keith Warner, editor, Rural Sociological Society, University of Wisconsin, Madison, Wisconsin, 1936.

Covers all aspects of rural life in the United States and other countries—including the economic, cultural, social and demographic components. There are five to seven research articles per issue, averaging 8 to 16 pages. These have dealt with migration and settlement patterns; educational and occupational aspirations and achievements; social characteristics of rural people and areas; the adoption of agricultural practices; and the relations of rural and urban areas and peoples. The authors are associated with departments of sociology and rural sociology, rural education, or agricultural economics.

Social Forces: A Scientific Medium of Social Study and Interpretation, Guy B. Johnson and Rupert B. Vance, editors, University of North Carolina Press, Chapel Hill, North Carolina.

Brief, scholarly articles report research over the entire range of theoretical and applied sociology. Related subjects include the family, social psychology, regionalism, public opinion and population. Emphasis is placed on the motivation and reasons behind social action, developments and mobility and such features as job satisfaction; occupational groups and reasons for participation in community activities; and the relation of educational expectations and parents' occupations. There are research notes, comments, and short but numerous book reviews. Of value since it deals with the social forces motivating the behavior of the average individual.

Sociology of Education, Charles E. Bidwell, editor, American Sociological Association, Washington, D.C., 1927.

Serves as a forum for the study of education by scholars in all the social sciences. The editorial board reflects this international and interdisciplinary nature, and the presentations use the perspectives of history, anthropology, education, political science, psychology, and sociology to analyze educational institutions. The four 15 to 25-page articles are research studies on such subjects as investment in education and economic growth; teacher attitudes toward academic freedom; the relation of education, mobility, social values, and expectations. Until 1963, it was entitled *Journal of Educational Sociology.*

Sociology and Social Research: an International Journal, Martin H. Neumeyer, editor, University of Southern California, Los Angeles, California, 1916.

The results of recent research on special aspects of current sociological problems and occasional articles on theory are presented. Coverage is international, with studies made in New Zealand, South Africa, Iraq, and other nations, as well as the United States. Each issue has about nine 15 to 20-page articles. These include historical surveys and articles on the contributions of individuals, empirical research designs in the area of such social problems as juvenile delinquency, and reports of attitudes toward these problems and programs for their solution. There are also presentations concerning the philosophy of sociology and social theories.

Sociological Review, W. M. Williams, editor, The University of Keele, Staffordshire, England, 1908.

A British journal presenting articles on a wide range of general sociological topics, along with short notes on sociological research and critical comments on previous articles. Occasionally pieces summarize work in a particular area, e.g., the role of education in national development, or the positivist movement and the development of English sociology. The five or six research articles cover all areas: the relation of change to demographic factors, the role of ideology in determining behavior, the influence of ecological factors, and comparisons of various matched groups. The book reviews emphasize British publications.

Studies in Comparative International Development, Irving Louis Horowitz, editor. Trans-action, New Brunswick, N.J., 1966.

Each publication is one comprehensive article on a development topic; the emphasis generally is sociological and the coverage is extensive and diverse.*

The Journal of Developing Areas, Spencer H. Brown, editor, Western Illinois University Press, Macomb, Illinois, 1966.

Concerned with underdeveloped countries, this journal carries articles on general types of development problems rather than the problems of particular countries. The approach is not purely economic, but attempts to deal with all potentially relevant aspects of changing societies, from tangible variables such as wage structures, schools, the military, unions, and trade to intangible ones such as goal orientation and values in their relations to change. There is much data given on many different areas and a regular news and notes section.

Youth and Society, A. W. McEachern, editor, Sage Publications, Beverly Hills, California, 1969.

An interdisciplinary journal concerned with the social and political implications of youth culture and development, this periodical attempts to bring together significant empirical studies and theoretical positions relevant to the process of youth development, political socialization, the impact of youth on society, and patterns of acquisition of adult roles. To provide flexibility, the journal defines youth broadly as those young people in middle adolescence through young adulthood. Contributions from the disciplines of anthropology, sociology, psychology, political science, history, and economics are included in this publication.*

INDEX

INDEX

Agency for International Development, 12, 167-179 passim
AID, see Agency for International Development
Almond, G., 133 n. 14
Apter, D. E., 104

Banfield, E. C., 103
Barnard, C., 114
Bayley, D., 108 n. 23
Birkhead, G. B., 143-144
Black, C. E., 95
Blaise, H. C., 22, 39 n. 1, 143, 155, 158-159
Blueprint, see Mapping; Planning
Bruhns, F. C., 39 n. 4
Buckley, W., 160 n. 5

Caiden, G., 143
Change, see Social change; Mapping; Planning
Change agents, 22, 25-27, 34, 43, 46, 48-50, 52-53, 55, 91, 96, 102, 105, 171;
    see also Technical assistance
Change processes, 13-14, 24, 26, 28-29

Dewey, J., 96
Diamant, A., 131 n. 1

Tillman, R. O., 103
Time in planning, 67-68, 73, 80, 84, 113-131 passim, 139, 183-184, 189
Transaction linkages, see Linkages, transaction

Uphoff, N., 39 n. 5

Values in institution building, see Institution building, values
Variables mapping, see Mapping
Von Neumann, J., 106

Ward, R. E., 109 n. 24
Weber, M., 98, 142
Welch, P., 107 n. 6
Wood, G., 60

Znaniecki, F., 142

DATE   DUE

RETURNED